The Gratitude Book Project

Celebrating

365

Days of

Gratitude

© 2010 Donna Kozik, Donna Kozik & Associates, Inc.

ISBN: 978-0-615-42354-8

Publisher: Donna Kozik & Associates, Inc.
3780 Arnold Ave.
San Diego CA 92104

Cover design by Susan Veach and Maureen Day

Want to be a published author?

Book writing, publishing and consulting services provided by Donna Kozik & Associates, Inc.

Write Your Book

"Write a Book in a Weekend" is an online, virtual course that guides you in writing a "short and powerful" book in two days with pre-formatted templates, how-to information, and expert guidance. Find out more and get a FREE AUDIO "12 Strategies to Publishing Success" at WriteWithDonna.com.

Publish Your Book

"Done for You" Publishing Services offers everything from editing, proofreading, interior formatting, and cover design, while providing personal connection and top-rate customer service. Find out more at DoneForYouPublishing.com.

Get Answers to Your Book Writing and Publishing Questions

If you're struggling with what to write about or organizing your material, or if you're frustrated because you can't find answers about how the book publishing process works, get a "Big Breakthrough Session" with two-time award-winning author and publishing expert Donna Kozik. More at MyBigBreakthroughSession.com.

Not sure what you need?

Email business manager Dina Rocha with your questions at Dina@MyBigBusinessCard.com or call us anytime at 619-923-3082 to talk about it.

More about
"The Gratitude Book Project"

From the beginning, I knew "The Gratitude Book Project" would be more than the sum of its parts. It started with a seed of an idea that blossomed forth with an amazing speed to touch my life and the lives of my team and the hundreds of co-authors who simply wanted to say "thank you."

In this same spirit, I thank you for picking up this book. It's through your actions that the "attitude of gratitude" started in our San Diego offices continues to go across the desert, over the mountains, and ripple through the oceans to encompass the world.

In keeping with the essence of the book, proceeds from national bookseller sales of *The Gratitude Book Project: Celebrating 365 Days of Gratitude* go to support:

- FeedAmerica
- The Make-a-Wish Foundation
- The American Society for the Prevention of Cruelty to Animals (ASPCA)
- Women for Women International

We hope you will join us in supporting these deserving organizations.

Finally, if a piece moves you to laughter or happy tears, you can share your thoughts and connect with the book's co-authors and readers at the **TheGratitudeBookProject.com**.

Want to tell a particular author what his or her contribution meant to you? Send an email to **FanMail@TheGratitudeBookProject.com** and we'll make sure the author receives it.

~ Donna Kozik, Editor

Contents

February

June

July

October

November

December

Acknowledgments

They say it takes a village to make something extraordinary happen. This book was no exception. From conception to bookshelves in just over three months, it took the combined efforts of many gifted and giving people.

But anyone in the business of writing and publishing books knows there are many faceless individuals behind the scenes working tirelessly to turn a manuscript into a tangible and professional book readers can hold in their hands. All too often those people go unnoticed, and they are rarely given the recognition they deserve.

"The Gratitude Book Project" represents the importance of expressing our gratitude aloud—for things big and small—and if we failed to mention the following people for making this come together we would be missing the very point of this collaboration of thoughts on gratitude:

Dina Rocha, "The Gratitude Book Project" Publication Manager and Go-To Person for everything from customer service to capital ideas. Without your organizational skills, your insistence we meet our own deadlines, your ability to crunch numbers, and your unwavering dedication, we would have been lost out of the starting gate. But most importantly, Dina, we thank you for your encouragement to "dig deep" and all the laughter-in-the-right-places to ease tension and stress around the office.

Michelle Dimsey, "The Gratitude Book Project" Associate Editor and Resident Doppelganger. Much appreciation for saying "roger" to whatever's been asked of you—from joining in a teleseminar with hundreds of co-authors to being our writing backbone.

Thanks also for reaching out to others who celebrate the power of gratitude, too, and putting the Law of Attraction to work. (By the way, are you around? How about for some ketchup and scrambled eggs?)

Deanna McAdams, Submission Coordinator and Queen of All Things Survey Monkey. We cannot thank you enough for making sure every single contribution from our submission site was transferred to another document for editing and proofing. But for navigating your way through each author's date request, we will forever be in your debt. Without you there would be no need for the subtitle, "Celebrating 365 Days of Gratitude," because no one's entry would appear on any specific day.

Jodi Brandon, Proofreader and Governess of Details. Your job requires painstaking attention to detail and often requires multiple readings of a manuscript. Your willingness to proof the submissions of hundreds of authors for a single project, while working to meet our ambitious deadlines, goes unparalleled. You are truly one of the unsung heroes working behind the scenes to make everyone look their best.

Susan Veach, Cover Designer and Layout Artist. Most people do not understand or have an appreciation for the professionalism required to turn a manuscript into a visually appealing book. From cover colors to font size, line spacing, placement of page numbers, and alignment issues, you handled it all. Amazingly, you did this with hundreds of authors—many of whom had specific formatting requests to add impact to their submissions. Without you, this book would look like one big run-on sentence!

Becky Cohen, Assistant Formatter. You joined us in midst of this project whirlwind and never looked back. Your willingness to fill in wherever needed and your beautifully designed Contributor and Ambassador Badges have been a wonderful addition to this project.

Carey Powell, Promotion Director and Leader of the Army of Ambassadors. Without you no one but the authors and our team would know this book exists. With only a month before its launch, you volunteered to coordinate our ambassadors and drive the promotion train. You are forever in our hearts.

The Army of Ambassadors and Believers of the Project. Not only did you submit contributions to this book, you heeded the call when we asked for support to help get the book into the hands of people everywhere. Each and every one of you stepped up to the plate with your best, and we couldn't appreciate you more.

We stand on the shoulders of giants, those people who inspired us with their work and messages that set the stage for a project such as this, including Gary Blair, Jack Canfield, Dr. William Donnelly, Mark Victor Hansen, Mary Manin Morrissey, and others who have, knowingly or not, fanned the flames of ideas into action.

Finally, we would like to express our deep appreciation to every contributing author. You and your submissions are by far the most important component of this project, and without you this book would just have remained another cool idea.

Introduction

My boss and my friend, Donna Kozik, is known for a number of things. She loves and excels at helping people to fulfill their dreams of becoming authors. She finds joy in making complicated things easy. She is a devoted fan of all things Padres baseball. She believes in the Law of Attraction and the power of positive thinking. Thanksgiving is her favorite holiday. And around the offices she has also become known for her "showers of inspiration."

Let me explain that one, because it's probably not what you think. Although we all find Donna inspirational and uplifting on a daily basis, that's not what I mean by her "showers of inspiration." She literally has her best ideas while in the shower. So whenever a conversation starts with "I was in the shower this morning and I was thinking...," we all know something big is coming.

"The Gratitude Book Project" was one of those ideas. Her tireless quest to show aspiring writers how to become authors combined with her favorite holiday rapidly approaching was bound to lead to one of those showers.

The concept of bringing people together to share their thoughts and feelings about the subject of gratitude was one we all fell in love with instantly. Her idea to have one entry for each day of the year is a fabulous and fun way for us all to remember to count our blessings every day—not just during the Thanksgiving season. And what a great way to give lots of writers an opportunity to see their name in published—without having to write a whole book.

There's no doubt having an attitude of gratitude has many benefits.

But there's a reason we say "thank you" out loud. Sometimes silent gratitude isn't enough. When we take the time to express our gratefulness in words, written or verbal, or in deeds, big or small, we put the power of gratitude in motion. And gratitude in motion can be a life-changing experience.

All of us know expressing gratefulness when things are going according to plan is much easier than doing it when things seem to be falling apart. Being grateful for the bumps in the road, the losses in our lives, and the setbacks we all endure can be challenging, and it takes practice to be thankful for less-than-desirable circumstances.

Richard Bach, author of *Illusions*, said, "There is no such thing as a problem without a gift for you in its hands. You seek problems because you need their gifts." Those of us involved in the production of this book have been gratefully overwhelmed by the enthusiastic response to this project, and we have immense appreciation for each and every entry. But those who shared their stories of finding the gifts hidden in the struggles—and took the time to express it "out loud" on these pages—have humbled, amazed, inspired, and encouraged us all to new heights of gratitude awareness.

However this book landed in your hands, we appreciate having you here to share this moment. We hope you drink deeply and often from the well of gratitude contained within. And we encourage you to keep gratitude in motion by remembering to express it out loud!

~ Michelle Dimsey, Associate Editor

January

"We can only be said to be alive in those moments when our hearts are conscious of our treasures."

~Thornton Wilder

January 1

Using the Power of Focus to Make a Better Day

My gratitude is for an inspirational writing that flowed from my pen one day as if by magic:

We are all perfection expressed in an imperfect way. We can choose to focus on each other's imperfection and suppress the perfection,

or

we can choose to focus on each other's perfection and support its unfoldment.

This gift opens up new horizons for me. It allows me to look at people in a new light and be less judgmental. It prompts me to ask, "Where's my focus?" as I go through my life, day by day, moment by moment.

I now always focus on people at their highest and best, no matter how they are acting to the contrary. This process also seems to support myself and others in regaining our sense of balance and self-control. When parents use this process while facing the challenges of parenthood, they experience a personal "time out," which can be much more beneficial than making their kids take a "time out."

Using this as a framework for my own behavior has allowed me to receive other well-known magical writings, such as "The Gift of Love."

~ Jerome DeShazo

January 2

We don't have much if we don't have our health.

"Some people spend their health gaining their wealth, and then have to spend their wealth to regain their health."

~ A.J. Reb Materi

I have been so blessed to have become aware of how thankful I am to have good health and not to take it for granted. I have seen my mother and several family members and friends die of cancer, and I do not wish to ever experience that.

After having the good fortune of overcoming some of my own health issues, and seeing my children overcome health issues, I can only be grateful each day for the health we do have. I am grateful that I have learned that we do have control over our health and how we feel each day, and that we do have the power to change it.

Also, in my eighteen years as a physical therapist and three years of health coaching, I have seen hundreds of people with debilitating injuries, diseases, and ailments that have changed their lives forever.

We never know what the future will hold, so we can only appreciate and enjoy the present. I am continually inspired by my clients and patients, who remind me that there is always someone worse off than they are, and that they are grateful for what they have in the present moment.

~ *Deanna Mandichak*

January 3

My Gratitude Journal

When I was a little girl, my mom would ask me, "What are you grateful for?" During this time I started my first gratitude journal to assist myself in finding the positive actions happening in my life.

My gratitude journal is a chronicle where I'm only authorized to write positive thoughts. At the end of each day, I write at least seven things I'm grateful for. This is a powerful tool to use at the end of the day, right before bedtime, as it provides positive thoughts right before going to sleep.

We all know it's easier to journal when you've had a wonderful day, but what if you've had a not-so-good day? Take a look at the things that have happened, and see if you can find the blessings in the not-so-good activities. Once you've taken a deeper look, write down seven positive thoughts. I believe this creates a win-win situation, as it empowers you to design something beautiful with your life.

My gratitude journal has been a much-needed tool. I challenge you to start one today, to remind you of all the fabulous and positive things in your life.

~ Laynita Cichy

January 4

Thank You, Tucker!

I'm outside with Tucker. The bright white disk of the full moon is high in the northwestern sky. The soft yellow sun is still low in the east. Orange-pink clouds connect the two like a sash. I can't stop looking, east to west and back again.

My mind wanders to all the bits and pieces of life I've become aware of in the last ten months. There's been a re-emergence of parts of me almost forgotten. But that's all BT: "Before Tucker."

A permanently disheveled bundle of energy, Tucker is my miniature Schnoodle. Tucker moved in just before Christmas 2009. Instead of getting busier, life has become better. I'm so grateful for not missing the highlights of this year:

- Twinkling fireflies.
- Eastern cottontails, waiting until we are almost upon them.
- Fluttering leaves.
- Butterflies and bees (oww!).
- Sunrises, sunsets.
- Snow glittering like diamonds under the stars.
- Gentle breezes.
- Dog park friends.
- Smells of rain, worms, and earth.
- Miss Wendy, dog trainer extraordinaire.
- Phases of the moon.
- Strangers who want to know, "What kind of dog is that? He's so cute!"
- Long walks.
- Dog-friendly establishments.
- The joyful, loving, body-wagging exuberant greeting I get just for being me.

Thank you, Tucker!

~ Laura Lynn Westerberg

January 5

Grateful for Hope and Smiles in My Life

I have found a special link between hope and smiles. Growing up, my dad was my best example of one who would freely share smiles, and a spirit of hope to all around him. Even though times would get very tough, he would find a way to control the chaos, by looking at things differently, smiling, laughing, and staying hopeful (and things always changed!)!

When I was about 7 years old, there was a man in the neighborhood that all the kids were scared of because he seemed "grumpy." I tried my "experiment" of just smiling and saying "Hello" each time I passed him.

Soon, he looked for me, and met me with a big smiling response! He wasn't grumpy! He was lonely — and wanted to feel special like we all do!

Despite all struggles, family, friends, and scriptures provide examples of hope to lift me though my darkest hours.

Hope found in a sincere smile has awesome power!

Keep smiling, and never give up hope!

~ Doreen Susan McGrath-Smith

January 6

In Gratitude and Memory of My Cousin

"How can I assist you?" I asked her. She responded, "Just pray for me." After I explained to her that I could lead her through some processes that could benefit her, she agreed to do them. After an hour and a half of working together, she was able to release a lifetime of guilt and the fear of dying.

I am grateful to my cousin for allowing me to guide her through this process and to trust me to witness her transformation. I am grateful that she had the courage to open her heart and to allow the healing to take place so that the last few weeks of her life were filled with joy, peace, and tranquility.

I am grateful that she taught me to live life to its fullest—to do things that I enjoy and stop working just for money so I can "enjoy" the future because there may not be a future. She, who was a couple of years older than I, left when she was ready to enjoy life. Thus, thanks to her, I learned that every moment counts, and now is the time to follow my passions and to enjoy every moment of life.

~ Dr. Luz Liliana Garcia

January 7

Life Shows the Way

Some time ago, the normality of our life suddenly unraveled. We were struck by a series of challenges, including financial ones, which coincided with the birth of our first child.

One day we came across a book about real people's encounters with the divine. We learned that angels can only help us if we would ask —because of their respect to human free will.

We did ask, and things gradually fell into place.

I took up a daycare job, watching another child together with my own. Additionally, a "coincidence" reminded me of the joy my creativity brings to others.

Now, I handcraft gem angel jewelry and pursue my writing passion by posting informative as well as inspirational articles about angels and healing crystals on my website and blog. My husband has a rewarding new job he loves.

So what are we grateful for? We are grateful for the loving support offered by God and the angels. We are grateful for the love that flows between us, and the love we share with others. We are grateful for the inner knowing that, whatever happens, life will show us the way.

~ River Grace

January 8

I'm Grateful for Being Grateful

Shifting gears, personally or professionally, can be rewarding, but it can also be challenging.

In 2003, I began a journey of career transition. From the security of a full-time, established career in professional communications, I stepped into the dynamic and still-evolving world of professional coaching. My work-life is rewarding on so many levels, yet at times also oh-so-challenging! What keeps me resilient, optimistic, and focused when life goes into overload is my gift of gratitude.

In good times, gratitude amplifies what is already good — like adding ice cream to an already-delicious apple pie. When times feel tough, paying attention to what is right helps me see the forest from the trees.

I'm grateful for so much....

For all the opportunities that allow me to use my authentic gifts and make a difference to others;

For my growing personal toolbox of gifts, strengths, and skills that continually expand my own capacity to work and live meaningfully and help others do the same;

For the enormous classroom called "life" that provides a bottomless supply of lessons, inspiration, and awakening.

Mostly, it's my gift of gratitude. It's one thing to have gifts in life; it's quite another to notice and appreciate them. I guess you can say that I am grateful for being grateful.

~ Eileen Chadnick

January 9

Grappling with Gratitude

"We often take for granted the very things that most deserve our gratitude."
~ Cynthia Ozick

I am grateful for my life, love, laughter, health, happiness, family, friends, faith, freedom, country, nature, etc. The list is long.

Today I am especially grateful for my customers, clients, and network.

For business owners, entrepreneurs, and sales professionals, maintaining client relationships that matter takes effort. We know that saying thank you is important. Our clients have many choices. We never want to take them for granted.

Showing gratitude and sincere appreciation is conveyed by what we do, say, or send. While it is important to vocalize gratitude, taking unexpected action makes a statement.

Here's a "Gratitude List" to spark ways of expressing appreciation:
1. Sharing your knowledge, research, resources, etc.
2. Being creative: sending a pizza, hiring a babysitter, showing up when it matters.
3. Delivering bagels to the office.
4. Introducing them to a contact.
5. Inviting them to an event.
6. Buying a subscription.
7. Making a donation.
8. Going to their children's school play.
9. Giving a hug.
10. Adding your own. Do it!

Our professional "family" shapes our livelihood.

Thank you to my customers, clients, and network.

~ Barb Girson

January 10

God, Grace, and Gratitude

I am grateful for the twelve-step program that gave me so much more than mere recovery from an eating disorder. I have:

1. Tools to embrace my strengths and fearlessly face my limitations.
2. The ability to see myself clearly and love all that I am.
3. The willingness to own my power without the need to defend, explain, or apologize.
4. A close walk with God, who accepts and loves me unconditionally.
5. Lifelong friendships with people I otherwise would never have met.
6. A foundation for service that continues to expand throughout my life.

From that foundation, I was able to risk and overcome these challenges:

I faced my childhood demons.
I extricated myself from an abusive marriage.
I re-entered the workplace and built a successful career.
I launched three children into college and productive adulthood.
I completed bachelor's and master's degrees after the age of 50.
I remarried and navigated the choppy waters of blended families.
I reinvented myself again in midlife to become an author and entrepreneur.

I love that that my Higher Power came to me in such a gentle, compassionate way and have committed my life to helping others find a God they can trust regardless of their denominational backgrounds.

~ Kim Halsey

January 11

I Want a Different Life!

"Do you want a different life? Then change your mind!" ~ Anonymous

Are you miserably unhappy, experiencing failing health, with a habit of constantly complaining? I was. Do you want to live a happy, fulfilling, and more confident life? Yes? Me, too!

What can you do to create that different, happier life? What did I do? I changed my mind.

How? I discovered the life-changing experience of gratitude! Who knew something so simple could have such an enormous power.

When asked "What are you most grateful for?" my response was "the ability to express gratitude." That simple little action transformed my life.

Now, I live a fulfilling life of happiness, my health has greatly improved, and rarely do I complain. Yes, there are up days and down days. I find gratitude and something to be grateful for in both.

Thanks to the ability to express gratitude, I have "changed my mind" and now live a vastly different life. And you can, too!

How easy can it be? Just fill in the blank. "I am grateful for _____."

Pick up a pen and express some gratitude!

~ Gwen L. Lepard

January 12

Gray

What am I grateful for?

Gray, as in the gray in my hair. Growing up poor gave me a strong desire to succeed, which is seen by some as a real asset. After all, I climbed up and out of poverty like a rocket, hitting and surpassing any goal ever set before me.

But the problem with rockets is they go so fast you can't see what you're passing by: soccer games, school plays, long talks about broken hearts, the pain and suffering of everyone around me and what they're facing. And not just my family, but strangers — I mean, where did they fit into my life?

Well, the fast times and black hair are coming to an end. At a time when jobs are scarce and things are hard, I decided to leave a high-six-figure corporate banking job to go make a difference. Everyone who knows me thinks I've lost it. But I disagree: I believe I finally found it.

It's not about money and success. It's about people; it's about relationships. Sure, people will remember the wealthy but more so the one who stopped to help them along their way. I want to be remembered for the latter.

~ Robert L. Day

January 13

To My Mom

The first thing I'm grateful for is that you love me. The fact that I know this makes you a great mom! That you devotedly cared for me and my brothers and sister makes you an awesome mom!

I am sure you had many dreams and goals that you gave up for us. That you put your needs aside so you could meet ours and didn't lose your mind, makes you a wonder mom! And then, of course more recently, there is you staying strong while our family struggled to survive through addiction.

During all this time, you managed to hold us together, while working and keeping a smile on your face. This just proves that you are one of the strongest, most awesome, and wonderful moms in the galaxy! I admire you hugely for everything you have done for me and our family, and I am truly grateful for your love every day.

Do not be surprised that, when I have a family of my own, your phone keeps ringing and it's me. I already know I am going to need a lot of advice from you, my magnificent mother!

~ Michelle E. Dupar

January 14

What Makes
My Life Complete

Living on a gorgeous river

Seeing Mt. Hood every day from my window

The way my partner says "Good morning, Sweetie!" when I wake up

My two dogs, who love me no matter how cranky I may be

A Sunday afternoon nap

A mother who is brave and strong, raising four children on her own with next to nothing

The freedom to work from home and run a business I am passionate about

The anticipation of being a new mother someday soon

Good friends who have known me for many years

A big belly laugh

Knowing that tomorrow is always a new day

~ Carey Powell

January 15

Gratitude: It's a Good Thing

I was devastated on the day my husband and best friend, Rory, passed away at the young age of 39. My little 3-year-old son, Ryan, and I were left to find our new life's path together as a family of two.

Eventually I had a revelation. Ultimately this was one of the most important and mindset-changing actions of my life, which was to practice the act of gratitude. Each morning before getting out of bed I would speak from my heart and recite my gratitude for all the people and things for which I was grateful. This daily ritual helped me focus on the blessings in life versus what I had lost. Thus began my process of healing and thriving again.

Today I am so grateful that I have been able to put the pieces of my life and work together in creative ways. My son is thriving; hearing his laughter is the best sound in the world! My work and business are meaningful; I have the opportunity to help others.

I am energized, healthy, and happy. I have found love again! It all began with becoming and being very grateful.

~ Colleen C. Phillips

January 16

On My Special Day

On my special day I thank God for:
Being alive and healthy.
The resources I have and use, making others happy.
The talents used to make money, and to enjoy life to the fullest.
The gifts of self-awareness, wisdom, and the power of my mind.
My inner power during the hard times.
Meeting the people, teaching me the life.
Moving to and living in Ireland.
All my achievements.
All the dreams that have become the reality.
The nature that I can enjoy and eternalize, filming or taking photos.
The pets visiting my house.

Gratitude to my heroes:
Parents for preparing me to the adult life
All my true friends, on-line and in the real world, for their support and advice
Joey Tempest for his wisdom and "The Final Countdown"
Europe, Beata Kozidrak, and Bajm for their brilliant music
Anthony Robbins, Napoleon Hill, Tadeusz Niwiński, Nathaniel Branden, Robert Allen, Stephen Covey, and Brian Tracy for self-help education
Wanda Loskot, Mirek Szmajda, Peter Majwski, Kamil Cebulski, and Tony Ennis for professional support
Robert Kiyosaki for financial education

All not mentioned here, yet contributing something to my life.

~ Victoria Herocten

January 17

There's Something About Kelsi

Parenting is one of those figure-it-out-as-you-go jobs. By the time you learn all the important skills, your cute little bundle has grown into an independent woman.

The hospital provided a beanie to keep your head warm, but they didn't give your mom a manual.

So I knew I would make mistakes along the way—hence the therapy fund.

Friends, family, even strangers knew early on there was something special about you.

But whatever that something is—seems impossible to describe.

It's true you're smart, compassionate, courageous, funny, unbiased, and beautiful… (I could go on—but I've got a word limit here.)

Some people call you an old soul.

Others say anything you touch turns to gold.

Whatever that something is, people just feel better when you're around.

I know I do.

Here's the bottom line, Monkeybutt—I don't know if I had anything to do with you growing into the amazing person you are—but I'd like to say thank you for making me look so damn good.

And thanks for providing me with so much love and laughter.

It's an absolute pleasure to be known as Kelsi's mom.

Happy 18th!

I love you!

G.U.Y.C.C.

~ Michelle Dimsey

January 18

So Many Things

So many things I am grateful for:

1. The first breath of each day
2. A quiet morning meditation
3. The luxury of staying under the covers for five more minutes
4. The view out my window
5. My happy son
6. A hot, lavender-scented bath
7. Comfortable clothes
8. The strength of my body
9. The healing of soup
10. Love and friendship
11. The smell of puppy breath
12. Fresh, cool air and the beauty of the planet
13. The ability to pay my bills
14. Seeing a moose eat in a lake while I was in a boat rowing
15. An amazing performance or piece of art
16. Hearing that song that makes me cry
17. Any act of kindness
18. A good cry
19. A good laugh
20. A challenge
21. Deep passion
22. My ability to connect with Spirit in service
23. The sun and the moon

Thank you, also, Dear God. In addition, please include every single little blessing that I forgot to be grateful for. I might as well cover all the bases!

~ Marsha Lee Bressack

January 19

A Life of "Aliveness" and Meaning

I am profoundly grateful to Marshall Rosenberg for developing the skills and consciousness of non-violent communication, or what I professionally call "Speaking Peace, Hearing Peace" (SHP). Below are some of the reasons why!

My life up until I discovered SHP was an experience of confusion and unhappiness. I needed a turnaround but didn't know how, regardless of all the workshops, books, searching, and money spent.

Since 2006, I have been supporting people in building the skills and consciousness of speaking, hearing, thinking, and acting from their deepest values. I am grateful for my clients' determination to work toward this new way of living, and watching it enrich their lives.

My clients report how powerful it is to have the support that they need to break through to having their dreams be reachable, tangible, and exciting experiences for them. I am so grateful. My life is so much richer for being able to contribute to them in this powerful way.

Both my clients and I now have experiences of lives filled with more "aliveness," meaning, and empowerment. Trusting ourselves and trusting life. A life filled with more peace. I am truly grateful for that!

What are you grateful for?

~ Rachel Monde

January 20

Grateful to Be an Aunt

I am grateful every day for the babies, children, and young adults in my life: my nieces and nephews. I'm also grateful to their parents for letting me be such a big part of their lives on a daily basis.

The first baby I lost was due on January 20th. My journey to motherhood has not gone as my husband and I planned—though it is still a work in progress—and we mark each of our due dates with a candle and a prayer. Some days it's hard not to focus on the empty nursery or conveying true happiness for a friend telling me she's expecting, but even on the hard days, I am thankful for my nieces and nephews. They fill my heart and home with love, they make me feel less empty inside, and they remind me that I do matter in the lives of many children, whether they are my children or not.

~ Jodi Brandon

January 21

Birthday Wishes

It's a Thursday morning in 1999, and I'm on my way to the hospital. Eric has decided he is ready to meet us. Once there things start moving really fast; I have never been so nervous. After some time the nurses agree it's time.

The doctor comes in, and after a brief examination hushed voices are passed among the staff. We are told we need an emergency procedure, as our baby is in distress. Quickly paperwork is signed, and we are off to the operating room.

He's here now but something is wrong. Why is he still blue? Why isn't he breathing? I silently pray, "Let him be okay. I'll do anything." I tell her he's fine, but I don't convince myself. After what seems like an eternity he takes his first struggled breath but is not out of the woods. Over the next week nothing in the world is as important as getting a chance to know my son. All the petty things in my life are washed away, and I am laid bare.

Today Eric turns 12 and is a happy, healthy boy. I have been grateful every day since then that I was given this gift of love wrapped up in an innocent child.

~ Joseph Garcia

January 22

Gratitude: A Lifetime Gift for You and Others

Gratitude is one of the most joyous and constant gifts we can give ourselves and others. And it doesn't require any special circumstances. And it's highly contagious.

You can have and express gratitude the whole time you're driving your car (in Los Angeles that's a lot of time!):

- For every green light, to speed you on your way

- For every red light and stop sign, to remind you to slow down, take a deep breath, and just relax and be present

- And in between, for even having a car to drive

After a while, you're having so much joy, you're in gratitude for having gratitude!

A meditation: Watch your breathing and notice the life-giving air moving through your body. Get in touch with how the air nourishes you, how vital your breath is to your very life, and how it connects you to all life forms everywhere.

In Higher Consciousness gratitude is a state of being – a place to come from and to bring to everything you think, say, do—and are. Like love and joy, it doesn't depend on your relationships or situations. It simply is.

You can be in gratitude always.

~ Joyce Kenyon

January 23

Earth Angels

What have I got to be grateful for? Let me tell you, life has not always been kind to me. Yet, there was always a reason to smile. You see, growing up, there was one I could always count on. He would listen patiently to my concerns. When I was ill, he would settle down on my tummy and purr. No matter what was going on in my world, he was there for me.

Sadness ensued after he passed, but I was blessed by another loving being. She brought joy and laughter into a childless marriage. Her cooing sounded like puppy growls; shrieks of delight were excited barks. When she grew up, she gifted us with a girl who came out of the chute yipping and yowling—full of energy and spirit.

Suddenly, only we three girls remained. Then there were two. Then there was one. Now I have a new one who purrs on my tummy.

There is a special bond between man and beast that's been present since time began. I do so miss the ones who left such deep impressions on my heart. Yes, I am very grateful for my earth angels.

~ Monika Huppertz

January 24

Reflections of
a Grateful Heart

I am grateful for :
The sun that gives daylight while on this journey called life.
The darkness that signals "it's time to sleep and rest."
The wind that causes the leaves to dance on an autumn day.
The flowers that offer their beauty and splendor to the world.
The trees that bear their fruit in "due season" for all to enjoy.

I am grateful for having the use of:

My eyes, to see the deer that graze in my backyard,
the rabbits that hop along "oh so carefree," and
the squirrels that run playfully to and from.
My ears to hear the birds that "tweet tweet" sweet melodies.
My arms to hug and embrace.
My hands to gather and then release the blessings.

I am grateful for family and friends that:

Stand with me through "the thick and the thin."
Provide a shoulder to cry on.
Pray for me in times of adversity.
Support me in my vision and dreams.
Love me unconditionally.

For all these things and so much more, I am really grateful for.

~ LaVerne M. Byrd

January 25

Gratitude Is Attitude

I am absolutely grateful for the life I give myself and for the choices I have made. If I fail, it is my failure to learn from. For that I am blessed. Using my knowledge and my skills daily to build momentum in my life, I feel grateful for having the courage to take on new physical challenges. A 50K, a 100K, whatever — I love tackling new challenges! This is my journey; this is my life!

Simple things I am thankful for (in no particular order):

My wife

My view of Mt. Hood

The taste of fall

Walking to our Saturday farmers' market

A good book

Great conversation

My family

My friends

Trail running

Walking barefoot in the sand

Reflections off of the river

"Gratitude is the best attitude."

~ Author Unknown

~ *Michele Flamer*

January 26

God Works Within Me, Beside Me, Through Me

My mother suffered in a black cycle of negativity: chronic pain and illness, emotional scars, and self-defeating religious beliefs that left her hopeless and powerless. Day after day, year after year, she would watch a televangelist handing out miracles to his viewers by name, but never to her. I endured her threats of suicide and fits of rage as she cursed God, yet insisted I be a "good Christian."

Determined not to repeat her patterns in my own life, I made the difficult decision to forgive her, but nonetheless break ties with her, at age 22.

Over the past ten years, brilliant spiritual teachers have helped me heal emotionally and spiritually. I am grateful that I now know I'm only one thought away from his miraculous healing, creative power, and divine wisdom. He works within me, beside me, and through me to help me glow with the white light of his presence, peace, and purpose. I no longer confuse religion with spirituality, nor people with God. My confident meditations now replace insecure prayers.

Today I empower others as a spiritual author, speaker, and counselor, spreading the good news of self-healing, self-love, and self-truth. Celebrate with me!

~ KD Fox

January 27
Gratitude:
Life's Most Rewarding Lesson!

I am grateful for:

My parents instilling confidence in me, and teaching me to believe in myself and to never give up!

My wife, best friend, and lifetime partner, Kelly. Thank you for loving me, for believing in me, and for being by my side!

The courage to live my dream, which is to motivate, teach, inspire, and make a difference in people's fitness lifestyles!

Surrounding myself with successful people who have been there and done that — people who like teaching me by sharing their journey and for gratefully accepting their help!

All of my clients throughout the years. Thanks for teaching me about life!

Enjoying the expansion of self and wanting to personally grow and search for any way possible to become the best that I can be!

Completing a marathon. It has changed my life forever!

Laughing and crying and experiencing all kinds of emotions and feelings, for this is our true guide to happiness!

Experiencing the unconditional love of every dog that has been in my life. What a wonderful gift! We love you, "Bay-Bay Girl!"

Enjoying the journey of life by actually stopping and smelling the roses!

~ Jeffrey W. Brandes

January 28

Awareness Is Key

I am grateful for the awareness of my ability to affect my life and my environment by how I view, think, feel, and act in relation to them.

In this world everything is connected energetically, each to all other; my very presence makes a difference. Because I have the power to create good or ill with my intentions, thoughts, words, and deeds, I have a responsibility to be conscious and consistent with them, clarifying what is desired.

In the past, my choices shifted when I saw my life and health worsen by repeated thoughts of "I'm sick and tired of __" Even my anger or grudges affect the energy space around me.

Now I revise my language and images using positive and open-ended ideas. I visualize an optimal setting with me in it, having the greatest experience I can imagine. With friends, I am creating miracles of healing, smooth flow for securing better jobs, buying cars, finding items, and changing hearts. My life and surroundings are far richer as I intentionally create a more preferred outcome for myself, others, and our world.

Being aware of my power to affect things is awesome; I appreciate this gift.

~ Carol B. Gailey

January 29

My Alive Day

I am grateful for my Alive Day: January 29, 2004. This is different from a birthday; it's the day that my life was spared and I was given another chance.

It's the night when insurgents sent three rockets blindly into Baghdad International Airport. No one, not the insurgents or the frightened soldiers scurrying for cover, knew where they would end up. By the grace of God, these three nasty projectiles missed my eight-story building by one hundred yards, while tearing huge holes in the parking lot directly in front of it. Not ten minutes before, I had debated whether or not to go running around the parking lot that night. Something or someone made me choose not to, and this is why I am able to sit here and type this.

To say I have a guardian angel watching over me is an understatement.

It was a chance to return home and see my two young sons again. It was a chance to continue on with my life, as so many others will never have the chance to do. It was a chance to chase my dreams and make something of myself.

I will never take this life for granted.

~ John Ready

January 30

Inspired by Their Passion

I'm grateful for nurses. Not for the reasons you may think. Yes, nurses are important to our healing, and they step up to do the things that most won't—and I love them for it. My recovery from appendix surgery could not have happened without them.

After coaching thousands of nurses over the years to help them obtain their nursing degrees online, I realize that I love them most for their passion.

It has been my privilege to get to know so many nurses as they go for their associate's or bachelor's degree of nursing through my online methods. The light in their eyes when they talk about learning and doing more, and the concern you can feel as they discuss their patients — they're very inspiring.

Nurses have incredible dedication as they juggle their families, crazy work schedules, and the educational and paperwork demands placed on them. Many make huge sacrifices to be there for you when you are ill, or to help your parents in a nursing facility, or to take your pulse at the doctor's office.

It takes great devotion for nurses to remain in the profession, and they constantly remind me to be passionate and giving in my own life!

~ Joy Porter

January 31

The Blessings of Decisions

I am grateful God gave me the ability to make decisions.

The decision to have my children filled my life with unconditional love. The decision to take responsibility for my own life changed my life forever. The decision to always make positive choices in my life has brought me happiness and joy. The decision to learn how to dance and then compete in country western dance competitions gave me self-esteem and pride.

The decision to join Mary Kay and then become a sales director taught me that I am a powerful leader and brought me lifelong friendships. The decision to get remarried gave me a loving man to spend the rest of my life with. The decision to take a social media course in the summer of 2009 started a whole new life for me and a new business.

The decision to invest in my business by taking classes and joining a mastermind group helped me build my business at a much more rapid rate. The decision to write my book brought me recognition.

Although all the decisions in my life have not been perfect, I am excited to have the ability to make decisions. And remember: Indecision is a decision, too!

~ Michele A. Scism

February

"Dare to deeply desire love.
Align yourself with God and return to the
practice of loving, again and again. You will
find that love will call you to reach out and
help people in need. Your whole life, and the
lives of others, will change. You, will, in the
words of Henry David Thoreau, '...live with
license of a higher order of beings.'"

~ Rev. Mary Manin Morrissey

February 1

Write On!

Every day I am grateful for many things, but among them, what stands out: I am grateful for my ability to write, to publish what I write, and to get feedback from my readers that what I have written has been meaningful to them.

Writing is not hard for me: My poems write themselves; my books flow easily, or, as someone said, "God writes all the books."

What I am especially grateful for is that I have recently gained confidence in my ability to get published what I write, by one means or another: traditional publishing or self-publishing.

I have been helped enormously by writing teachers, books coaches, and editors, through their encouragement and their examples. And success breeds success.

One teacher, way back in college, told me, "Eric, you are a poet." An editor told me I wrote well and clearly. A reader told me what I had written helped her enormously. What could be better?

Every day I pen a few more pages. I now know I can write a chapter a day, a book in a month (a new definition of a book-of the-month club), and ten books in ten years. I am grateful for this.

~ Dr. Eric Pfeiffer

February 2

Grateful for Groundhog Day

When you're a farmer, Groundhog Day is your favorite holiday.

At least that's how my dad, Walter M. Kozik, saw it. "If you had at least half your feed left now, then you knew you'd make it through the winter," he told me.

Even after that snowy January night when our barn fell in and put Dad out of the farming business for good, the day remained his holiday. When my sister and I were in elementary school we showered him with homemade cards made out of blue construction paper and our rendition of a brown groundhog peeking out of its hole. Later Hallmark got on board with fancy cartoon character depictions of this harbinger of spring.

Always an optimist, and whether or not Punxatawny Phil saw his shadow on February 2nd, Dad would say, "Spring's around the corner, 'DonnaTeresa.' (His universal name for my sister and me.)"

Long before the movie led to Groundhog Day being synonymous with Bill Murray, déjà vu, and repetitive behavior, it meant something special at our house.

And I celebrate Groundhog Day now, grateful for the optimism Dad passed on to me that "spring is always around the corner."

~ Donna Kozik

February 3

A Cup of Tea

Today I am grateful for my morning cup of tea. The naturally sweet flavor of the green leaves floats over my tongue, awakening my taste buds and flooding my body with its comforting presence. One hand carefully holds the mug handle, while the other wraps itself around the outside of the cup, allowing the warmth to seep deep into my flesh.

Sometimes I wander down the trail of gratitude, thanking those who participated in making my cup of tea possible. I might start with the people who planted, harvested, dried, and rolled the tea, then move on to the packagers and transportation that brought the tea to my location. From there I might think about the source of the water I make my tea with or the hydro that helped me heat it. I might think about my teapot or my favorite mug that I drink from, giving silent thoughts of gratitude to all who had a hand in its creation.

Other times, I just drink my tea and enjoy the sensations that flow through me.

~ Debbie Pokornik

February 4

In Honor of World Cancer Day: February 4

When life is good to us, it is easy to take all the good things for granted. Not everyone is so fortunate. All around us there are people putting up a valiant fight. Among them are those who bravely fight cancer. They fight for each day they can have with dignity, resiliency, and humor. I am thankful for these brave ones and all they endure, because they inspire me and those around them. They remind me that I am so fortunate. For that, I am grateful.

Some survive their long battles. I am so grateful. Others may prepare to leave this world. With profound sadness, I give thanks for the time I had with them. Both leave their mark on us. They inspire us with the enduring strength of their spirit at life's most difficult moments. I am grateful. They touch my heart. I am grateful. They are brave; I am not. I am grateful for their courage. I am grateful for each moment they share with me. I am grateful for the conversations and the silence. I am grateful to be in the presence of those who have learned what's most important in life.

~ *Susan Brownell*

February 5

Gratitude Can Grow from Loss

We have been through years of fertility treatments that have given us two pregnancies that both ended in miscarriage. It's been the highest highs, and the lowest lows. This experience changed how I think, what I believe, and, more importantly, how I love.

The second pregnancy lasted into the fourteenth week. Every day I fell more in love with our baby. Once we knew there were problems with the baby, that love grew with the hope that our baby would be okay. Before this pregnancy I would try to hold back my emotions to save myself some pain during a difficult time, but the opposite happened with this pregnancy. Our little one was struggling and we were scared, but there was a bond between us that no one could break.

When our doctor couldn't find the heartbeat, I felt broken. My body, mind, and spirit hurt. As time passed the pain eased and I healed. I grew stronger, loved more, and learned to appreciate the little things in life. That loss gave me a new outlook on life. I am grateful that our baby taught me more about life and love than I ever knew before.

~ Amy B. Windham

February 6

Chinese Good Fortune

I was the director of the Program to China at a university in Connecticut ten years ago. One day the leader in China who sent students to our university sent a special messenger to tell me his son was coming to America—and he wanted him to live with me and my family.

I thought that if I refused the leader from China would stop sending us students, so I said yes. It has proven to be one of the best decisions I have ever made.

Every year we take in new students, and every year I feel my family grows.

This year I have three students and wish I had space for more. One of the girls calls me "hommom," her rendition of "home stay" combined with "mom." We laugh together. We cry together. We celebrate all of the victories in their lives as they learn to bridge the gap between their Chinese life and life in America.

Although they eventually leave my home, they never leave my life. Since I believe peace happens one person at a time, I feel I am having a positive impact on the next generation of leaders in China. It has been an experience for which I am truly grateful.

~ Angela I. Schutz

February 7

Turning Trauma to Triumph

I'm eternally grateful for:

- the privilege of being born into a family with a mix of dysfunctional and functional attributes.

- the legacy of generational assets and liabilities. The assets have given me good values, education, and an attitude of contributing to community. The liabilities have pushed me to search and to understand how trauma and distress help to build people into the richness of their full potential.

- living beside a river, next to and opposite state forest, walking in which provides daily inspiration for my life and work.

- the privilege of having a husband and two wonderful daughters who have developed into inspiring, lovable, strong adults, striving for authenticity. All of them have been my teachers, sometimes through considerable challenges.

- the opportunity to live according to my values, and for friends and associates who share them.

- the young people who lost their lives through suicide, providing the impetus for me to develop and run a trauma recovery program with my husband. Leading from Within (Greater Shepparton) has created opportunities for hundreds of others to recover from trauma and give back to community. The dream of creating growth from trauma is emerging from their sacrifice.

~ Jennifer O'Connell

February 8

Gratitude: It's a Choice We Make

I am grateful for the love and support of family and friends. I am always amazed at their constant encouragement, which seems to flow forth unconditionally, fueling my passion and purpose.

It is often hard to focus on what's right in our lives when we hear so much negative chatter on the TV and Internet, but the one thing I know to be true is that we all have choices to make in our lives, and I am grateful for the ability and the freedom to make those choices.

I choose to be grateful for the gifts and talents God has given me to make a difference in the lives of others. I choose to be grateful for life's ups and downs, as I know they are part of my journey. I choose to embrace adversity, as I know opportunity will soon follow. I choose to see the good in others even when they may not be at their best.

Today I share with you what I am grateful for: to inspire, empower, and encourage you to be all you were created to be! Today is your day. It's time to embrace life, and choose to let your light shine!

~ Dana Dunn

February 9

The Crazy Life

When I first met Kathy Bowes, I thought she was crazy. She told me that, in her experience and self-education, sugar and wheat could be addictive. She recommended I stop eating it. Period.

No more fettuccini alfredo. No more pizza. No more ice cream, candy bars, or sugared soft drinks.

No more.

"You don't have to do it forever," she said. "Just try it for twenty-eight days. Then, if you want, you can go back."

So I did. On February 9, 2004, I went "sugar and wheat free." Seven years later, I'm happy to still be living a life of "no more."

No more food cravings. No more foggy thinking. No more mood swings. No more!

And, yes, it's led to much, much more, too.

More focus. More calmness. More laughter. More happiness. And more personal success than I ever dreamed possible.

I am grateful for the prayer I spoke aloud that led me to Kathy and her program. And I am grateful I took a chance of trying "the crazy life" for myself.

~ Donna Kozik

February 10

Feeding the Heart

I am extremely grateful not only to family, friends, clients, and people close to me, but also to others who may never know how they touched my life.

Years ago, as a young model/spokesperson, I was hospitalized for exhaustion. An elderly man across the hall was having trouble eating his bowl of mushy food. I volunteered to help him. He ate slowly and told me of a life well-lived — a life of helping and meaning. He was so frail, yet so strong. He touched my heart. I wanted to help others, too. I went back to graduate school to become a psychologist/success coach so I could help people make positive changes in their lives.

Through sharing his wisdom with me, that elderly man in the hospital changed my life and the lives of many others. How ironic — all the time I thought I was feeding him, but actually he was feeding me.

I am grateful that we are all connected in this universe and we help each other. Little do we know how far-reaching our words and actions may go.

With deep appreciation and gratitude for all who have fed my heart.

~ Lynn Workman Nodland

February 11

The Women Who Walked Before Me

I am grateful for the women who paved the way for me. Each connected to my soul and contributed a piece of her wit and wisdom.

I speak of my grandmothers and their sisters. Known individually as Alma, Louise, Madge, Aylene, Geraldine, and Hazel, they were all women of great strength and grace. They shared Southern roots and a unique combination of Dixie charm with unabashed truth-telling. All born in the second decade of the 20th century, they lived full lives, even though three left our world too early and three have continued past the turn of the century.

Provoked by the right things, they stood for what really mattered in a changing world and cared for others as only Southern women can. Baking pies for new neighbors, hemming dresses for friends, or needle-pointing pillows for church bazaars, they harnessed their gifts to benefit those around them. Their actions spoke louder than their words, and I do my best to follow their lead.

I'm grateful for their gifts of strong roots and blazed trails. When my future granddaughters reflect on what they are grateful for in their lives, I hope they think the same of me.

~ Julie Edge

February 12

Twists, Turns, and Corkscrews

Today I am grateful for the twists and turns that life brings to me. It's like a roller coaster where being at the crest is breathtaking; my heart skips a beat when I'm on the brink; the speed makes me dizzy; and the free fall makes my stomach drop. In just two minutes I go from being terrified to exhilarated. I un-strap myself and step out of the car, feeling triumphant and wanting more.

The thrill of those rides makes me thankful for all that life has in store for me. Every high and low has brought me to the sweetness of today. I've walked in breathtaking beauty; my heart has been broken and on the brink; there's been dizzying laughter and joy; loss and grief have made my stomach drop. I've grown into myself while riding through every crazy corkscrew along life's track.

Through the years I've experienced terror and exhilaration, along with every emotion in between. Those memories bring deep appreciation for the life that's mine and mine alone. It takes courage to ride this ride of life, and today the thrill of all my life experiences leaves me feeling grateful, triumphant, and wanting more!

~ JJ Frederickson

February 13

Appreciating Our Radiance

"As my outside ages, my intention is to become stunningly beautiful on the inside."

~ Tamara Gerlach

I am grateful for any moment that I spend taking care of myself. So much of our lives is filled with taking care of everyone and everything else, that sometimes we forget to take care of ourselves and feel disconnected.

Taking time to nurture myself became vital to my happiness when I discovered that, rather than feeling selfish, it actually feels awesome. I create more energy and am able to serve others at a much higher level.

The gratitude that I feel when I care for my whole self creates the radiance that I generously share through living a passionate, inspired life. It brings with it a sense of ease, harmony, and balance. I feel bigger than my problems and ready to shake my world into greatness.

I am grateful that I get to rediscover my radiance every day, because, as I cultivate my connection, I am capable of so much more.

Whether it is a few minutes of mediation, taking a yoga class, eating a healthy meal, or setting a boundary around what I can realistically do, these times of self-care are cherished.

~ Tamara Gerlach

February 14

An Unexpected Soul Mate

In 1996, I unexpectedly left my friend Tammy's house with an eight-year-old cat named Princess. As Tammy put it, Princess claimed me as her "person" as soon as I walked in the door. Princess Little (she was so special I needed to give her a surname) was a "people cat," and I used to think when Brad and I were dating that he came over to see her as much as to see me.

She followed me everywhere, slept with me every night, and was simply a joy. Being part Siamese, she did a lot of talking. Indeed, she was never shy about letting all the other cats (and us) know she was in charge. She also snorted due to chronic sinus problems, and we had special songs about her that she liked us to sing to her. But mostly, she did a lot of purring.

Princess Little died in January 2007, and I miss her fiercely. I am so lucky she was part of my world. I have not been in touch with Tammy in years. Wherever you are, Tammy, I am grateful to you for giving me the gift of Princess Little. She was my heart.

~ *Teresa A. Castleman*

February 15

Through Every Tear There Shines a Rainbow

I am truly grateful for so many things in my wonderful life, but since today is the day that my mother passed over, St. Valentine's night, 1994, I'm choosing to reflect on the many gifts that she left me and our family that continue to this day.

During her short illness (she had pancreatic cancer), I learned so much more about beauty, love, and laughter than ever before.

Her final journey — her journey into her dying — changed the way I live my life and the whole way I practice my medicine. We laughed, we sang, we prayed together, and I watched as she grew more whole, more Jane, and more fully into life. I watched as deep, old, frozen lifelong wounds melted away.

By night I would cry with unbearable anguish, sobbing from deep within my soul, and by day I could be more open and present with her. When she was complete she left, with a smile on her face.

When I let go of trying to save her, the most incredible, loving, fun, gifted support team surrounded her and helped her heal. Beauty heals, love heals, and laughter heals. Gratitude!

~ Dr. Susan Lange

February 16

Message for Me

I am grateful for the day I opened my mail and read a newsletter from the Humane Farming Association. The articles and pictures of animals on factory farms were devastating to me. I stood in my kitchen and cried. That day changed my life.

I told my husband I was now a vegetarian, and he could join me if he wanted to. He did! Joyfully, we began to explore the wonderful world of meatless eating. I started researching the subject of vegetarianism.

As a result of my research, I discovered the health and weight-loss benefits of eating a plant-based diet. When my husband went to the doctor, his blood pressure, cholesterol, and triglycerides were all normal for the first time ever! We both lost weight and started feeling better. I was so inspired I wrote a mini-book on the subject and got it published.

Although the newsletter I read that day was sad and distressing, I am truly grateful for its message. It has given me a mission in life: to educate others on the health, environmental, and humane benefits of eating a vegetarian diet!

~ Tricia Ebert

February 17

No Matter What

Have you ever had someone in your life who stood by you no matter what?

There when you failed. There when you made bad relationship choices. There even when you were wrong — and took up for you anyway. My list is long, and she continued to be by my side.

As long as I live, I can never thank my mom enough for giving me her unconditional love — no matter what. I love you, Mom.

~ *Tamara Brimm Miranda*

February 18

When Life Is Filled

When life is filled with too many demands to accomplish — I am grateful for simplicity, calm, and an hour with nothing to do.

When life is filled with those who distrust, lie, and deceive — I am grateful for authenticity, integrity, honesty, and generosity.

When life is filled with people who care only about looking good or being right — I am grateful for those who know how to just be themselves, show spontaneity, admit their mistakes, and practice living in the moment.

When others have misjudged or wronged me — I am grateful for John, Catherine, and all my family and friends who let me laugh out loud and sing my favorite tunes off-key.

When my body has an infection or a disease, breaks down, or has an ailment — I am grateful for scientific break-throughs and the miracle of the body's ability to heal.

When a day is filled with fear, doubt, impossibilities, and hopelessness — I am grateful that I have the power to choose how and what I think and feel, and that I possess the tools to make it so.

I am grateful the sun will rise tomorrow.

Most of all, I am grateful for God's many blessings.

~ Judy A. LaCroix

February 19

Simple Gratitude

As I think about what I'm most thankful for, the five senses come to mind.

The gift of sight: seeing the faces of my precious babies for the first time, catching a glimpse of a colorful rainbow, watching a sunset as it glistens over the water, a crystal blue sky as far as the eye can see.

The gift of smell: warm baked apple pie, waking up to fresh-brewed coffee, burning an aromatic candle, a sweet fragrant perfume.

The gift of hearing: listening to my favorite song on the radio, the sound of rain on the rooftop, the blissful laughter of my children, the purr of my cat.

The gift of taste: eating a hot meal on a cold day, a glass of red wine at dinner, drinking clean water.

The gift of touch: embracing my loved ones, a relaxing shower, my cozy robe and PJs, the bright sun on my face, a brisk walk in the cool air.

I am truly grateful for the ability to see, smell, hear, taste, and touch.

Life offers an abundance of small blessings each day, and for me, the simple things are without a doubt the most meaningful!

~ Michelle Heinselman

February 20

"Wonder Who Lives Here?"

Traveling through West Texas to our sheep ranch, we turn onto dirt road.

When we bump across our cattle guard my husband asks, "Wonder who lives here?"

I answer, "What a beautiful place. They are so blessed to live here."

Husband replies, "They should be happy as kings."

I answer, "I think they are."

When I see the mountains silhouetted against the sunset I am filled with gratitude for our parents and grandparents, who made choices allowing us to live in this wonderful place.

~ Margaret G. Holmes

February 21

This Moment

I am grateful for this moment. As I breathe into it, I get nourishment from it. I know that this moment is all I have, and in that I am safe and loved, and all things are possible.

A few years ago I trembled as I looked up at the clock from the gurney I was on. The future was my only concern. Then I heard a sound that was beyond the sounds of nurses, doctors, and machines beginning their process to help me: I was hearing people who weren't in the room. No drugs had been administered yet, so I knew that wasn't a factor. Listening carefully, I realized that I was hearing my loved ones praying for me. I catapulted out of the future and plummeted into the present. I felt love washing over me and entering my body. I had always known that I was loved, but I had never felt it before. In that moment there were no more questions to be answered and no more problems to be solved. Both living and dying were okay with me. I let go.

Miraculously I am here now, sharing this moment with you.

I am grateful for this moment.

~ Carol Lynn Fletcher

February 22

For Colin, Claire, and Laura

My mentor, Jack Canfield, says gratitude is a joyful and selfless expression of thankfulness from within. I am deeply thankful for my three wonderful children. I have a sincere heartfelt love, appreciation, and gratitude for who they really are.

As each of them attained the age of 3 years, it seemed clear to me how each would progress on their journeys throughout life. My son has always had a knack for thinking about exactly what is needed and wanted. Colin Peter thinks his way through life. Now he thinks about research to provide businesses with products. My eldest daughter has always worked diligently, whatever the task. Claire Louise works her way through life. Now she works to improve the way businesses evolve. My youngest child has always been photogenic. Laura Catherine is the one with flair. She is improving the way businesses present themselves to the world.

There is no finer legacy than to have made a positive and lasting difference in the world. I get to watch it being done before my thankful eyes by three magnificent souls. Thank you, Colin Peter, Claire Louise, and Laura Catherine, for the positive and lasting differences that you make in the world.

~ Ron J. West

February 23

Life Changing

I am grateful for my life, my family, friends, and this country we live in.

My life turned upside down overnight in 2008. Our single-parent daughter serving in the United States Air Force deployed to Afghanistan, and my husband and I became the guardians to her two school-age children. My husband and I had been working empty nesters for the previous thirteen years.

I did not know it then, but my entire life and career would change when our daughter returned from her tour of duty. When my daughter deployed, I searched for information to better understand my mixed feelings, new responsibilities, how to cope with deployment, military procedures, dealing with raising children today versus thirty years ago. When my daughter returned, I was unprepared of the changes in my daughter and how to reconnect her to her family.

I wrote a personal story of what I went through. I published it and shared it with others. The reception has been positive, and I feel I'm on my way to a whole new world of writing and speaking.

I am so grateful my daughter's career changed my life.

~ Debbie Nichols

February 24

Savor the Sweetness of Everyday Life

Love, as softly as a sigh,
infuses life with such sweetness
that every moment is a blessing.

I am profoundly grateful for the "four Cs," each an essential ingredient that adds sweetness to my life on a daily basis:

The aliveness of **curiosity**: diving into the mystery of a new relationship, relishing the nervous excitement of doing something that stretches and grows me, unraveling the puzzle of what makes a successful blog, soufflé, marriage

The adventure of **creativity**: feeling the fire of inspiration flow through me, exploring the wonder of words, filling a blank canvas with color and life, adding new ingredients to a family recipe

The joy of **celebration**: honoring every small step forward, valuing (and experiencing the thrill of) my clients' accomplishments as deeply as my own, appreciating precious time spent with friends

The deliciousness of **chocolate** (and other favorite foods): savoring the last luscious spoonful of a creamy chocolate mousse, reaching for the warm comfort of a crisp, tasty tuna melt on a cold winter's day, surprising people I love with their favorite dessert to say "I'm thinking of you"

All are aspects of love — of life's infinite bounty and potential. Embrace them. Embody them. Enjoy them.

~ Julie Isaac

February 25

Lakeside Learnings

When I was growing up, our family vacations were week-long trips to the lake. It was cooking over the campfire. It was bathing in a clear cove with Ivory soap (because it floated). It's easy to see thirty years later how those vacations shaped me.

In the 1970s, there wasn't much overseas travel in my midwest life. Today, my family doesn't think twice about our world being limited by the boundaries of the United States. My husband seems to collect passport stamps in his job. My 11-year-old daughter is traveling to Europe with a student travel group. We have truly become a global society, and I see that every day.

Yet, each summer, we take a week off and travel to the lake as one of our summer vacations. It brings all of us back to what matters the most in our lives, to what we are grateful for. It reminds us that, even as we become global citizens and travelers, we are also local citizens. I am grateful that the sense of connecting with family and nature was settled within me so young—and grateful that we are able to give that same gift to our kids.

~ Jennifer Peek

February 26

That Magic Moment

We met on February 26, 1987, when she walked into the "How to Flirt" class (seriously!). I later found out she had endured three postponements of the class to end up there that night, so some mysterious forces were at work.

Something made us sit side-by-side, to chat, to flirt. Whatever it was that made our two lives intersect at that moment changed everything for me.

And now, not only am I grateful for the circumstances, but also for the outcome. A life together with my Contessa, il mio amore, Luisa.

I am grateful for those moments when life-changing blessings come about. Call them fate, coincidences, serendipity, destiny, magic — you don't even recognize how big they are at the moment they occur. It's in looking back that the wondrous power becomes evident.

I am grateful.

~ John Rasiej

February 27

Gratitude: The Great Gift of Transformation from the Creator

In my first career in the fashion industry of New York City, I remember expressing gratitude for the pleasures and satisfaction of that exciting life.

But unexpectedly, I began to experience some deep crises that started me on a journey to look for new meaning in my life.

I can now express great gratitude for the "gift" of those crises, because they took me on a quest that brought me to the Sukyo Mahikari Centers for Spiritual Development. Their practice of offering light energy to awaken the radiant soul and the practice of attitude change allowed me to learn new, profound answers to the meaning of life. The greatest gift was to experience the true existence of the Creator and the power of Gratitude.

GRATITUDE has:

- Awakened me again to the inspiration of my childhood faith of Judiaism and the altruistic love of my family.
- Created profound beauty in my relationships with others.
- Taught me how to transform my anger into open communication and respect.
- Helped me to forgive myself for my perceived mistakes and build hope for the future by giving thanks for even my smallest successes.

~ Louise Ann Cohen

February 28

Gratitude: Celebrate the Gifts

As a nurturer, caregiver, friend, and curious seeker of science, spirituality, and the meaning of life, I am grateful for the following:

- To be able to use my gifts as a trusted healthcare provider. Every day I see people's lives transformed in both simple and dramatic ways. I am grateful that some good came through me and that people trusted me with their lives.

- Nature teaches that change is evolutionary, and transitions prepare us for the next season. Blossoms spring forth from what appears to be desolate. Nothing lasts forever, and something better is ahead when you expect good things.

- Support always comes when you need it and ask for it. It does not necessarily come from whom you gave it; it can come from a different and unexpected source.

Whatever you give comes back to you multiplied, and I am appreciative of those who appreciate me for who I am, not what I do, who love unconditionally, and who smile even when it's hard. The effort and energy of faith and trust in the goodness of life attract more good, and for that I am grateful.

Look for the good and you will find it.

~ Lorraine Maita, MD

February 29

An Extra Day

What will you do with your extra day today?
Call someone and express your love?
Clean that clutter drawer?
Finish reading that good book?
Start writing another good book?

Take yourself out to lunch?
Blow dust off a "to-do?"
Think of something new to do?

What will you do with this extra day?

~ Anonymous

March

"I've learned the hard way that some poems don't rhyme, and some stories don't have a clear beginning, middle, and end.
Life is about not knowing, having to change, taking the moment and making the best of it, without knowing what's going to happen next."

~ Gilda Radner

Fresh Starts and Connections

For yesterday is but a dream,
And tomorrow is only a vision,
But Today, well lived,
Makes every Yesterday a Dream of Happiness
And every Tomorrow a Vision of Hope

~ ancient Sanskrit writings

I am so thankful for fresh starts. Each year, each month, each day, and each moment are new God-given opportunities to make a connection and make a difference.

My Gratitude Pledge for Today:

- In gratitude for my spouse, I will give him an extra hug and pay attention whenever he speaks to me.

- In gratitude for my children, I will write them a note or send an e-mail.

- In gratitude for my parents, I will give them a call.

- In gratitude for my home, I will make a donation to the local homeless shelter.

- In gratitude for my health, I will make healthy eating choices and exercise.

- In gratitude for my life, I will breathe deeply, observe keenly, and pay attention to the blessings all around me.

Like love, gratitude is one of those rare things that multiply by giving it away. And for that, too, I am eternally grateful.

~ *Elizabeth Herbert Cottrell*

March 2

Uniqueness

As a child growing up, I was taught that I was to be seen and not heard; therefore, I listened. It was easy for me to listen. I had inherited huge ears — at least they certainly looked huge on my tiny, skinny body. Ears, like fingerprints, are unique to every person. I could not hide them under my fine hair. They always seemed to be poking through as a constant reminder that I was to listen.

I was drawn to the unconditional love of animals. It didn't matter to them what I looked like. I could talk to them, and they would listen. We bonded with love and respect for each other. They were my mirror and reflected back God's love for us all.

Through living in the moment with animals, I have learned to love and have compassion for other people as I listened to their life stories. God has also spoken, and I have heard Him in my heart tell me to act upon what I hear, so that He can be glorified. I am grateful for these unique ears, for it is through them that I have listened, acted, and received so many blessings.

~ Amelia Hartfelder-Johnson

You Can Do It!

Our children and our grandchildren never cease to amaze me.

A few months ago we had our then-4-year-old grandson visiting us, and I was having a tooth problem. Attached to my side like Velcro, he followed me to the bathroom, where I went to apply some medicine. I would have preferred to be alone, as I knew it was going to hurt and I did not want him to worry about me.

This scene is especially poignant because this darling little boy was born with physical limitations. He has had more surgeries in his four years than many of us have in an entire lifetime (with more to come). He knows about pain and having to do tough things to heal. He knows that encouragement augments bravery.

So there he stood at the sink, bent over with his little hands resting on his knees while looking up with his big, brown eyes saying, "You can do it, Gramma! You can do it!" And I did. Somehow it was a lot easier to be brave with him there.

I am also grateful for the mirror they hold up to us, especially when it reflects the good they absorb!

~ Margie Cole

March 4

My Heart Lifted

During the long, cold, dreary winter, I'd fallen into one of my deep funks. Most everything seemed dull and gray. I felt as though I was slogging through my life, rather than living it.

And then, one early March morning, I glanced out the kitchen window into the cheerless fog and saw the slender stalk: tall, straight, and elegant, with a tiny sliver of hope and joy peeking through! The daffodils were close to blooming! The tiny glimpse of yellow lifted my heart like a bird taking flight. Spring was near!

I am ever grateful for the color yellow that lifts my spirit — and for daffodils, those most amazing gifts of the Creator that remind me to stand tall and straight, with elegance, dignity, and unique beauty.

~ Kamala Murphey

March 5

Life Lessons from My Little Ones

I am completely grateful for the gift of seeing the world through the eyes of my children, who open me up to so much understanding....

Waiting, two girls in the back seat of my car, eyes squeezed shut, one curious, the other patronizing, listened carefully as I painted for them a challenge.

"Imagine you are in a small white room with no windows, no furniture, no toys, and no friends to play with. How do you create your own fun?"

Since the question was posed after a lengthy whining session from my older daughter, whose demands were being completely ignored by her fanciful younger sister, she wasted no more time in letting me know exactly how she felt.

"There is nothing to do! I am alone and I am bored!"

I completely expected that from her, so I addressed the little one. "What are you doing in the room for fun?"

"Ooh, Mommy! I am singing and I am dancing and I am playing hand puppets!" she giggled.

If we want to live an extreme life adventure, full of joy, connection, and success, we need to play full out, no holds barred. Take the world by the hands and just dance!

~ Heather K. Meglasson

March 6

A Letter of Thanks

Dear Chancellor of the University of Hard Knocks,

I would like to take this opportunity to thank you and all of the teachers who took me through many lessons thus far in my lifetime.

I learned how to take the worst circumstances and turn them into times of opportunity for personal growth. For instance, how first impressions may not always be right and to give the other person a second chance, as we both might be having a less-than-perfect day.

Other learning experiences include: Having a nemesis in your life can be good, as it breeds inner strength; losing a loved one you were dependent on breeds self-sufficiency, and being displaced in the workplace after decades of employment can set you free.

I've received many opportunities from those who believe in me—too many to name here. But what else I want you to know, Chancellor, is how important the support of family and friends were during these challenging times, continuing to be so. My children are fantastic cheerleaders, along with my best friend, Colleen; however, it is my husband, Mark, who I am most grateful for in standing beside me these thirty-plus years.

Sincerely,

Peggy Lee Hanson

March 7

Technology: Priceless!

"Today I got texts from Monique, Dan, and Michelle! Yay! They're coming to the family reunion!" my mother-in-law e-mailed my husband. And so it is. With our families spread all over the United States, I am so grateful for the technology that lets us stay in touch with each other in ways that were unheard of not so many years ago.

I tried three times to get to my father's 80th birthday celebration, and the weather simply was not cooperating. My flights to Boston and Providence were canceled because of snow. Finally we had the inspiration to Skype me into the party. What fun it was to "visit" with Dad, my brother from Arizona, my sister from New Hampshire, and all the other family members attending this event. The family picture with me Skyped in on my sister's television is definitely a modern family picture!

With one daughter living in Colorado and one living in New Jersey, we had a virtual wedding shower and a virtual baby shower for them — recorded with my video camera and seen real-time on our computers! How cool is that?

My most cherished blessings: our families and friends — plus technology is priceless!

~ Leona M. La Perriere

March 8

Listen Carefully!

A few days ago my wonderful little daughter told me a great story of her own creation.

When finished, she asked, "Did you like it?"

I answered, "Yes, I love it!"

I could have never expected her reply. With a great smile she said, "See? That's how you make me feel with your stories!"

She is a master in the art of living. So young, she already knows how to get the best from life, create the same experience for others, and keep it flowing.

If you listen carefully, you will realize all the marvelous and mysterious ways in which life is always telling us how important we are, how intensely we are loved, and how easily we can use all our outstanding gifts and potential to transform and uplift ourselves, our lives, and our world.

I am deeply grateful as I'm beginning to hear life whispering her beautiful message in my ear every moment.

~ Yardena Krongold

March 9

My Greatest Gift

I'm grateful for family and friends, and am especially grateful for my most precious gifts: my three sons.

These three young men have taught me more than I could ever have taught them. The truth is that I didn't raise them — they raised me — and I'm grateful for their patience with me, for their sense of humor, and for the persons they have turned out to be.

As children they brought me joy, tears, angst, loads of laughter, and all those things that come with being a mom.

Yet, like polishing a stone, they chipped away at my rough edges of impatience, my need to control, my inability to understand the workings of the male species, and my need to learn flexibility. Their energy and interests, such as sports, snakes, spiders, dogs, and sailboats, and thirst for adventure opened my world beyond what I ever knew existed.

They're like the gift that keeps on giving, and now they have their own most precious gifts. I pray that they will appreciate their own children as much as I appreciate them.

I'm grateful that I can enjoy my grandchildren and to know that those little ones are in good hands.

~ Dolores T. Hagen

March 10

Girl. Father.

She is 5 or 6 years old, a glowing girl, sitting next to me in the waiting room, her father on her other side.

I am peeling off a small candy from a mini-box I just purchased. There is no mistaking the desire on her face.

"Want one?" I ask, offering her a candy, smiling.

She turns her look away, shy.

I try again, this time with empathy, peeling a candy for her. "Embarrassed? You're not used to this kind of offer?"

The glow is now directed at me! I "saw" her!

The little hand reaches out.

"When you have a chance, give something of yours to someone, will you?" I add.

Now the look goes to her daddy, who, moved by the act, tells me how generous she already is.

My father didn't tell such stories about me.

My father thought education was about punishment.

My father thought I was amazing, but spoke about how I should improve.

So I learned to outgrow his spell.

And found out who I really am.

I am grateful for his share in my journey into myself.

I am grateful for what I found.

I am grateful to all fathers, however they show their love.

~ Arnina Kashtan

March 11

Practicing Gratitude

There I was, in the summer of 2003, asking my friend for advice—again: Why am I so unhappy, and what can I do about it? This time he told me I needed professionals: a minister, a coach, and a therapist. He also urged exercise, better nutrition, and focusing on helping others.

The therapist and the minister taught me that gratitude is an important skill for improving one's life. I had no understanding that gratitude works this way: First you get conscious about and grateful for what you have, and then you are given more.

In the fall of 2005, blessed with student loans, I found my way to grad school. The four-hour commute gave me lots of time to consciously practice the new tools I was learning, especially gratitude. I really started looking around, deliberately acting grateful for the ordinary things in my life, and the small blessings of not having the problems others have.

By January 2008 I became manager of the massage department at a local resort. I graduated from grad school in May 2008. I've made lots of new friends. At 55 years young, I'm ready for adventure and beauty around every corner!

~ Robin West

March 12

Sunshine

I am grateful for sunshine. The "oh my goodness, the sun is out!" kind of sunshine that comes after a long season of cold. Sunshine that returns just when I thought I'd never be warm again.

I am grateful for sunshine. That single ray of light drawing me outside to turn my face upward, soaking it up with eyes closed, stretching like a sunflower.

I am grateful for sunshine. Its warmth thawing my bones, elevating my mood, illuminating my life, and stirring my passion to live.

I am grateful for sunshine. The promise of renewal, for a new season, for spring!

~ Kathy "HiKath" Preston

March 13

18 Power Words and Thoughts that Inspire Gratitude

Wealth: Appreciate the wealth you have received.

Honor: Honor and recognize who you are in life.

Appreciation: Show appreciation toward others by accepting them as they are.

Thankfulness: There's always something to be thankful for. Show gratitude by speaking kind words.

Astounding: Life is astounding and beautiful; open your mind to experience it.

Motivate: What motivates one person, may not motivate another.

Inspire: Design your inner and outer vessel to inspire gratitude. Shine your light as bright as you can.

Generous: From gratitude comes generous giving.

Renew: Attitude renews the spirit of gratitude.

Admire: Gratitude teaches us to admire those around us.

Tranquil: Being grateful helps you to see the tranquil beauty in all things.

Express: Expressing gratitude is food for the heart. Feed it daily.

Faith: Having faith calls for gratitude.

Unity: Creating unity builds a foundation for love.

Love: Gratitude opens your heart to receive love.

Fortune: Giving thanks for everyday luxuries and blessings creates a fortune mindset.

One: All it takes is one kind thought, or one kind word to express your gratefulness.

Resources: Spirit has given us an abundance of resources to see gratefulness in our lives.

~ Laynita Cichy

March 14

Expand into Gratitude

We are grateful to those pioneers who never gave up. They held on to a dream that life could be better. Their vision may have been lost on most folks. Still, they continued to climb mountains, forge new paths, and map out uncharted waters so that we might stand on their shoulders and expand the frontiers of their vision. They reached down and held a hand out to us from their evolutionary perch. And, in gratitude, we promise to do the same.

~ *Christine Marie and Julie*

March 15

The Everyday

I get up hours before dawn. I lace up my running shoes. I kiss my husband and dog. I own the road. I roll down the windows. I pass a coyote. I smile at sweaty faces on treadmills. I run like I'm on fire. I shower. I let my hair be curly. I put on pink lips. I drive to work. I almost get hit. I admire the mountains. I see the Strip. I arrive at the Y. I have full arms. I thank the member who holds the door. I brew coffee. I work. I laugh. I work. I sigh. I work. I smile. I work. I lose my work. I reboot. I work. I get a text from Dad. I get a call from my husband. I smile some more. I leave. I call Mom. I pass a man on horseback. I get home. I play fetch with my dog. I Skype my niece. I call my best bud. I eat ice cream. I pay bills. I make dinner. I eat with my husband. I prepare to do it all over again. I fall asleep in loving arms.

I am grateful for this life.

~ Tara Maras

March 16

For One More Day

A few years ago I was able to squirrel away enough money to buy three plane tickets to Spain to celebrate my oldest daughter's graduation from high school.

I had recently gotten out of debt and did not want to put all of our travel expenses on a credit card, so I asked my angels for a financial blessing. Also at that time, I was dreading a visit to see my mother, who suffered from Alzheimer's and alcoholism. It was possibly the last time I would see her.

One afternoon a flyer appeared on my front door. The Harpo Film Company wanted to use my home as a set for a TV movie called *For One More Day*. The movie was about a family illness like mine—alcoholism. It was serendipitous, and encouraged me to have closure with my mom, and it allowed my daughters and me a memorable trip.

I know in my heart when in recovery if you take a few steps toward God, you had better get ready for an angel's blessing with feathers all over it!

~ Allegra S. Harrington

March 17

Rebirthing My Mind

Turbulent years, adolescence, compounded with being exiled from one's native land. Thus I landed in London at age 16, scared, closed off, belligerent, rebellious. Enter Miss Mary Bradley, the woman who changed my life.

Miss Bradley was the English teacher at the British school I attended. The other kids were terrified of her, but I adored her. She was a strict, tough disciplinarian who held high expectations for all of us. She didn't just teach us literature; we experienced it. Twice a month we read a Shakespeare play, or perhaps Ibsen or Moliere, and then saw the production at one of the London theatres. Our 1,000-word weekly essays had to be perfect. She would not even accept a mediocre paper until it was done well. She taught us organization, pithiness, comparing, and contrasting, all applicable to literature and life!

And yet the real lesson was in how to open our minds and use them wisely while being true to ourselves. In all things she was strict yet fair, tough yet caring, prodding yet helpful. She opened not only my mind but my heart. Because of her I became a teacher and gratefully learned to love to learn.

~ Dr. Liana L. Carbón

March 18

My Gifts

Animals are gifts to the universe. I am grateful that they have been a meaningful part of my life. In childhood, dogs and cats gave me comfort and solace in a chaotic, dysfunctional world. Throughout adolescence and adulthood they became companions, friends, healers, and spiritual mentors.

When I moved to Maine in 1993, I was walking into an animal haven. Joining the ranks of dogs and cats were deer, moose, fox, beaver, bear, hawks, and eagles. Then came the intimacy of working in an animal shelter, attending to neglected animals' bodily and emotional needs. Sneakers and Tauri were my first Maine "four-footers" and had come home with me from the shelter. Then came Benji, my spirit dog, who touched the lives of everyone he came into contact with — a therapy dog without the training. Tasha and Shilo are currently my family.

My latest gift has come from Tasha, who led me to doing Reiki for pets, my current labor of love and my new livelihood.

Each animal, whether domestic or wild, has gifted me with comfort, joy, understanding, empathy, a sense of awe, lessons of life, and, most importantly, unconditional love.

~ Karen J. McCarthy

March 19

Call Me When You Get Home!

My maternal grandparents, Joseph and Nellie Oldenski, were quite the characters.

My grandfather always called us dzieci (the Polish word for "children") even after we grew up. I can still hear him saying, "Dzieci, stay on everyone's good side." My sister and I often remind each other of that gem during our telephone chats. In addition, whenever I traveled more than five miles, he would worry about the weather even if it was June. I was required to call him and let him know I was home safely.

Now, my grandmother, who was in excellent health until her early eighties, walked all over town. She was a modest, even shy, woman, and she usually kept her head down while walking. As a result, she had an incredible collection of found coins she shared with us.

My grandparents were an excellent team and shared kitchen duty. My grandfather's specialty was soup, and my favorites were his chicken soup and his beet soup. My grandmother was a skilled baker, and her secret to excellent pie crust was the liberal use of lard. I miss chatting with them in their kitchen or on the patio.

I cherish the memories of my wonderful Dziadzia and Bushie.

~ *Teresa A. Castleman*

March 20

Gratitude: The Quintessential Happy Pill

I've determined that gratitude is the quintessential "happy pill." Whenever I'm in a bad mood, if I can allow myself a pause to bring to mind thoughts of gratitude, my spirit always lifts.

The next time you're a little annoyed standing in line or sitting in traffic, pause and bring to mind something you are grateful to have in your life. It might be something relevant to the situation: *I'm thankful I have this car. I'm thankful to have a job to go to.* But it can be an unrelated item: *I'm thankful for soy lattes. I'm thankful for the sweet feeling of my bunny licking my toes. If two aren't enough, keep going.*

Not only does gratitude improve your mental condition, it also improves your physical condition by calming your parasympathetic activity, positively impacting your blood pressure, heart rate, and breath.

Gratitude is a mighty power. It is like sending love out to the infinite Universe and then the Universe sending it right back tenfold. It fills your heart!

Imagine all the headaches, missed events, and bad days shrunken to mere moments by the happy pill called gratitude.

~ *Marjorie W. Old*

March 21

Love Song to the Universe

My heart is so full of appreciation that I might burst with love.

Tears come to my eyes throughout the day, because I am full to overflowing with abundant grace.

I get to breathe, move, experience, and live for one more moment.

I get to feel a variable wind, a soft blanket. and a loved one's tender kiss against my skin.

I get to hear the sweet music of birdsong, the supportive voice of my friend, and the rhythmic purr of my cat with my ears.

I get to taste the tang of strawberries, the crunch of potato chips, and the cold goodness of ice cream with my tongue.

I get to smell the warm invitation of home-baked bread, the centering scent of sandalwood, and the comfort of coffee with my nose.

My blind eyes do not see the color of your skin, the quality of your clothes, or the size of your body.

I see the beauty of your soul with my Spirit-Eyes.

I get to touch lives with words, thoughts, and inspiration every day.

All is One, and I feel blessed!

~ Ronda Del Boccio

March 22

Loving Life—Just as it Is!

When I first found out that I would be a part of this amazing book, I thought, "This is what I am grateful for! What more could I possibly want?"

As I sat thinking, I realized that I, of course, did not want to be like everyone else! It's easy to write about wonderful things, such as "I am grateful for my family, friends, job, health, etc.," but that just wouldn't be me. So what is it that I am grateful for?

Well, let's see...

* I am grateful for all the animals that I have rescued, met, worked with, and lived with. Each one of them has taught me a unique and valuable lesson. They filled my heart with love, compassion, and gratitude.

* I am grateful for all the pain and suffering I had to endure from my ex-husband, ex-partners, ex-friends, ex-bosses, ex-coworkers, and anyone else who has dispensed hurt in my life. Without those experiences, I would not have grown, and learned self-love and self-reliance. Most of all I would not have realized that after each moment of darkness there is a moment of enlightenment and gratitude.

* Finally, I am grateful to wake up each day and say "I am alive!"

~ Milana Vinokur

March 23

I've Learned What I'm Grateful For

I'm grateful that:

There's no expiration date on the milk of human kindness.

I'm not a celebrity, so my mistakes don't make headlines in the grocery store tabloids.

I get undeserved and unconditional love from my wife, family, friends, and God.

I've learned that life is mostly both/and — not either/or.

We get second chances and second childhoods.

Children are the best teachers on how to love and laugh and live.

God has unlimited patience and mercy — and a great sense of humor.

All my electronic communication devices have a marvelous app called an "off" switch!

My precious granddaughter shares freely her heart-melting, with-all-her-being smiles.

I'm learning to accept affirmations from others and actually believe them.

Summer ends — because then yard work does, too.

God keeps secrets better than gossiping Aunt Gertrude.

Mortality teaches me to value every day as a gift.

The season for harvesting wisdom from life experience is year-round.

I've learned the wisest and most honest answer is often "I don't know."

~ Steve Harsh

March 24

The Childhood Adventure that Changed My Life

In 1976, aged 13, I boarded a plane from Stuttgart, Germany, to London. My parents' idea to send me abroad for the summer to learn English, embrace a different culture, and make friends with foreigners was radical at the time. I was equally nervous and excited at the prospect of living with a British family I had never met before. Thankfully, my hosts, the Cotter family, made me feel at home straight away. I had such a wonderful time that I revisited them often during my teenage years.

Learning about different cultures has remained an important part of my life: I moved to England, married a Briton, and became the proud mother of two culturally adept children. And as an international career consultant, I feel privileged to support my clients' expatriate journeys to the UK and beyond.

My childhood trip taught me an important lesson: When human beings suspend judgment—when they show empathy, curiosity, and respect for each other—cultural and language barriers shrink, and true friendships across geographical borders can flourish.

I am so grateful to my parents, Marianne and Richard Winden. Their everlasting support, generosity, and wisdom helped me find my own place in the world.

~ Ruth Winden

March 25

Rising from the Ashes

The officer stood solemnly with hat in hand. "I'm sorry to inform you that your son was killed in a fatal accident this morning...." Words no parent ever wants to hear. My first-born, my beloved son, was dead.

You're probably wondering what this traumatic event has to do with gratitude, but I have much to be grateful for.

At the top of my list is that the last communication I had with my son was full of love and laughter.

I'm grateful that I'm supremely steady in an emergency and that my brain seems to go into a place of overdrive where I know exactly what to do:

Get Emergency Trauma Solution into everyone!

Call the medical examiner's office and arrange for organ and tissue donation.

Call the University Honors' Program and arrange for student support.

I'm grateful for the amazing community who brought us food, massaged our over-stressed bodies, and celebrated with us a memorial that included two choirs, a theater troupe, and over five hundred people.

And I'm grateful that my son's last gift was to fulfill my dreams as a writer, speaker, health coach, and singer.

Thank you, son. Life's good.

~ Joan Hathaway-Sheldon

March 26

Magnitude of Blessings, Each and Every Day!

I thank God each and every day for his love, guidance, protection, and my incredible journey of life!

Love. Beauty. Peace. Joy. Bliss. Success. Inspiration. Intuition. Reflection. Vision. Family. Friends. Memories. Exploration. Strength. Vulnerability. Illness. Loss. Injury. Tragedy. Abuse. Failure. Sadness. Loneliness. I am grateful for all!

Each moment, person, place, feeling, and thought bring me new understanding of the path that is uniquely mine.

Knowing I am a byproduct of all I've experienced, allows me gratitude for good times and challenging times, and brings me peace that I'm blessed with abilities to always move forward, the spirit of an overcomer and great success on my journey!

Contemplating all I've experienced brings solace, *knowing* God's arms surround me and my loved ones!

I am most grateful for, proud of, and blessed by my children, Jeremy, Samantha, and Danielle: my greatest accomplishments and passion, always inspiring and encouraging me to be my best self, catalysts of my greatest achievements.

They are where I see the greatest manifestation of God in my life, *my heaven on Earth!*

That soft place where unconditional love, support, and my greatest joy resides.

What more could I be grateful for than all that is my life!

~ *Anne M. Skinner*

March 27

Connections

"None of us can exist in isolation. Our lives and existence are supported by others in seen and unseen ways, be it by parents, mentors or society at large. To be aware of these connections, to feel appreciation for them, and to strive to give something back to society in a spirit of gratitude is the proper way for human beings to live."

~ Daisaku Ikeda

We meet all kinds of people in life. I appreciate inspirational individuals such as Gandhi, Martin Luther King, Jr., Daisaku Ikeda, Mother Teresa, John Lennon, and the like, who dedicated their lives to promoting inner and world peace. I am also grateful to:

My parents for nurturing and supporting me.

My sister for sharing happy and sad times with me.

My teachers for helping me learn and think.

My friends for being kind and understanding.

My cats for being loving and cute.

Moreover, I am thankful to those who gave me a hard time, as I learned from the interactions and became more resilient and stronger. I also want to thank the Universe for my existence and the amazing connections I have with all living beings.

~ Cherry Hsu

March 28

Just Imagine...

I close my eyes and imagine the quiet beach with palm trees swaying in the gentle breeze of my inner sanctum. Even the sounds of traffic outside the New York City apartment do not distract me.

This ability to imagine and transport myself anywhere I want at any moment is a magnificent gift for which I am deeply grateful. I remember as a child, when left alone to do dishes and clean the kitchen, how I would invent stories where I was invariably the heroine. I escaped all emotional and physical pain, and entered a world created solely by my imagination.

This is the place where I continue to imagine and create who I am. It is where worlds are made and dreams are dreamed before they become reality.

What is your dream? Just imagine...

~ Luisa Rasiej

March 29

The Light Switch Is On!

Gratitude is an attitude I choose every day. I am grateful for the unconditional love, encouragement, and support of my family and friends. I am grateful for the valuable lessons learned from experiences, both good and bad. Interestingly, I learn more about myself from the challenging experiences than the joyful ones.

I was blessed, at age 44, to give birth to a beautiful, healthy daughter. Every day, I gain greater insight and grow to be a better person as a result of being Alyssa's mommy.

My desire is to teach Alyssa valuable concepts, empowering her to use tools necessary to keep moving forward and live her dreams. One concept she recently learned was that when she says the phrase "I know," it's like a light switch in her brain shuts off and she can't process new information. Alyssa demonstrated her new understanding by telling her preschool teacher that the teacher's brain shut down when she responded with "I know that" to another student.

Alyssa also learned that by saying "Oops!" she can interrupt the pattern, which then turns the light switch back on, and learning resumes.

Every day, I remind myself that I control whether or not my light switch is turned on.

~ Phyllis A. Klein-Buonocore

March 30

Need a Gratitude Adjustment?

For each new morning with its light,
For rest and shelter of the night,
For health and food, for love and friends,
For everything Thy goodness sends.

~ Ralph Waldo Emerson

How fast we forge. I caught myself grumbling this morning because I was out of the "right kind" of coffee milk. And the kids were complaining because we didn't have pancake mix. I turned on the news, and had to turn it off, because it was too depressing. It's times like this when we need a "gratitude adjustment."

If you have clothes to wear, a place to sleep, food to eat, and a roof over your head, you are richer than seventy-five percent of the world.

Can you read this? Over two billion people in this world can't read at all.

Have your health? There are millions who will not make it through the week.

Are you and your family safe from battle, torture, starvation, oppression?

Have friends and family who love you?

Gratitude is all-encompassing. There is so much to be grateful for. When you catch yourself grumbling, get a "gratitude adjustment." Take time to appreciate your surroundings and loved ones. It will put a smile back on your face.

~ Patty Hedrick

March 31

Why Are You Crying?

"Why are you crying?" I hear a voice ask.

"My father just died," I answer.

"And that makes you sad?" the voice asks again.

"Of course it does!" I reply angrily.

"But why?" is the calm response. "I thought you were not on good terms."

"Because he left me," I respond with a sobbing voice.

"So you are telling me that knowing his end was near and that time was running out, you were able to overcome all of your conflicts and bond with him the way you always wanted to?"

"Yes."

"He held your hands and looked you into your eyes and told you that he loved you?"

"Yes."

"And you told him that you loved him?"

"Oh yes."

"Aren't you grateful for these moments?"

"Yes, I am."

"Aren't you grateful for seizing the opportunity for love to prevail?"

"Yes."

"Aren't you grateful that for the rest of your life you will be carrying these bonding moments in your heart, replacing all the earlier struggles you have had?"

"Oh absolutely!" I exclaimed with a smile on my face, as I rolled over and fell back into a deep and peaceful sleep again.

~ Q Moayad

April

"Sometimes the questions are complicated and the answers are simple."

~ Dr. Seuss (Theodor Seuss Geisel)

April 1

It's in the Knowing

I t's in the knowing...
I am grateful for knowing that God is the orchestrator of my life and He has it under control.

Whenever I get nervous about a new speaking engagement or business venture, I say to myself, "God gave me this opportunity, and He is not going to let me fail." This gives me strength and an unwavering belief in myself to move forward with courage.

One of my favorite quotes is from Marianne Williamson: *"Our deepest fear is not that we are inadequate. Our deepest fear is that we are powerful beyond measure. It is our light, not our darkness that most frightens us. We ask ourselves, Who am I to be brilliant, gorgeous, talented, fabulous? Actually, who are you not to be? You are a child of God."*

It is in the knowing that makes me strong. It is in the knowing that brings peace to my life. If you knew you could not fail, what would you try?

Know this: You were born for greatness! Make today the day you start to believe in your dreams. You are more powerful than you know.

~ Heather Clarke-Peckerman

April 2

What Makes God Smile?

"Having gifts that differ according to the grace given to us, let us use them."

~ Romans 12:6

I awoke this morning from a dream where I went to visit someone who was completely paralyzed. I was asked to visit her because she loved to hear people sing.

When I arrived at her room, someone was already with her, so I waited outside the door. From inside the room I heard a woman sing the song "Sing Alleluia to the Lord." Without realizing it I found myself joining in singing harmony. I couldn't help myself. I felt compelled to sing even though I rarely sing harmony.

I continued to wait outside the patient's room for my opportunity to enter and sing for her, but suddenly realized I had to leave to find pen and paper to capture what I was thinking and feeling. In that moment, I heard a voice whisper to me and was inspired to write a song.

I'm fully awake now. I'm grateful to God for blessing me with an outer voice that brings joy to people when I sing, entrusting me with an inner voice that inspires me to write songs, and the ears and patience to quietly listen.

~ *Peg Roach Loyd*

The Biggest Gift I Have, I Get to Share

When asked what I am grateful for I realized it would take a lot to explain the abundance I have experienced over my lifetime. But as I recount all I have received, I find my biggest gift is actually a part of me, and through this gift I have received so much more.

I have always had the ability to communicate and connect with people outside my age group, my social-economic status, my academic level, and other differences most would find insurmountable.

I've always been comfortable talking to everyone on a level where they can feel heard. I have memories as a teen of sitting in the office with the catering boss drinking coffee while other girls were out giggling in foolish cliques. I remember feeling as comfortable talking with Ph.D.s as I did to high school students. Executives, CEOs, teachers, students, and parents — they are all interesting and I find value in the relationships. Being able to listen to and relate with all types of people has been a wonderful gift.

I am so grateful to be able to communicate with others in a way that has given me the time to spend with my children recounting the day or planning my future with my husband, Brian. Thank you!

~ Barbara Stuhlemmer

April 4

A Moment with Tea

As the sun rises, I ponder green foam on the top of my bowl of matcha, and am thankful:

- For a community of friends on their way to enlightenment.
- For the mist that falls on a foggy, gray morning.
- That those closest who know everything about me, treat me with love and grace.
- That those who do not know everything about me, treat me with love and grace.
- That God gives us both the desire and ability to heal from emotional and spiritual wounds.
- That we all have within us the ability to lead.
- That I can cultivate the "being-ness" of my true self.
- And that there are those who can assist me to do so along the way.

Full of gratefulness, I finish my tea and begin my day, knowing that:

I *am* the full extension of God in my sphere.

My way is peace; my journey is mastery.

My power comes not from me but through me.

I am filled with the love and joy of my being always, in every moment.

For this, I am truly thankful.

~ *Jeremy M. Bennett*

Emergence

I was riding my bicycle to work and hit by a car in July 2001. Even though I was wearing a helmet, I sustained a traumatic brain injury.

Psychologists suggest people who have been through a traumatic brain injury experience have a funeral for the person they were before the injury and acknowledge that person is no more.

If you are familiar with such injuries, you understand the person can have a dramatic shift in personality and abilities, which hinders full recovery as the person wishes his or her old life back.

It has been nine years since my injury accident. I postponed having the funeral for the "old Mia," thinking it was weird.

Then I recognized it was time to let the new Mia emerge. To observe the butterfly who has been forming and was ready to arrive.

I had the funeral for the old Mia at the beach in September 2010. Alone with the fire pit and a box full of papers and memorabilia, I left the beach with an empty container, a clean slate, and the use of a new name, one that reminds me this life I am in is a beautiful expression of life in motion, my definition of Avi!

~ Avi Dalene

April 6

Life's Colorful Messages

Life brings us colorful messages from our soul in all tones, hues, and shades, in all shapes and sizes, in human form, disease, or incident. Some colors need our tears to come to light or shine just from joy and laughter.

I had self-imposed restrictions and limitations from auto-immune disease, back pain, frozen shoulder, marriage problems, financial worries, and some more. All the walls I hit are only colorful road signs and not out to get me. The certifications to prove my "life-worthiness" are only a bland piece of paper.

We gather colors and spread them on the canvas of our life with joy, bitterness, rage, boredom, passion, or perfection. With hope, love, compassion, and an inner knowingness where they go, we paint and create with all that we are and have a picture so unique and beautiful, so strong and passionate for all to see, to share, and to enjoy. We express our inner and outer fireworks of life and love.

I love butterflies and rainbows, the grains of sand, and the wide ocean.

I'm grateful for the variety, miracles, and wonders, the richness of all of life's colors, and for each one of us.

I'm grateful for life.

~ Jutta Kastner Leahy

April 7

Ranchers and Farmers

He embodies a man of the earth. He watches the weather, the seasons, the signs. He possesses an uncanny alertness not found in others. My husband is a fourth-generation rancher. Wild deer wait for morning rations of corn near the water trough. He observes the sheep making daily migration for sustenance: counting, checking, comparing. Once a colleague referred to farmers and ranchers as those who can't make a living with their brain. What a wrong judgment. Ranching and farming involve genetic studies, Internet selling, and market knowledge. I'm thankful for an agriculture industry providing food for our country. I'm grateful for my husband.

~ *Margaret G. Holmes*

April 8

Grateful Is as Grateful Does

Reluctantly I noticed it was already a feeling "blah" kind of day. You know the kind. It just took one bad incident after getting out of bed. A negative mental image formed and joined with another from before, and then another. The chain made an attitude, and my attitude was just "blah"!

I told myself, "Hold on. Not so fast. I have a remedy for this." I spied it on the shelf and picked it up — a purplish-hued, well-worn, wide-ruled volume of my handwritten pages — and opened to a random page of four or five one-line entries. Rereading each instantly brought a lightness of being into my body and shifted my attitude. Transformation happened like magic as I read. The present infused with joy. I was standing again in moments of fleeting pleasures and smiling.

The Daily Gratitude Journal let me relive once more what I had been grateful for before. From a negative neural path of "blah!" to joy, delight, and saying "thanks," my train was switched to the happiness track.

~ Dr. Liz Zed

On a Razor's Edge

My husband left me. For months I reeled. To manage my world, I worked every day and drank every night, until one night I found myself on the floor with a razor blade in my hand. For that I am grateful.

Feeling like a hopeless loser, I called my father and said, "I just need to know that you don't think of me as a failure." Every cell of my body was poised to hear "Well, what else are you? You couldn't even keep your marriage together!"

His answer stunned me. "Lovey, it sounds like you've done all you can. Sometimes it's just time to move on." Two simple sentences. One giant reorientation for me.

To my husband I say:

"For the pain that drove me to reach out to my father, I am grateful. For the poignancy of hearing his love for me, I am grateful. For the changed relationship with him, I am grateful. For releasing me from the prison of my self-perceptions, I am grateful.

"By having the courage to do what was best for you, you absolutely did what was very best for me. For that I am grateful."

~ Jolina Karen

April 10

Unexpected Job Benefits

A deciding factor that led me to becoming a life coach was imagining all the people that I could help with reshaping their lives and ensuring they find more success, deeper fulfillment, inner peace, simplicity, and sheer happiness. Not once did I envision the joy and self-growth that touching their lives would bring to my own. I have learned so much from every person who has granted me access to his or her dreams, frustrations, passions, and accomplishments.

I am grateful for the trust that is given so freely to me, for the opportunity to be a part of their lives, and for the relationships that ground and connect me to our shared universe. I am most grateful for having a career with benefits like no other I've ever experienced.

~ Delores Mason

Grateful for Life and Liberties

On the afternoon of April 11, 1945, Abe Korn was lying in his barracks extremely weak from fighting a foot infection without nourishment or medical attention. He thought he heard singing. It became louder and more distinct. The barracks door swung open and Abe beheld a sight he'd never forget. There were German SS soldiers, bound with rope, being followed by some of Abe's fellow Jewish prisoners holding guns and bayonets. Behind the singing prisoners came the American soldiers. Abe was seeing a miracle that he had prayed for, over six years of persecution, of being pushed around, of hunger and deprivation beyond description, of whippings and psychological torture, of being treated worse than an animal.

On that day, the American army broke through the Buchenwald gates. Abe was finally liberated from a life worse than death. "Our American heroes stood like giants before our eyes," Abe wrote before he died in 1972.

I am grateful to be married to Abe's oldest son, Joseph (Joey). We are constantly inspired by Abe's story. We love and appreciate our family, our life, and our liberties. We are forever grateful to be a part of this great country, the United States of America.

~ Jill M. Korn

April 12

Who Would've Known?

I made a seven-hundred mile drive to Minnesota in early April, encountering a winter storm on the way. Family and friends who were flying in were grounded halfway and forced to hop in rental cars, braving the blizzard in unfamiliar territory, to arrive on time. Tuxes and dresses in tow, everyone finally graced us with their presence, and my wedding went off without a hitch. Now, two years later, we have a house, a dog, and two beautiful children. Twins at that! The only thing that's missing is the white picket fence, which I can happily do without. Who has time to paint?

~ Heidi Danos

Grandmothers

Every day I am inspired to be an amazing woman. I am grateful for my grandmothers, who have each made me the woman I am today.

Grandma is a homemaker, and a good one at that. I have enjoyed many unique adventures with her. I have always admired her, but her amazing strength and humility shine through while she battles cancer; I have never heard her complain. I am thankful for her lessons, and her courage.

Nana was a successful businesswoman who paved the road for ladies in her industry. As a widow of two husbands, she continues to live as if age is just a number. I am thankful for her entrepreneurial spirit and her energy.

My Nanny-in-love (my husband's grandmother) has been a blessing in my life, and a great friend. She is one of the most generous souls I know, putting everyone ahead of herself. I am thankful for her kind heart and helping hand.

Life is a gift. I am grateful for the privilege to be inspired by my role models, and the freedom to pursue my dreams. Who inspires you? I dare you to live an inspired, amazing life!

~ *Robyn Beazley*

April 14

Humor Transcends Generations

I treasure the memory of my dad laughing, often so hard he could barely finish whatever story he was trying to tell. He could get to a punch line and then not be able to say it because he was laughing so hard and just couldn't get it out.

There's something special about laughing; it transcends generations. My husband and I were able to use humor with our boys when their ages made it seem as if we had little in common. No matter what the family occasion, we always seemed to top off it off with laughter. To this day, when our family shares a humorous story, listens to a comedian, or sits together in a darkened movie theater, we can't help but look over and acknowledge each other moments after the punch line. It's a look of pure joy you just don't get to see on other occasions. I've always thought that if the day comes when my husband doesn't use that time to look at me, it's time to worry.

Humor is a loving gesture for which I'm grateful. It allows me to not take myself too seriously. It's the glue that has sealed many lasting relationships.

~ Standolyn Kerr Robertson

What I Know Now

Little did I know as a young child, when my parents divorced, that I would need and use all that I learned from that difficult experience to handle my own divorce in a positive, loving way. For that I am grateful.

Little did I know as a parent, when I got divorced, that I would need and use all that I learned from that challenging experience to start my own coaching business to help others through divorce. For that I am grateful.

Little did I know as a coach, when I started working with clients and hearing their stories, that I would need and use all that I learned to write a book about divorce. For that I am grateful.

What I do know now as a human being is that every time I experience a challenge in my life, something wonderful and unexpected will come as a result. It might be immediate and it might come years down the road — but it will come. And for that I am incredibly grateful.

~ Marlene Clay

April 16

Living in Awe

"We can only be said to be alive in those moments when our hearts are conscious of our treasures."

~ Thornton Wilder

Livia — your name became an acronym to me for "living in awe." You see preciousness and beauty in everything you lay your big beautiful brown eyes on — in nature just as well as in people. Your laughter is contagious, your sensitivity is touching, and your charming mischievousness is heart-warming.

What inspires me most is your joy of life, the abundance from the heart you live by every single day. From the moment I first saw you — a tiny dot on the ultrasound screen — you captured my heart completely and changed my life forever.

I am eternally grateful to be blessed with a little daughter who exudes enthusiasm, kindness, happiness, and love. You teach me to feel and give unconditional love, courageously, in all vulnerability, every day, regardless of circumstances, and to become more playful, curious, and immersed in life than ever.

Because of you, I can feel my soul more deeply. My gratitude about this gift goes out to the Universe and to my husband for co-creating and co-raising this wonderful human being with me.

~ Elisabeth Balcarczyk

Divine Gratitude

Divine gratitude is a thought or a simple "thank you." It's gratitude that comes from the heart — from the innermost sanctity of your being.

Divine gratitude is not just in or of the mind; divine gratitude fills you up and spills out of your being like a shower of beautiful rainbows splashing over the beautiful essence of you.

Today I am filled with gratitude from the tips of my toes to the top of my head. I live and breathe gratitude. Gratitude flows through the very essence of my being.

I am so very grateful for the many people — the divine relationships — that have touched my life and left an indelible imprint on my soul: my children, my friends, my co-workers, the light workers, the angels, and, truthfully, every sentient being here on planet Earth.

I am grateful, and I give thanks for I am blessed. I am blessed in abundant ways.

I am blessed. I am loved. I am.

~ Barbara G. Wainwright

April 18

Coming Home

I am grateful to a young woman whose search for me on Facebook reminds me that we can never truly lose what we once had.

Stacy was my younger son Bob's high school sweetheart. And I adored her. She was, and still, is a kindred spirit to me—thoughtful, kind, considerate, and loving.

Having borne two wonderful sons, I had always wanted a daughter. And in some ways, Stacy and all the young ladies that my sons dated were those daughters.

After nearly twenty years, Stacy found me. Her words to me were, "You were always so kind to me. I always felt welcome when I came to your home. And I've been looking for you on Facebook."

So, thank you, Stacy. I am honored to be a part of your life today!

~ Sandi Cornez

Appreciating Cancer

My best spiritual teachers were my breast cancer and leukemia. For many years of my life I felt exhausted. I was not listening to my body, and I was living my life completely for others. Some studies suggest that repressed anger and resentment are associated with the development of cancer. For me, I know that was true.

So I learned the importance of saying what I needed to say, such as "I apologize," "I love you," "No, I choose not to do that," and "Yes, I'm going for a massage." The airline's oxygen mask instructions of putting mine on first and then helping others became my example.

Forgiving others and myself had tremendous healing power, and now I am very grateful to be cancer-free for over nine years.

These illnesses were my wake-up call that began my journey back to joy. When I'm feeling joy I know that I am honoring myself, and when I honor myself I can truly begin to be of service to others. I am truly grateful.

~ Donna J. Davis

April 20

Grateful for Life's Abundant Treasures

My cornucopia runneth over! I am grateful for:

The feel of my grandson's breath on my neck as I rock him.

The tickle in my nose after smelling fresh roses.

The feel of my granddaughter's little hand in mine as we walk.

The sight of wrinkles and age spots on my mother-in-law, because it reminds me how lucky we are that she's still here.

The compassionate, caring daughter I am so proud of.

The tender, loving father my son has become.

The juice of a large peach running down my cheeks.

The fleeting glimpse of a bluebird at my bird bath.

The smooth, silky feel of a good chocolate on my tongue.

Things that make me laugh when I carry a heavy burden on my heart.

My husband, my best friend, my soul mate, through all of life's ups and downs.

Family that pulls together when life throws us a curve ball.

A son-in-law and daughter-in-law who give me joy and pride.

Siblings and their families, whom I cherish.

Friends who are there when I need them.

Faith that sustains me through life's trials.

I must never forget to be grateful for my overflowing cornucopia. I am truly blessed.

~ Susan Brownell

Museums

"Why did we come to see all this old, broken stuff?" the young girl questioned. I struggled to explain why I love museums: the Getty, the Met, the local ones. I am grateful for the lessons learned in museums. The furniture, paintings, and costumes at the Getty transport us to another time and culture. These are wonderful lessons to learn for the willing heart.

Local museums recall a town's history; Iraan was named for Ira Yates and his wife, Ann, thus the name Ira-An. Museums docents gush with stories, facts, and lore about each piece displayed. I am grateful when my son serves as my private guide to world-renowned collections.

On family trips we always managed to include a trip to museum to browse the guns, jewelry, or pump jacks of a bygone era. I am thankful for those who preserve the past so that a new generation learns to live more wisely in the present.

~ Margaret G. Holmes

April 22

Grateful to Call Her Mom

Mr. B and I will celebrate twenty-three years together, this year. I am very grateful for the journey we've shared together, with its many ups and downs, detours, and turnarounds. I could sing his many praises, and I am sure I will one day, but today I choose to write about the special woman who shares his birthday and raised him. Sadly, mothers-in-law bear the brunt of endless jokes and ribbing. But I got lucky and won the mother-in-law lottery when I married her son.

She's a classy lady who knows her own mind. We don't always see eye to eye. We don't agree on either politics or religion, and quite probably many other things. Those differences have never seemed to matter or get in the way.

She is upbeat and fun. She sees the good in everyone, but she has been especially good at seeing and validating me even with all my warts. I never envisioned myself calling another lady Mom, but I am honored and grateful to call her that. I am privileged to know her and hope to do the mother-in-law dance half as well.

My own child got married this month. I have a wonderful role model. So maybe there's a chance I'll get it right.

~ Jan Blount

The Letters

My world had fallen apart. It was August 2004, and, after numerous requests to move out, I separated from my wife and three children.

Feeling unfairly treated and living in a small basement room, my faith in the future, in life itself, was shattered. I desperately searched for some clarity and direction, trying to re-construct my faith in God and go forward.

My wife had written me letters during the time of our strained relationship, and I kept them with the intent to get her future apology for the accusations she made in them.

Years later, I came across these letters. I was dumbstruck and humbled as I read them again. This time, with my changed perspective coming from a more mature heart free of resentment, I understood every word she had written was true! Every defect and limitation she had mentioned was spot-on. What she had wanted me to see before was now clear to me.

Since then, I've repaired the relationship with my ex-wife and have regular contact with my three almost-adult children.

Now I can look back and feel tremendous gratitude for my experience and to God, who opened my heart to appreciate life more.

~ Bernard Naughton

April 24

In All Circumstances Give Thanks

"In all circumstances give thanks, for this is the will of God."
~ Saint Paul, 1 Thessalonians 5:18

I am a young widow; my husband died unexpectedly at the age of 46. Yet I have joy in all circumstances that comes from my faith in God, through Jesus Christ.

Bob was a practical man of science, never putting much stock in spiritual things, yet on his deathbed in the ICU, he was given a choice. One day a sudden look of fear gripped his face, and I asked him, "Where are you?" He snapped out of his trance and asked me, "Do you have a cross?" After praying for this man for twenty years, I certainly had one to give him! He held it to his lips and then over his heart. He seemed totally at peace. That would be the last time we ever spoke.

Later, after his passing, Bob came to me in a dreamlike state. He gave me a glimpse into the afterlife, where all things are equal and all people live at peace, joyfully praising the Lord of life!

This is the source of my gratitude: I worship a God whose love is everlasting!

~ Dr. Karen L. Gray

April 25

My Birthday Club Group

Sometimes we need to reinvent our life. I have had to do this twice.

The first time I started over was in 1978, when I moved from Seattle, Washington, to San Diego, California, as a 30-year-old single mom with two young children in school.

I knew only two people in town: my mom and my brother. My mom helped me enormously and supported me in finding a good new career that fit my interests and personality. The new career allowed me to meet some really cool women. The really cool women became my Birthday Club Group.

Over the years the Birthday Club Group and I have gone through everything together: births, illnesses, deaths, divorces, celebrations, jobs lost, jobs found, and meeting for each other's birthdays, celebrations, and holidays. My life would have been lonely without the laughs and love this marvelous group of women has given to me.

Today, I am so GRATEFUL for each one of them and look forward to spending the rest of my life in their friendships and love.

God bless my girlfriends!

And God bless my wonderful mom who is still a great support and a great friend.

~ Kathy Nelson

April 26

All Blessings

Being grateful means counting all your blessings.

These things I am grateful for: God, the earth, the stars, the sky; my family, friends, and long goodbyes. For animals and rainbows, too; for flowers, trees, and oceans blue. For films and music, books and dance; for kisses, love, and true romance. For sushi, art, and mint ice cream; for laughter, sports, and happy dreams.

I'm grateful for my hands that heal, and true emotions that I feel. For simple pleasures, hugs and touch, and everything I love so much. For nature, travel, and the birth of every culture on this earth. For truth, compassion, and good deeds; for understanding human needs. For service, handshakes, and a smile, and giggles from a little child.

There's just so much—I could add more, of everything I'm grateful for. I count my blessings every day, and "thank you God," is what I pray.

~ Kim M. Baldwin

The Broken Road

On April 27, 2007, I took my son and left my second marriage with little more than I received on supplemental security income (SSI).

I was in the last few semesters of earning my bachelor's degree in journalism at San Diego State University and taking five classes at the time. I had to serve my husband with a restraining order and go through a court hearing, where I was told I had forty-five days to get out of my house. This was just weeks before finals. Perfect timing, right? Not!

Recovery was long, painful, and anything but smooth. I am, however, grateful for the broken road that brought out strengths in me I never knew I possessed.

For the first time in my life, I'm gainfully employed and supporting myself. I've managed to get off of SSI and food stamps. All of this has elevated my confidence as a blind woman who has come out of an emotionally abusive marriage.

Today I'm more goal-oriented and I look forward to an exciting future. Life is great, perhaps even better than it would have been had I not lived through the pain. So here's to a brighter tomorrow!

~ Nicole Bissett

April 28

What a Wonderful Day!

Thank you for the love I got and the love I give! I am grateful for being able to open my heart!

Having been hurt a lot and having cried a lot, I found a way to trust in love, in God, the universe, emptiness, or however you call it. I trust myself, happy to be able to risk love, wherever love takes me.

I learned to let go of anxieties and to listen to my inner voice. I am grateful for the change that took place in me. I want to say thank you for, with his help, I have stopped putting pressure on the man I love. I am responsible for myself, for fulfilling my dreams, responsible for my satisfaction. I am responsible for what I feel, what I imagine, what I think, what I say, what I do, what comes along in my life, and what happens to me. It is always fruits of these seeds: my feelings, my imagination, my thoughts, my words, what I do, and the mercy of love.

I am grateful for trusting that the harvest will be rich, and I enjoy true success in whatever I pray for.

What a wonderful day!

~ Eva Maria Wiesenthal

This Life of Mine

At age 17, I found out my mother tried to have an abortion while pregnant with me. I was angry, hurt, and disappointed. What do you say to that? I wasn't wanted in this world, yet I survived.

I joined the U.S. Army, ran away from my past, and forgot who I was. Being older now, I realize I have touched the lives of thousands of people. As a motivational speaker, healer, and life and fitness coach, I have inspired people to accomplish goals they never knew they could, saved lives, and helped people heal emotionally and physically. I didn't die because God's plan for me was bigger and better than I could have ever imagined.

My relationship with my mother and family couldn't be better now. I love my mother. I am her pillar of support; she leans on me for everything. I am successful and happy, and continue to inspire people to set and reach new goals and heal themselves. I have found my purpose, and I am grateful every day for replacing anger, hurt, and disappointment with unconditional love. I give thanks for this great life of mine and the opportunity to make this world a better place.

~ Willie Marrero LaBonne

April 30

Gratitude for My Refrigerator

I do the big clean on my refrigerator twice a year or when I just can't ignore the grunge any longer. I completely empty it, scrub it down, and then replace the inventory. (That is after having ruthlessly tossed the jar of jalapeno jelly that seemed like a good idea at the time, the mustard that is crusty around the rim, and the unidentifiable gray stuff in the margarine container.)

I love my fridge. It's not a behemoth, and it doesn't have a water dispenser in the door, but it is rather sleek and modern, and it runs perfectly. I really love it when it's sparkling and organized. Yet I still found myself whining when it came time to do the big clean, until I remembered the "kitchens" in the village I visited in Guatemala. Most of the cooking was done on an open fire inside their shanty. Yes, a camp fire. No stove. No refrigeration. A family to feed.

Now the big clean is simply my reminder to be grateful for my refrigerator, the food inside, and the ease with which I live my life.

~ Sandra Ahten

May

"*Wake at dawn with a winged heart and give thanks for another day of loving.*"

~ Kahlil Gibran

May 1

Gratitude as an Action

Gratitude has both an attitudinal and a behavioral component, and truly lacks depth and weight unless both are present.

We may feel grateful, and the experience of that feeling is wonderful, but unless that feeling is matched by behavior and motivates behavior, it is not complete.

If I say I am grateful for my health, and then do not take care of myself, or if I say that I am grateful for my wife, and then do not behave in a manner that reflects that gratitude, then there is a hollowness to my claim of gratitude. Feeling gratitude for getting to know others, without allowing them to know me, is not a grateful stance.

As with many other aspects of life, words and feelings are nice, but the true measure of those words and feelings is in our behavior. Act in a manner that reflects and expresses your gratitude.

~ Jay Westbrook

May 2

Being Grateful for Nature and Our Blessings

W hat! What! What!
Oh no, I can't believe this (says my voice).
I get up in the morning and I ask myself,
"What happened when I was sleeping?
Who took care of me?"

Am I able to figure out what happens? *No.*
Do I appreciate the changes from one stage to another without risk of loss, danger or death? *Yes!*

I am grateful for the gift of nature and the free things we take for granted: air, water, trees, changes in weather, time, music from birds.

I am grateful that I have food, to keep my energy and health strong.

I am grateful for my family and friends whom I have built throughout my journey of life.

I am grateful for the countless blessings I have received over the years and being able to share those blessings with those around me.

I am grateful for serving and being able to help when needed.

I am grateful for being there to make a difference in the world.

We have to be grateful for the things we have, things that are given to us, or just gift of natures, for in so doing we will make the world a better place.

~ Florence Onochie

Ports of Communication: Gratitude to the Men in My Life

I received a Christmas cactus as a gift when my fraternal grand-mother died in 1994. It never bloomed, but I kept it, watered it, and even brought it with me when I moved from Virginia to Ohio.

In eleven years, that plant never once bloomed.

Until one day.

The day I returned home from my dad's funeral, tired, sad, and grieving, there it was—a Christmas cactus that had never bloomed before, much less bloomed in May, in full bloom, when it should have been dormant.

Quite literally, it took my breath away.

Just a few days earlier, I told my dad that I would still talk to him when he was gone. His response was, "Ports of communication will remain open." Spoken like a true professor.

I told my husband that I really wanted to believe that the blooms were a message from my dad. A message of hope, love, joy, and peace. A sign that he was okay. Better than okay, he was finally able to make a joyful noise once again.

Then I heard the two words I'm most grateful for. My husband said, "Then do."

And so I do.

~ Meredith Liepelt

May 4

You Are What You Pack

I arrived at my hotel in San Francisco with two large, overstuffed suitcases, a briefcase brimming with work, a purse overflowing with clutter, and sunglasses hanging around my neck, and wearing a trench coat complete with zip-out lining. I was sweating, exhausted, stiff, huffing, puffing, and disgruntled. All this for a three-day conference!

As I unzipped my burdensome bundles, a jumble of clothing sprung out. Suffering from "perfect moment syndrome," I was prepared for anything and everything. Within the cramped corners of my suitcase were dreams waiting to be tried on and hopes longing to be fulfilled.

When overwhelmed in life, my suitcase was cumbersome, heavy, and overstuffed with little thought to planning. Too busy and consumed to pause to identify my values, needs, or priorities, I brought everything — including regret.

Yet I remembered a twelve-day trip to Scotland that was completely satisfying with only carry-on luggage. I had the ability to be clear, decisive, content, and light!

Thus began my journey of looking at contentment and satisfaction in my life through the porthole of what I packed in my suitcase. My excess baggage had something to teach me.

I am grateful for discovering that "you are what you pack"!

~ Dr. Leslie A. Loubier

May 5

Count Your Blessings

"I wept because I had no shoes, until I saw a man who had no feet."
~ Persian saying

It was a sweltering day, with temperatures reaching 110 degrees, when I saw them: a homeless man and his dog walking along the highway in the desert heat. With torn shoes, a backpack bigger than he was, and the scorching cement blistering his feet, I drove past, hoping someone would pick them up. I then thought, "Why can't that person be me?" Before turning around, I bought lunch (burgers and water) and took them to the man.

"Where are you headed?" I asked.

"To the Indian Canyons," he said.

His name was Jim; his dog was Goldie. They had walked for days, over one hundred miles, so I offered them a ride. I spent the day with them shopping for new clothes, shoes, and personal items, and then dropped them off in the mountains.

I took their picture, and Jim said, "How can I ever thank you?"

"You already did," I replied. "God bless."

Gratitude is a full circle of giving and receiving love, and being thankful for our blessings. That day, for me and Jim, our blessings were each other — and we were grateful.

~ *Kim Marie Baldwin*

May 6

It's All in How You Look at It

When I think of things I'm grateful for, certain special people come to mind. Carolyn Scharkey and Sandy Hargrove, two dear friends and prayer partners of mine. Krystina Stressman, my best friend since I was 15. My son, Eddie, who is now 15 himself and thriving both as a student and as a wonderful young man. I'm especially grateful for the relationship I enjoy today with my Lord and Savior, Jesus Christ.

I may never have known any of these blessings had I been born with sight.

You see, I met Carolyn and my son's dad at a center for the blind, Sandy on a phone system that blind people use to correspond. I met Krystina through a mutual friend who was in my adaptive physical education (PE) class in junior high. I was taught about God at a summer camp for the blind at age 7.

I could actually write a book on everything I'm grateful for that can be traced back to my blindness. Sure, life without sight has its drawbacks, but the bottom line is, it's all in how you look at it.

~ Nicole Bissett

May 7

What *You* Show Me

As cliché as it sounds, I am incredibly grateful for my family and friends. To know there are people who care enough to brighten my day when it seems dim is something special. The really cool thing is, sometimes, a total stranger will do the same!

But today, I am grateful for something more: my gift and my awareness of it. Somewhere along the way, I received the gift of really seeing people. Through this gift, I see their greatness. Every single day, I get to experience the power of others through what I hear, feel, and see in them. It is kind of like opening your eyes to a dazzling brilliance. How cool is that? Whether it is the coffee shop girl who stops what she's doing to ask me how my day is (with a sparkle in her eye) or the actor in the play who pours all of his passion into his next line to draw that tear down my cheek, it is greatness. Maybe it is the woman from Zimbabwe who empowers other women despite her obstacles.

Big or small, profound or subtle, it is all Divine. So, I am grateful for what you show me.

~ *Michelle A. Beitzel*

May 8

"It Just Needed to Be Said"

The year after my son Chris left for college, I got the best Mother's Day message ever.

Usually he's an articulate and somewhat verbose young man with a leaning toward purple prose and unusual, handmade greeting cards. But this day he called on the telephone to wish me happy Mother's Day. He said, "I just wanted you to know how much I appreciate what you've given me."

I replied with some humility and apology, "Oh, it wasn't that much." Like most moms, I felt I should have done more.

He continued, "You gave me everything. You gave me life. Without that, I wouldn't have anything."

I was speechless. Fumbling around for a reply, I managed a weak "You're welcome" and a "Well, you sure know how to go right to the heart. You've got leverage for the next ten years, son."

I added, "I'm very proud of what you've done with what I got started. What made you call and say this?"

"It just needed to be said," he replied. "Bye, Mom. I'll talk to you later."

He was back on course to his own life, leaving me in grateful tears.

~ *Veronica Weeks-Basham*

May 9

Quiet Bliss

I'm grateful for moments of quiet bliss with my dog, Rincon. Especially the game of Apple. On summer evenings I pick an apple from the tree in our back yard, bite off a piece, and throw it across the yard. Rincon tears after it.

While he's gobbling up that piece, I take a quick bite for myself.

Then I throw the next piece to the other side of the yard, and Rincon is a streak of yellow Labrador lightning flashing in that direction.

And so the game goes. I get roughly every other piece while Rincon zig-zags his way across the yard chasing down his share. When the game is over, we are both beaming.

In Apple, there is nothing happening but beauty and fun.

It's the simple stuff. The apple is juicy, the grass is green, the sky at sunset. A dog running is gorgeous and fluid, and the dog you love running is over-the-moon beautiful. Nothing is happening that is not the game of Apple and the tiny backyard oasis that is the stadium for it — not even in my head.

I am never thinking any further than the next bite. That's bliss. The quiet kind.

~ Martia Nelson

May 10

The Best Is Coming

"When you wonder what is coming, tell yourself the best is coming. The very best life and love have to offer, the best God and His universe have to send. Then open your hands to receive it. Claim it and it is yours."

~ Melody Beattie

I'm grateful for "the best," no matter how it looks when it first arrives.

I'm glad for the chances I've taken hoping for "the best" and, many times, being fine with the "okay" or even "the worst" as it looked when it first appeared.

After many years of experience, and just like a GPS system that eventually leads me home even if I get off track, I know the "okay" and "the worst" are just stops—pauses to breathe—along the way to "the best."

In fact, "the best" is around me every day, waiting with its eternal patience for me to notice it with wonder.

And today—in this very moment—I do.

~ *Donna Kozik*

Deep Universal Human Values

I am profoundly grateful to know that I have deep "universal human values" that are always motivating me. What? Okay, let me explain!

If there is a fire in your house, do you say to yourself, "I feel tired. I think I'll go to bed." No, you don't. That's because there is something inside you motivating you toward safety!

In the past, if I was unhappy, I didn't know what to do about it other than to have some coffee or chocolate, go shopping, or read a book, but these strategies weren't helping my long-term happiness. Now that I understand that we all have deep inner values that are always motivating us (usually unconsciously), I can brainstorm some strategies that are more likely to fulfill my deep values.

For example, I was unhappy because I wanted more meaning from my work. So I kept thinking about, and meditating on, how to have more meaning. I discovered that I love teaching and coaching people how to recognize, and make choices toward, their deepest values. I watch it change their lives, and — surprise, surprise — that is deeply meaningful to me. And I am happily grateful for that!

What are you grateful for?

~ Rachel Monde

May 12

Gratitude Is an Action

When I think of gratitude, I have the urge to express. I put my thinking cap on to gather the things together in my mind that cause me to feel joy.

As I sit here this morning, I realize I have two choices. One is to focus on the things that are not the way I want them to be. The other is to focus on the fulfilling things I have so handy in this moment.

Why would I choose to go in the direction of discontent if I am able to find joy?

I take action in thanking God, accepting the joy He is providing right here and now. It takes a conscious effort on my behalf, knowing that I am worthy of the splendor and joy that bubble around me.

I express my gratitude for the presence of my loving husband sleeping on the couch, the sound of the dishwasher taking care of my household duty, the "feel good" music reaching my ears, the calmness and beauty of the nature scene beholding me as I look outside my patio doors.

My ability to choose provides an open door to the joy of gratitude.

~ Nancy McNaughton

In Memory of Delores

My mom, Delores, possessed a love of life that was infectious. She worked hard and tried to find the good in life everywhere she could. We lost her in 2009 to breast cancer, so in her memory I want to share one of her favorite stories.

Many years ago she attended a holiday celebration when she was nine months pregnant. She was noticeably uncomfortable and could barely move around. I was born right after Christmas that year. By New Year's Day she was ready to celebrate and show me off. One of my young cousins asked what on earth she had received for Christmas that made her look so much better. It made Mom laugh every time she told it.

I am so unquestionably grateful for every day I enjoyed with my mom in this world. She loved and believed in me every step of the way. I would give anything if I could call her right now and tell her I am writing this.

So if your mom hasn't heard from you in a while, why not give her a call? Tell her Delores says "Hi." Then I know she will be proud of both of us.

~ Darlene Janke Horwath

May 14

The Caregivers

Horrific images daily bombard our senses: earthquakes, pandemics, and war. Counterbalancing that are loving images of caregivers. They are a hidden majority. Most labor in homes, shut away from notice, self-sacrificing.

I entered this world when my mother needed me. Her daily calls from her nursing home became desperate. She told of being left alone in a bathroom and screaming for help. No one came. She couldn't walk, and her speech was indecipherable. A passerby would just think she was just another elderly woman readying for death.

I decided to bring her home. I had no experience in care-giving, but I was lucky. Thanks to many people, I learned about special equipment, how to move her, how to bathe her, and so much more. A year later she walks, reads, swims, and even bakes brownies for the troops. She has come back from the dead.

So many caregivers get no recognition, no pat on the back for a job well done, but stand duty 24/7 out of love, compassion, and hope. If you are one of these angels, I want to whisper in your ear every night as you sleep, "Bless you!"

~ Kathleen Dakota Parker

May 15

Affirm-itudes of Inspiration

Affirm-itude: A synthesis of affirmation and gratitude; an affirmation with an attitude of gratitude.

I begin every day with "rebelicious" thoughts and affirm-itudes of Inspiration. They fill my heart with love and gratitude for the people, things, and blessings in my life. It feels fabulous!

Affirm along with me:

"I love and trust myself completely and unconditionally just the way I am, in all of my power and magnificence. I am inspired by my passion, purpose, and large sense of play!

"I feel good. I feel fine. I feel this way all the time. I'm alive. I'm awake, and I feel great!

"Today is the beginning of a new day. I've been given this day to use as I will. I can waste it or use it for good. What I do today is important because I am exchanging a day of my life for it. Let it be good."

"Thank you for the 'rebelicious' abundance in my life."

An attitude of gratitude inspires. It creates positive emotion.

What does positive emotion attract? Why, fabulous things, of course!

Affirm-itudes of inspiration. They open my heart, inspire my mind, and enthuse me with boatloads of gratitude.

I'm inspired! I'm off to affirm....

~ Tuck Self

May 16

Simple but Magnificent Gratefulness

Gratefulness is in the simple things of my life that are truly magnificent:

• Having wonderful parents who stayed together and modeled marriage, love, and family

- Loving my sister and now remembering her to her children
- Loving my father and now remembering him as he is in Heaven with my sister
- Moving my mother in with us for her twilight years and being able to give back to her as she (and my dad) always gave to us
- Being greeted every time I come home with bounding licks, hugs, and cooing from my Pomeranian, Sadie
- Having the most wonderful husband, who is always there for me
- Being able to raise three sons, two nephews, and one goddaughter, and watch their uniqueness and gifts grow
- Having the best job in the world as an event planner and the most wonderful team members, Lisa and Alana
- Getting to travel and meet delightful people making a difference in the world, such as Jack Canfield, co-author of the *Chicken Soup for the Soul* series
- Living in America, where opportunities abound and freedom rings
- Being able to play in the ocean, ski the river, hike the mountains, and enjoy my family

~ Linda Elaine Cain

May 17

Hopelessness to Happiness

The year was 1979. I was married to my best friend and expecting my first child.

In May, my son was born with severe health and motor skills problems. By Christmas I was divorced, a single mom, and feeling hopeless.

I didn't know it then, but my divorce and the twenty-one years of being a single mom are the highlights of my life! Why? I wouldn't be the woman I am today if the events of 1979 hadn't happened. They made me realize that I was stronger than I thought.

Instead of rushing out to qualify for food stamps or to find a husband, I decided to stand on my own and be a good example for my son. I got student loans and went back to college. Sometimes I worked multiple jobs, but I always strove to balance my rising career with my "Mom" responsibilities. My son and I faced his health and academic problems together. We laughed, explored, and learned new things. Now he's an adult with his own productive life.

I am proud of him and proud of me, and I think he is proud of me, too. I am so very grateful for my life as a single mom.

~ Catherine Traywick

May 18

Commitment from the Heart

"The moment one definitely commits oneself, then providence moves, too."
~ J.W. von Goethe

May 18, 2004 marks the day when I learned a huge lesson about the power of commitment, community, and the courage to step up for making a difference in the world. On that day, I started a ten-month leadership program with a group of people who came from different countries and paths of life, and yet were like-minded.

My tribe, called "Antares," was named after one of the brightest stars in the Milky Way galaxy. And our leaders, Henry and Patrick, became close and precious friends with whom I am truly blessed.

Over time, I learned a lot about authentic leadership, taking responsibility for how I show up in the world, and the power of "we" instead of "I": the sum that is truly bigger than the parts.

And I learned what commitment really means — a lesson that has had a huge impact on my life ever since: true commitment as an engaged promise from the heart, which does not settle for doing what is convenient. It means making things possible even and especially when it is not convenient. The gift of this learning enriches my life, and I try my best to live up to this standard, every day.

~ Elisabeth Balcarczyk

The Aspiration of a Lifetime

What am I grateful for? The more provocative question to me is: What do I *aspire* to be grateful for? I aspire to be grateful for sorrow, sadness, grief, jealously, and other points of view. I aspire to be grateful for my suffering and unease at not having or being enough. I aspire to be grateful for the deep sense of separation I feel as a human being and for the inherent conflict between what is and what I want instead.

The truth is that if I'm not grateful for these things, then I'm not grateful for anything at all. If I'm not grateful for these things, can I really meet myself with compassion, understanding, and acceptance of my own humanity (or anyone else's, for that matter)?

See, it's easy to be grateful for what's wonderful. It's easy to love what you love already.

The real art and beauty of cultivating gratitude is to be grateful for what is in this moment and not waiting for the next moment to present you with something better.

These are my aspirations for gratitude — the aspirations of a lifetime.

~ Kelly Kim

May 20

Faith, Family, and Friends: The Blessings I'm Most Grateful For

First of all, I have tremendous gratitude for God and all the blessings he has given me, some of which I mention below.

I am grateful for all my clients helping me to get the hang of my private practice the past two years, especially during a "down economy"! Starting a new business is hard work, but it is also a lot of fun and really helps you learn what you are made of. I am happy to be keeping things under control, and I look forward to really living life as it should be in 2011.

I am thankful for my friends and family, including the unconditional love of my dog, Bear. I am particularly grateful for my husband, Dan, whom I consider my soul mate. Without Dan, I would have had to pay a lot more to get my website up and running!

I am also thankful for my health, my home, and my abilities. Though I was not able to compete in many races during the past two years, I did spend more time coaching and cheerleading. That gave me a whole new appreciation for people who spend their lifetimes being our coaches and cheerleaders!

~ Christine E. Marquette

May 21

Wounded Healer

Some may think that being grateful for chronic pain is sheer madness. That isn't true when you are able to put a purpose to your pain.

Having fibromyalgia has given my life additional meaning. It has provided me with a firsthand understanding and sparked my passion for research that has led me to devote myself to others with this condition. Because of my own pain, I am now able to help in a way I was never able to before. I'm grateful that I have become a "wounded healer." For each and every patient I have been able to help, and for those that I have yet to meet, I am grateful.

I have been completely blessed, and I am enormously grateful for my wife and son, who have given my life balance and have always supported me in everything I do. They have been my one true constant.

I have learned that life is not about what happens to us, but rather our reaction to those events. As each and every day comes to me fresh and new, so does my gratitude renew itself daily.

~ Dr. Mark Guariglia

May 22

Gifts of Life

Gratitude? I am grateful for every breath I take! Twice in my life surgeons gave me less than a fifty/fifty chance to live more than thirty days without a rare liver transplant. Twice in my life my family and I took that bet, and twice in my life we won!

Every day is a present! I can't wait to look inside! Every day I look to the heavens to thank God for allowing me to pass along my two "miracles," to pay forward my second chances.

Every day I am reminded of one of my heroes, Walter Payton, "Sweetness," the Hall of Fame Chicago Bears running back who died waiting for his second chance. He died waiting for a donor who never appeared. He died waiting for his life-saving liver transplant, while I have been blessed to receive these "gifts of life" — twice!

Thank you, Walter, for inspiring me! Thank you, kind strangers! I strive to honor every breath you have given me doing what I believe God has kept me on his earth to do. That is to "connect friends with friends who can help each other profit from their passions."

Every day is a present, and this present is truly a gift of life!

~ Thomas J. "Tom" Starr

May 23

It's Great to Be Grateful!

I am grateful for my beautiful bride, my better half, and the love of my life.

I am grateful for an incredible, supportive family that will always be by my side.

I am grateful for the wonderful friends whom I consider family.

I am grateful to have a roof over my head, food in the kitchen, and a bed to sleep in.

I am grateful to have the health, experiences, and wisdom to contribute to this incredible project.

I am grateful to have the sight to read it and the insight to learn from what others are grateful for.

~ Tom Buford

May 24

E-I-E-I-O

I did not grow up on "Old MacDonald's Farm," but I was lucky enough to grow up on Kozik Farm on Beaverdam Road near Union City, Pennsylvania.

Living in the country wasn't always easy. My father worked long hours, and my mother faced a never-ending battle with laundry, canning, and sweeping. My sister and I walked to end of the road to catch the school bus, and our summer activities including picking rocks out of fields, helping fix barbwire fences, and occasionally chasing cows back to the pasture. However, the good far outweighed the bad.

Here are a few of my favorite memories:

- Taking the tractor and trailer back to the woods to cut down our Christmas tree
- "Sleeping" outside to watch for shooting stars
- Picking blackberries with my grandmother
- Riding my bicycle up and down the dirt roads
- Having wiener roasts near our cabin
- Picking fresh vegetables out of our enormous garden
- Playing with our dog Annie's puppies
- Driving around the country block (five miles long) spotlighting for deer
- Lying under the big maple tree in the front yard and reading

I am blessed to have had a country upbringing!

~ Teresa A. Castleman

Finding Ms. Amy

Who knows who you will meet today who will change the course of your destiny. I was in nursing school and had an opportunity to take off and travel for a year. Sounds great, but I knew that, if I left school, I wouldn't go back. It was a tough decision, because traveling is one of my passions.

That is when Amy Cook, a 103-year-old spitfire at the nursing home where I was working, helped me solve my dilemma.

She told me that whenever she was in a crossroads in her life, she would make her major life decision as if she was in her death-bed. By reflecting back on her life, it showed her what was really important. Morbid, maybe, but she said there is no time in life for regrets.

I realized that if I didn't become a nurse I would always regret it. Since then, nursing has given me many travel opportunities, and I have met incredible people all over the world. I will be eternally grateful to Ms. Amy. She knew being a nurse is where my heart is.

~ Patty Hedrick

May 26

Always Enough

I give thanks for realizing there is always enough.

Over the years, I have woken with worries over finances, parenting, mortgage payments, how to pay for dance lessons, varsity jackets, and college; how to know the difference between what was wanted and what was needed.

Midnight worrying brought no relief.

Trying to discern the difference between wants and needs led to twisting confusion over how to survive. The churning in my belly and the spiral of worry ended when I realized there was always enough. Just as there was always enough love for more children, there was always enough energy, enough feeling, enough friendship, and enough financially to create a wonderful life. There is always enough when you let go of the struggle to control life and let circumstances prove:

There is always enough.

~ Kristine A. Friend

Growing Through Grief

The year 2010 was supposed to be my year! After all, I had a lot to celebrate: my 50th birthday, my dad's 75th, my grandmother's 95th, my daughter's graduation from high school, and my stepdaughter's wedding. Daddy's birthday was the day before the graduation, so a surprise party was part of the year's plans.

Sadly, my dad died unexpectedly in his sleep eleven days before my birthday. Turning 50 didn't seem like such a big deal after that. There would be no surprise party for Dad, graduation was bitter-sweet, and, to top things off, a few months later I lost my job.

Yet, I am grateful. I'm grateful for the people whose love got me through. I'm grateful for spiritual maturity. I am especially grateful for what I have learned:

Trust God.

It's okay for givers to receive sometimes. Be a gracious receiver.

Faith is an action word.

Keep life in its proper perspective.

God has a unique purpose for each of us.

It is through people that God bestows His blessings upon us.

I have been blessed beyond measure in unimaginable and awesome ways. I don't know how God does what He does, but I am grateful that He is God!

~ Bernée E. Long

May 28

My Sister, My Guru

When I consider what I am grateful for, I think first of my children, the miracle of life itself. Then I notice that the greatest cause for change, the moments of the clearest, sharpest, most compelling insights have often come in the throes of great pain.

My thoughts turn to my sister. We are so very different. Yet, we are siblings and have shared much. I call her my guru because, for all the love that lies at the foundation of our relationship, my sister is more adept at triggering my shadow — all the parts of myself that I have rejected — than anyone I know. And this acute, sometimes almost-intolerable pain has catapulted me into intense states of clarity, heightened understanding, and the re-integration of lost parts of myself.

She has been the greatest teacher to my illusions, to my criticisms, to the hardened places in my heart; a guide in my quest for wholeness. I am eternally grateful to her for being the magnificent mirror she has been into the wounding of my soul, giving me insight into how to heal. This is an immeasurable gift. My sister, my guru.

~ Betsy Shands

Michelle's Mom

Your unpretentious wisdom and bravery laid a foundation for fortitude.

Your uncommon gift of emotional intelligence created compassion and insight into what makes people tick.

Your creative discipline allowed me to begin grasping by age five that my body takes directions from the invisible me—the most valuable thing I now know.

Your reminders that no matter what life brought I'd always have choices—if only about my attitude—revealed life was happening through me—not to me.

Your guiding phrases such as "If doing the right thing was always easy, everyone would always do it," enabled me to calibrate my own moral barometer.

Your tolerance and open-mindedness fostered my ability to look at the world through a lens of appreciation and inquisitiveness.

You fed me. You clothed me. You housed me. So my body grew healthy and strong.

You educated me. You disciplined me. You challenged me. So my mind grew curious and sharp.

You encouraged me. You accepted me. You believed in me. So my spirit grew wide and free.

A good mom helps her kids grow up. A great mom helps them grow deep.

Thanks for being a great mom.

~ Michelle Dimsey

May 30

The Special People in My Life

I am grateful for the people I have met in my life:

The ones I have made friends with

The ones who showed up at the right time and place to point me to what was next

The ones who made my heart awaken and flood with love

The ones who, over the years, no matter what the physical distance between us, were always one phone call away

The ones who made me angry and resentful, for at the end they were my biggest teachers

The ones whose few words made me re-think who I am and what I bring forth and what I contribute to the world

The ones whose music and art connected me with universal beauty and helped me transcend the ordinary

And lastly, the ones whose presence inspired me to become more.

~ Liliane Mavridara

The Light at the End of the Tunnel

Some of the tunnels that we pass through can be very long indeed. Cancer and chemo are not only long tunnels but treacherously dangerous passages. Losses and fears of all kinds and relentless economic downturns test our gratitude to the limit.

What is a way to be heartfelt during such hurtful and difficult times? I offer one simple tool that has saved me more than once. When I feel uncertain and impatient, I "reframe" my experience with this new possibility:

Imagine you are standing in a thick fog. You cannot see ahead of you to take steps that will lead you to your future. You stand helplessly in uncertainty. Then, you realize you can detect a tiny light in the distance. You wonder if you can make your way safely through the dense fog to reach the distant light.

Then you realize the light is slowly moving toward you! The uncertainty changes; it becomes "Am I ready?"

In life, we cannot always know what is coming next. Frequently, the questions outnumber the answers.

Will your grateful heart be ready when the elements of "timing" set in motion that slow-moving light that will eventually reveal your greatest blessings?

~ Timi Gleason

June

"Gratitude is the memory of the heart."

~ Jean Baptiste Massieu

June 1

Damn, I'm Lucky

Well, "luck" might not really be what I'm trying to express. It's probably more like "blessed." You see, I've come to realize how grateful I am not to get everything I ask for.

My parents, for example. Some believe that we "choose" our mother and father for the lessons we need to learn. I have sometimes wished that my parents were different in the way they parented me, yet I now realize that they fostered so many of the qualities that helped me be strong and resilient. Because of them I have a fortitude that allows me to support others until they are ready to embrace their own inner strength.

Growing up I might not have always thought things were going as well as I wanted, but now I know how fortunate I was to receive all the gifts — even the ones that weren't "wrapped" as nicely as others! And I am grateful.

~ *Barbara L. Cummings*

June 2

Magnificence of All

I am grateful for the magnificence of All That Is.

I am grateful for my body—for the marvel of systems, organs, cells, and communications that make my life viable. I am grateful for my experiences and my emotions. I appreciate using the wisdom I have gained with added years and my journey choices; it helps me better enjoy all I am creating.

I am grateful for our Earth—for her beauty, nurture, generosity, abundance, grace, and forgiveness. I am thankful for the water, fire, air, and earth elements; and for the animal, plant, and mineral kingdoms. I love the way Earth's atmosphere perfectly supports us, with light, warmth, cloud, and rain.

I am grateful for our Sun—the center of this solar system, for its energy and power that enable our habitation. I like the way the Sun holds together our neighborhood of planets with their moons and traveling companions.

I am grateful for our Milky Way galaxy—for its elegance and dance within the Cosmos. I enjoy looking up at night to see stars and constellations, and wonder what else, and who, might be out there.

I smile my love toward that which created All.

~ Carol B. Gailey

Unconditional Love

Today is my birthday. It's also the day I learned my former mother-in-law is receiving hospice care and has little time left, so she is on my mind.

I was 16 when I married her son in a "shotgun wedding." Two years later my own mother died tragically at 36. I spent the next few years like a wounded animal, "hiding" in self-destructive ways. I lashed out and pushed away anyone who tried to get close to me, costing me not only my marriage, but also custody of my child.

My gratitude today is for the woman, my former mother-in-law, who, despite my temporary insanity, "left the light on" and continued to consider me family. That's rare in any divorce, and even more so because I was so unlovable at the time. More than that, she raised my oldest child when I couldn't, to be the loving, compassionate person she is today.

The person I knew as Louise has been gone for a while—both her unique self and her memories taken by Alzheimer's—but I'll never forget that she stood by me when I was really hard to love.

Today, I'm grateful for unconditional love. Wherever and whenever you find it, it's a precious gift.

~ Helen Sue Walker

June 4

All Things Work Together for Good

"And we know that all things work together for good..."
~ Romans 8:28 KJV

I have so much to be thankful for today. One blessing that I'm so grateful for is my dear husband, Gary, who I married at age 49 after being single for years.

Throughout my life, I experienced a lot of heartache, pain, grief, and depression. I was just 12 when my father unexpectedly died of a heart attack.

Because of my father's death, I began an intense study, learning all I could about preventative health and, at age 54, I started my business of coaching and consulting. I am passionate about educating and encouraging Christian women in the area of health and wellness. I also came to faith in Jesus at an early age. God gave me my greatest blessing, Gary, and in 2004, my life was changed by a miracle of God.

So much good came from those years of pain. I am most grateful to God for doing what is best: allowing the pain in my life and working all things together for good. It happened for me, and I know that God will bless those who patiently endure through the trials of life.

~ *Carol A. Boston*

I Am Grateful

My life so far has been wonderfully blessed and productive, replete with a loving husband and two delightful grown children. I truly have many gifts that I gratefully count among my blessings. Very recently I was graced with a gift so magnanimous that in describing my experience, words simply cannot give it the proper justice it deserves.

Upon awakening each morning, I turn my attention upwardly to God, giving praise and thanks for the new opportunities each day provides. One morning, I was graced by a vision of a most divinely beautiful being residing over my head, which I have come to know as my "*I Am*" presence. It stands in magnificent glory, bathing me in a protective pillar of pure white, sparkling light that fills me to overflowing with oceans of unconditional love and joy.

Growing daily in my ability to sustain focus upon it, at first I noticed a small threefold flame within my heart, that radiated soft, delicate pink, gold, and blue. These flames are now ever expanding within me, filling my consciousness with utmost peace and harmony that seem to come straight from the heart of God.

I am truly filled to overflowing with gratitude!

~ Lois Posner

June 6

What Gratitude Means to Me

I am most grateful for being a teacher, coach, and parent. I have come to realize that my greatest joy in life is in giving to others and helping others, for it is in giving that I feel most satisfied. Gratitude comes from giving, and it is in giving that we enjoy abundance.

I am wildly grateful for my wonderful husband and our two sons who, through their eyes, show my husband and me the whole world with wonder again. I am grateful knowing that I can share with them my life full of experience and lessons I've learned about living a life of possibilities. These are some of the sterling lessons I'm grateful for having learned:

Acknowledge where you are in your life now (gratitude leads to happiness).

Be happy right where you are (happiness leads to success).

Connect with what you would love to do all day long if you had no limitations.

Dare to dream (think of the possibilities, not of the impossibilities).

Empower yourself; own that you can do whatever you set out to do.

Find that you can make every ordinary day an extra-ordinary day!

Give. Give what you discover about yourself to the world. Share your gifts.

~ Marian Edvardsen

June 7

Grateful for the Blessing of Work

The pain was excruciating. The diagnosis? Carpal tunnel syndrome. The impact? Devastating. Being a workaholic with two jobs, I was crushed. Surgery and therapy did not help. The pain increased. I had muscle spasms.

I had difficulty doing manual tasks. Fibromyalgia compounded the problems. My husband was doing the housework. I was worried. I returned to work, only to experience more difficulty.

Management approached me about going on disability. I was scared beyond belief. My life goals were to teach computers and write—both of which required the use of my hands. I was devastated. How could they even think of bringing up disability? Yet, I knew in my heart that I was running out of options.

It was a long recovery as I struggled to continue to work. With perseverance, I accomplished my goals. I have been teaching for fourteen years, and I write as well. On those days when I jokingly say, "Oh boy, it's back to work tomorrow," it's really not a complaint. I am so grateful for the blessing of work. I love the feel of the keyboard under my fingers! I can't imagine life without the blessing of being productive and contributing to society.

~ Susan Brownell

June 8

Finding the Good Is Your Reward

"Look for the good in people and you will surely find it." (Rephrased from the movie Pollyanna.)

~ Wilhelmien van Nieuwenhuizen

I am grateful, for all the wonderful people I meet as I journey through life.

I was a little girl of 5 years old, living in South Africa in the early '60s, when I saw the movie *Pollyanna* for the first time. My young memory could only recall the quote above, and the principle became ingrained in my life.

Raising my children with this principle, I noticed how they excel, as their world view was formed to see possibilities, and to focus on the good. Though life has its quota of challenges, a possibility thinker has the strength to overcome them.

While going through a challenging time, I reflected upon my life and the way forward. Then it dawned on me: We are relationship people, and our life's purpose is realized through our relationships. My heart was filled with gratitude, and I became focused on helping people fulfill their purpose in life.

I am inspired by people who cross my path, and I value every new face on my life's journey. May I meet you soon!

~ Wilhelmien van Nieuwenhuizen

June 9

Unplugged!

There are moments when the necessity to once again experience and express life is more powerful than all depressing constraints. And magic happens.

Ten days "unplugged": to remember how to be me. My plans only prompted by serendipity and the date of the flight back home.

Breathing in a cloud of ocean spray, I walked among a tribe of long-legged Shorebirds and found hidden sand dollars and long wavy seaweeds that could have been a mermaid's headdress. There on the beach, even if I was but a dot, I felt immense: a part of the waves and the colors of the powerful landscape.

All the people I met were the manifestation of cheer, kindness, and success. My enthusiasm kept growing exponentially with each ranch and forest and town I visited; my trip was becoming surreal!

I never want to leave this surreal world where I am meeting fantastic new friends and possibilities graciously open their gates, inviting me to stay. My gratitude expands, looking for new ways to integrate and share this energy and joy with all that surrounds me. I feel alive again.

~ Alice R. Galassi

June 10

The Five Senses of Our Marriage

SMELLING: I am grateful for the spicy and sensual scents that we use to elicit the spirit of romance to embrace us.

HEARING: I am grateful for the vibrant voice of lively laughter, when our private joke pulsates between us and bellows in our bellies, resounding in our ears and reverberating in our hearts.

TOUCHING: I am grateful for the heavenly hugs, kisses, and caresses that have cascaded ever more in our thirty-eight years together, and most especially those that climax the closing of a conflict.

SEEING: I am grateful for witnessing and treasuring the accumulating and compounding of tangible wealth in our love bank account, from actively giving each other appreciation, attention, and affection.

TASTING: I am grateful for the sweet taste of applause, as we perform a steamy Samba on stage and savor the satisfying success.

I am grateful for the five senses of our marriage!

~ Annette Carpien

June 11

Finding Uncle Albert

Sometimes the Universe yells at us to get a move on or we'll miss the boat. Two years ago, that prod became a push; there was no other choice than to get on with it, even though my logical mind was telling me not to be so dumb. I'm so glad I listened!

We'd lost contact with Dad's five brothers after he died; everyone lived so far away. And yet over half a century later, I found myself inexplicably on-line, exploring my family tree...and found Uncle Albert, Dad's one surviving brother, now 90-plus.

I didn't get too long to know him; Albert's health was fading fast. And yet I found a wonderful gentleman who bore his frailty with the same spirit he had lived his life. A World War II veteran from the North Africa campaign and a POW in Italy, he managed to escape into Switzerland. A wonderful story-teller with a wicked twinkle in his eye, his anecdotes gave me back the Dad I didn't remember, and a sense of belonging to his family I had lost. I'm so grateful I listened to the promptings and found Uncle Albert.

~ Gillian Holland

June 12

Giving Thanks to Tenacity

If I have been humbled by anything over the last four years of my life, it has been the simple fact that the easiest way to fail is to quit. And I have wanted to.

Building a business is tough work. Being of service is consuming. Failing is expensive. Tenacity is free. For that I am most grateful.

Whatever you set out in life to achieve or whatever dream you hold dear, the gift that you have been given to prevail is tenacity. When all else fails, hustle. When all feels bleak, I am grateful that no matter the circumstances no one can take away my spirit or drive.

I am grateful that tenacity trumps intelligence seven days a week.

~ Suzanne Evans

Blessings in Disguise

I'm grateful for modern medicine and my son's second chance in life.

My first son was born on March 23, 1999. He weighed eight and a half pounds. He was healthy-looking with bright pink skin, lots of black hair, big brown eyes, olive skin, and a dimple in his chin.

It was love at first sight — a love you can't describe or understand unless you are a mother. I was about to embark on the most important journey of my life: to nurture, to love, to support my son, to help him grow up and be a happy, well adjusted, respectful adult.

After many months of not thriving, Nicholas was diagnosed at seven months of age with congenital renal failure. Both of his kidneys did not form properly. This was a shock to all of us. We didn't know if he would live or for how long. We were told he would need a kidney transplant one day.

After years of medication and growth hormones, at the age of 11½, Nicholas Adam Thomas Shugg received his father's kidney on September 6, 2010. I am so grateful for the gift of life Nicholas has received and for modern medicine.

~ Melissa Louise Groom

June 14

To Those Who Protect Our Freedom

"This nation will remain the land of the free only so long as it is the home of the brave."

~ Elmer Davis

I'm grateful to the brave men and women who ensure our freedom and way of life by serving on the front lines of our country's battlefields. These young service members sacrifice so much. They voluntarily leave the comfort of their own lives, put themselves in harm's way, and wage a dangerous and courageous fight to keep us safe at home.

Saying "thank you" is not enough. Mere words are never sufficient to show the depth of gratitude we owe our servicemen and women. But they're a start.

When you see members of the military in restaurants, pay for their meal, if you can, to show your gratitude. They'll be so appreciative. This simple exchange is powerful, and you'll always get much more than you could ever give.

I encourage you to show your support. And if you can do something for those who diligently serve us, do it. Their devotion to duty allows us to live the lives we cherish. Let's make sure they know they're appreciated.

~ *Deborah R. Avery*

June 15

Teaching Yoga Deepened My Faith

They say we teach what we need to learn. In teaching yoga, I ask questions that often stimulate my students to go deeper within — to listen and understand that how they are in their practice is how they will show up in the world. I am so grateful for my students. Their courage and tenacity to keep showing up for themselves show in their daily lives.

My initial intention for practicing yoga was to get still within and listen at the deeper level to what wanted to emerge to support my healing. This felt a little scary because I thought just having my faith should be enough and it wasn't, and it felt like admitting that was admitting failure.

It was my yoga practice that deepened my faith and allowed it to come alive. I began to realize that in order to fully accept the love of God I had to learn to accept myself, the dark and the light, and be in relationship with myself before I could fully be in relationship with the Divine and really live. I'm incredibly grateful to be teaching what I have learned from yoga.

~ Teresa C. Lea

June 16

The Wayshowers

"An attitude of gratitude is most salutary, and bespeaks the realization that we are now in heaven."

~ Ernest Holmes

I am grateful for all the spiritual teachers who have come to this world and handed down their legacy of Truth throughout the ages — those who have given up their personal lives, sometimes at the stake, to be the mouthpieces or scribes of the Divine in whatever faith or wisdom tradition they represented. I honor their commitment and their courage to take the straight and narrow path of their sacred interior compass, when to take the broader path of the masses would have been, perhaps, a more comfortable choice.

I am particularly grateful to Ernest Holmes, founder of the Science of Mind. This teaching resonated in the depths of my soul. It set me free from the erroneous conviction that I was a victim of forces beyond my control and led me to understand that, through the conscious, prayerful, cultivation of my thoughts, words, beliefs, and attitudes, I could command my fate.

Who knows where you and I would be today without those who went ahead of us to prepare the way....

~ Rev. Stephanie Clarke

A Matter of Trust

"To be trusted is a greater compliment than to be loved."
~ George MacDonald

A whole new dimension of trust opened up to me when I embarked on this miraculous, wild, amazing, and incredibly fulfilling journey called "coaching."

For a long time, my life had looked and felt like a race: chasing "the right job," what I thought was my true calling, taking the fast lane—and, paradoxically, finding myself moving even further away from my heart and soul's desire. Then I found my calling: coaching—or rather it found me.

I became a professional coach, and from that moment on, I was given the privilege of being with clients who show up in their entire humanity, with vulnerability, courage, hope — and their trust. Beyond treating conversations confidentially, they trust me to believe in them, and to see them in their greatness and their shining magnificence, even and especially when they cannot see their potential themselves.

To be gifted with this level of trust is invaluable, humbling, and a tremendous honor. It is this trust and courage to live their most fulfilling life that is a constant inspiration to my own life and growth.

~ *Elisabeth Balcarczyk*

June 18

I'm So Grateful You Were Born

Oh, little Missy, I am so grateful you were born. I am grateful for that little girl sparkle that climbed trees, played dress-up, and made messes (so many "artistic" messes that your brothers nicknamed you Messy). I love your free spirit that dances in the sunshine, sings loudly, and, yes, makes messes.

I am so grateful for your "I can do anything" attitude and your relentless desire to make things better. As a teacher I remember the program you started called DOT: "Do One Thing" that makes a difference for someone else or the environment every day. I felt proud of how it expanded from your classroom to the whole school. I love your optimism, knowing that we can make a difference, and your willingness to step forward to make it happen.

I am grateful for your loving, compassionate nature. In your presence it feels safe to open my heart, and share my wounds and my wonders. I love your ability to see the possibilities for other people, encouraging them to shine their light and to live their passions.

I am so grateful that you have grown up to be the woman you are: creative spirit, loving nature, passionate leader, making a difference...radiant Melissa.

~ Melissa Anne Lawson

A Life Surrendered

What am I grateful for? That is a big question, since I have so much to be thankful for at this point in my life. If you would have asked me ten years ago, I would not have felt the same way.

Being a single, Christian woman with morals that many didn't agree with or understand, I had experienced a lot of heartache and rejection in my life.

For many, many years I struggled on my own trying to make it through life. Although I was a Christian, I did not allow God to be in control of my life.

By November 2003, I had accumulated $39,000 in credit card debt. I was emotionally, physically, and spiritually exhausted. I desperately needed a miracle! Deciding to trust God completely, I surrendered my entire life to God and, in faith, began tithing to God's work.

Within five months of tithing, the $39,000 had been paid, and I met and then later married Gary, a wonderful, Christian man who is one of my greatest blessings. I was also able to retire. I am most grateful to God and that I surrendered my life to Him that day! God is good!

~ Carol A. Boston

June 20

Peace and a Smile

I am grateful that it is never too late to stop a thought or to change my mind. Review and redo my perspective so I feel better about it and me, my life, and all of you in it.

I am grateful to renew my commitment to remember that thoughts are things — that I get to choose which things run my seconds, minutes, and days on this journey called my life.

I am grateful my mind is under my control so I truly am the mistress of my fate and the captain of my soul. The way I see the world around me, even me myself and you yourself, is what I choose to believe we are.

I am grateful I have chosen to focus on the goodness, not the pain. The possibilities, not the dead ends.

I am grateful to know how the world really works. Enormous freedom. Tremendous potential. Peace and a smile.

~ Linda Cole

June 21

Busy "Be-ing"

"I am grateful for hot water that comes to my bathroom, burns the pain out of me and lets me work another day."

This simple prayer of gratitude uttered in primal tones spurts forth at the moment the shower water is almost too much to bear. It is at this edge of tolerance that the relief comes... and I am grateful!

I am a single woman, on my own, reaching mid-life with a multitude of injuries from the past. "What doesn't kill you makes you stronger."

I am a survivor.

I make a good, clean living digging dirt. I am a gardener. I tend God's gifts with a loving hand, encouraging the fruits and flowers to realize their full potential. The hummingbirds and bees co-exist with me as I kneel in their space and we all reap the benefits of the work being done.

Mother Nature is my boss, constantly challenging me with her extreme mood swings. Drought or deluge, she's a force to be reckoned with. Nature is my cubicle. A tank top and work boots round out my uniform. My tan and my exercise regime get worked on daily.

I'm busy "BE-ing"...and I am grateful.

~ Annie Ferrigno

June 22

True Love Everlasting

True love never dies; it just finds a new home!

With the holiday season quickly descending upon us like white on rice, I am reminded of my family's many blessings. The most profound and eternal blessing is the beautiful legacy that my mother, IlaMae, left us with, the year she departed from this earth.

Having recovered from the life-threatening disease polio in 1949, my mother was thankful for life: for every day, every minute, and literally every breath she took.

Her gratitude was like bright rays of sunshine that she wove into the tapestries of the lives of her four children and eight grandchildren. Although she was handicapped, through divine strength, she raised four children alone, while living with dignity, integrity, hope, inspiration, and unconditional love.

Life is like a tapestry that is constantly changing: a beautiful work of art filled with love, lessons, hope, and gratitude.

As my three children travel the sometimes-bumpy road through adulthood, I feel especially grateful to see their grandmother's rays of light unfolding in their tapestries of life.

The love and gratitude we share with others lives on long after we are gone. It just finds a new home!

~ Merrilee Johnson

The Cream of the Crop

We all have a choice for a wide range of sentimental emotions. Beliefs are ours to choose. Some are taught; some just are. They weave our life, and express our soul.

There are two feelings that are like gold — the cream of the crop. When you put them together they can produce enough power to heal the sick, move mountains, create miracles, motivate people, and conquer any problem. These feelings are free for all of us to have — a gift described in two simple words: love and faith.

Love and faith only become complex words when we make them so.

I have cried over a million tears from feeling love, yet have no regrets for opening my heart. As love's dear companion, faith has wiped my tears, comforting me to rise once again. How blessed I am to have loved and to have had unshakable faith.

With the many concerns for our dear mother earth, may we remember our freedom of free choice in our thoughts. To go for the gold, the cream of crop, and feel love and faith rise to the top.

~ Louise Rouse

June 24

What I Did on My Summer Vacation

My parents believed in family vacations. Each summer, we packed our tiny car and departed for a two-week road trip. In the mid-1960s, we drove one thousand miles to Florida. It was July — hot as blazes, and our car had no air conditioning.

There were no theme parks yet. Instead, we saw "mermaids" swimming underwater, a rocket launch pad, and a lunar lander. We rode on a glass-bottomed boat and looked at fish, while Mom suffered with seasickness. We drank chlorinated water from the Fountain of Youth. Dad proclaimed it would allow him to live to be one hundred. He's almost there.

Every day, Dad drove determinedly to the next destination. Bored, Mom counted the many mosquito bites on my sister's legs. My sister and I counted cars, played travel games, slept, and loudly whined, "Are we there yet? How much longer?" When we got too loud, Mom said tensely, "Dad, will you settle them?" "Settle!" Dad said, in a fake gruff voice. We all laughed, and peacefulness was restored.

There were no MP3 or DVD players, no video games—just imagination, my parents' endless patience, and memories to treasure for the rest of our lives. Thank you, Mom and Dad.

~ Susan Veach

Look for the Cake!

On my husband's birthday we were driving out of the downtown area and kept getting stopped by traffic jams and construction. After the third route change it became very apparent that he was struggling to remain positive.

I wondered if there could be a gift in this situation. There must be some reason for all these detours and delays in our travel. At that exact point in my thoughts, he heaved a frustrated sigh at being stopped by another red light. I looked up and saw a bakery. Knowing we didn't have a birthday cake for him, I convinced him to pull into the open parking spot in front of the bakery. I went in to see if they had any carrot cake (his favorite). Sure enough, there was one beautifully decorated carrot cake left! In a total of five minutes we were back on the road again, cake in hand, and, interestingly enough, there was not another traffic problem all the way home!

The minute we tasted the moist, delicious cake, we were both very grateful for the traffic problems. Now when I am stuck in traffic I offer my gratitude and look for the "cake"!

~ Deb Dawson-Dunn

June 26

Being Grateful

I'm grateful for my health and the health of my loved ones,

Grateful for my daughter's laughter,

Grateful for my husband's love and support,

Grateful for my family,

Grateful for my friends.

I'm grateful for the roof over my head and for the food I eat.

I'm grateful for the rain,

Grateful for the sun that follows the rain,

Grateful for the sounds,

Grateful for the sights.

I strive to be grateful for my losses, for it's better to have had and lost than not had at all.

I'm grateful to be alive.

I'm grateful to be grateful!

~ Maryam Nasr Sardari

June 27

My Parents' Love

I am grateful for the foundation that my parents instilled in me. My parents lived through the Depression and World War II. They developed standards that valued hard work, thrift, and respect for others.

I am grateful that they taught me a work ethic and the value of taking responsibility for the outcome of my life.

I am grateful that they taught me to help when possible, and to put others' interests above my own.

I am grateful that they taught me not to look to others for a handout, but to graciously accept assistance when appropriate.

I am grateful that they taught me to respect other people and to recognize their dignity in whatever circumstances in which they find themselves.

I am grateful that they taught me to give my best effort in service to others, in both personal and professional capacities.

I am grateful that they taught me to be loyal to my family and friends, and to appreciate the value of those relationships.

I am grateful for their love and caring, and their commitment to preparing me for my future as a son, brother, husband, father, and contributing member in business and in my community.

~ Douglas Brennecke

June 28

Life with Mom

I am ever grateful to my mother, Earth. She's the most beautiful world in the universe. I love being lost in the sway of her seasons and watching as life, both tender and mighty, springs from her.

With joy, I dance on her lap, waving my paintbrush, wowed by her contours and atmosphere. Her rhythms and moods flow through me onto the canvas. How grateful I am to be a landscape painter.

I'll stay by her side every day of my life, planting the seeds I've been given and sharing the lessons I've learned. How grateful I am to my students for their trust in the teaching I do. The art of each one blooms so uniquely. Their gardens of art spread much joy.

~ Lillian Kennedy

Full of Gratitude

Some days I forget to be grateful.

Most days I am reminded that I have so much to be grateful for.

I am grateful for a spirit that loves to learn.

I am grateful for many surprising teachers.

I am grateful for my husband, who is his beautiful soul self regardless of which self I am.

I am grateful for a handsome guardian lab, who is my soul keeper.

I am grateful for a sister who touches my heart and friends who never lose sight of me.

I am grateful for not knowing so that I keep looking.

I am grateful for a heart that hurts and heals and reaches out in love.

I am grateful for not giving up on me.

I am grateful for this opportunity.

~ Regina Eustace

June 30

On My Journey

I am grateful for the wisdom and all-embracing love of my maternal grandmother, the warmth and generosity of my mother's heart, the security and strength of my father's hand, the comfort of a lover's arms, and true friends.

I am grateful for the smile of a child, and the "hello!" of a stranger.

I am grateful for not needing to be "perfect" to be "good" and "exceptional."

I am grateful for the ability to heal from hurt and loss, remember and forgive, create, learn, care, teach, and give.

I am grateful for the ability and resources to create space I can call my own.

I am grateful for the courage, strength, and sacrifices of those who came before me: Jesus, Elizabeth I, Harriet Tubman, Frederick Douglas, Abraham Lincoln, Martin Luther King, James Baldwin, Barbara Jordan, E. Lynn Harris.

I am grateful for Bishop Desmond Tutu, Nelson Mandela, President and Mrs. Obama, Reverend Peter J. Gomes, Maya Angelou.

I am grateful for gay activists, especially those of color, and their allies.

I am grateful for the past, present, and future.

I am grateful for each new day!

I am grateful for you and me.

~ B. E. Thompson

July

"If the only prayer you said in your whole life was, 'thank you,' that would suffice."

~ Meister Eckhart

July 1

In Loving Memory of Jimmie and Inez Sunday

Throughout my childhood I sometimes felt my parents didn't understand me and that they weren't always on my side. My mother would sit down and pull me toward her, saying, "Dear, are you going through this situation or growing through it?"

Their comments back then always left me feeling bewildered, misunderstood, and that I wasn't heard.

My father, Jimmie Sunday, would assure me not to worry. For others to do something that wasn't right didn't give me a reason not to do right. He would tell me to do what I felt was right.

I am grateful I completely understand my parents' wisdom, and I now know that they loved and understood me. I am grateful they were patient to understand what I needed to hear, and did not simply tell me what to do. I became stronger as I grew since their advice did not change; it only evolved as I matured.

I am grateful for all of my challenging life experiences, for they strengthened my character and sense of self-worth.

~ Millie Sunday Jett

July 2

Immeasurable Gratitude

Each day brings infinite possibilities and opportunities for which I am appreciative. Counting my blessings is an impossible task that I have frequently tried. The tattered slip of paper in my wallet, a well-worn and well-read reminder from when I last attempted this feat, reads:

I am so grateful for...

1) my mental abilities because I can think unique and creative thoughts, have a quick wit, can devise solutions, and can think and feel deeply.

2) my physical health because I enjoy being an active participant in life and in my community.

3) my husband, Michael, because he is the best. He is patient and kind. He makes me laugh and think and dream.

4) my family because I felt safe and loved when I was a child.

5) the abundance of love in the world, my extended family, my in-laws, my friends, and my cats.

6) my careers for being flexible, fun, and financially rewarding, and for allowing me to make a difference in the lives of others

Now, as I gaze at my miraculous and beloved newborn daughter, she reminds me of the precious gift of time shared with loved ones in the here and now. Immeasurable gratitude.

~ Louise-Annette Burgess

July 3

The Law of Increase

Sir John Templeton, one of the most successful investors of all time, was asked the secret to creating success. He said, "Overcoming fear." "I understand that," said the interviewer, "but what's the secret to overcoming fear?" Sir John said, "Gratitude."

Why do you think he answered that way? How can gratitude help you overcome fear and be successful?

Sir John was expressing a principle of nature. Once we learn to be thankful for what we have been given, then we are willing to step out in faith — not fear — and ask for more. Gratitude works on the future, not the past. Success will come to those who overcome their fears while expecting abundance. This is the Law of Increase: Gratitude brings forth our desires, and it generates confidence, strengthens faith, and builds up an assurance for things to come. In other words, gratitude leads to both mental and physical increase.

Be grateful today!

~ Jeff Woodard

July 4

From Feeling Overwhelmed to Finding Joy and Purpose

Sometimes God has to get our attention through drastic measures.

Life had turned into one insane day after another, being overwhelmed and stressed out, and reacting to constant demands. I was running as fast as I could, striving to achieve.

When a conference call was moved four times, forcing me to cancel a rare lunch with my son so it could take place, I knew my life and priorities had to change. There was no joy in my life. When that call was over, I needed help. I turned to a guided meditation CD.

That simple act of slowing down and quieting my mind transformed my life. As a result, my priorities shifted from acquiring to serving. Freedom comes with not feeling overwhelmed and not reacting to what life brings. We are meant to create the life that God intended us to have filled with joy and purpose.

I quit my job and created a consulting business during extremely challenging economic times. But instead of focusing on lack, I focus on how rich I am to have loving family, friends, and clients that I can serve. Most of all, I'm grateful for a loving God that truly wants the best for us, if we will stop and pay attention.

~ Jackie Trottmann

July 5

At Home in the Body

Today I decide to be grateful for my body. This is a big step for me, because there was a time when I hated my body. I could only look at it or think about it, all of it, with judgment or shame. Today is different.

I do a body scan. What feels the easiest? My hands. I am grateful for my hands. They allow me to feel the softness of my cat's fur as I pet her. And as I gently lay my hands on her side I feel the reassurance of her breath that lets me know she is alive and well. My ears hear her gentle purr as she senses me. So I guess I am grateful for my ears, too. My eyes soften as I see her coat of white, checkered from the nose to across her back and tail, with pastel peach and light gray. She quietly opens her eyes, looks at me with complete trust and love, and then closes them gently. I'm grateful that I have my eyes to observe her in this quiet, serene space —a space in which I am learning to be more at home.

And for this I give thanks.

~ Teresa C. Lea

July 6

Expect Miracles—the Way My Teacher Taught Me

When listing the gratitudes of my life, my deepest and ongoing sense of gratitude stems from the transformative power that came into my life when I learned to expect miracles in the exact way that my teacher modeled while instructing me.

My teacher sits straight and still in simple elegance upon the floor. His eyes are locked in the purest quality of knowing. In this posture of ultimate awareness, he holds no hint of wishing, hoping, or doubt. Manifestation to the bowl before him is inevitable. His clear eyes and nearly perceivable smile present nothing but total omnipotence. Command of the universe remains solidly within his instant grasp. No one could resist the intensity of such pure and complete mastery of knowingness. As perfection of this meditative pose is complete, he curls his tail around his front feet.

His universe responds to his every desire. I have no ability to resist this enormous energy of intention and total expectation. I drop treats in to his cat bowl, and thus continues the meditative tradition of our daily lives together.

Every day EXPECT MIRACLES.

Every day MIRACLES expected will be delivered.

~ Louise Egan

July 7

Each Moment

"If you are anxious, you're living in the future. If you're depressed, you're living in the past."

~ Unknown

Each morning when I open my eyes, I am grateful, and each night when I close my eyes, I give thanks. But what I'm most grateful for are all the special moments that happen throughout the day, and my ability to be fully present in those moments—to be immersed in the here and now.

Realizing that living in the past or worrying about the future does not allow me the opportunity to be grateful for each unfolding moment, I have become more aware of focusing my attention in the present. Since yesterday is gone and tomorrow is not yet here, if I do not live in the moment, then eventually my life is lost, because I'm not really aware, I'm not truly experiencing each moment, nor am I living them fully and completely.

Being grateful for each moment allows me to enjoy every hour, every minute, every second of my day, and to be thankful for all my wonderful experiences—good and bad—and acknowledge them as they transpire.

I am incredibly grateful for the power of now!

~ Kim M. Baldwin

July 8

The Gratitude Lifestyle

I am most grateful for a recent understanding that there are levels of gratitude. For example, some people need reminders to say thank you. Others use it sparingly at obvious times. Still others devote time each day, acknowledging the things they are most grateful for. However, the ultimate practice is to live the gratitude lifestyle.

Just like living in the present, living in gratitude is a conscious choice. We choose to be aware of and grateful for all the bounty that we experience on a daily basis, no matter how small. Some examples of this lifestyle are:

- The words "thank you" come out spontaneously at the slightest hint of a courtesy or consideration.

- You find yourself waving at everyone who lets you cut into the driving lane, even as the passenger.

- You express appreciation to everyone who helps or serves you: grocery clerks, bus drivers, high-end jewelers — it's all the same.

- In the most intimate moments with your partner, you thank each other for the gift of life you've just received.

How to get started? Set a conscious intention to live in gratitude and begin by staying aware of opportunities for saying thank you. Try it; you'll like it!

~ Louise Morganti Kaelin

July 9

Support and Unconditional Love

I am most grateful for my family and friends who have shown support and unconditional love as I fulfill a twenty-year dream. At 40 years old, my husband and I, with our two children, three dogs, and two cats, moved from our birthplaces in Pennsylvania to Alaska. This meant leaving the security of our family, friends, home, and careers for uncertainty. For heaven's sake, we bought a house without stepping foot inside, and retired from our careers without having positions in Alaska.

This was truly a leap of faith (and totally uncharacteristic for me). Everyone kept saying they knew we would be fine; they believed in us. Deep down, I knew everything would fall into place at the right time.

As our departure day grew closer, it struck me one morning how grateful I am to have so many loving people in my life. As difficult as it was for everyone to say goodbye, they were supportive through their words of faith and encouragement for our happiness. If anyone had doubts, they were put aside to give me the support and unconditional love I needed to make the move. For this, I am forever grateful.

~ Gail M. Schuler

July 10

My Happy Thought

I am grateful for when you wake me up early every morning, pawing on the blanket and nudging me with your nose.

You are so happy to see me get up and walk toward the kitchen, constantly wagging your tail as if you are the one leading me toward the treat container.

I am grateful that you never cease to welcome a day without excitement, prancing on two paws and doing circles.

I am grateful that when I arrive home you anxiously wait for the garage door to open.

I am grateful when you help yourself to the bed and that, when I call out your name, I see the blanket move up and down to your tail wagging.

Happiness in your life is all about the simple things: meal time, walks, treats, playing fetch, belly rubs, sleeping under the blankets, soaking up the sun on a cold morning, and curiously following insects in the yard. You are my daily reminder that life is really not that bad.

Most importantly, I am grateful that no matter how happy, mad, busy, sad, stressed, tired, or down I get, I will unconditionally be the best part of your day.

They say that having a pet can extend your life. I believe a pet can save it.

~ Dina Rocha

July 11

Living a Blissful Life

There are so many things I could list to be grateful for in my life. Given the limitations of print, I've boiled it down to a few specific ones:

- My parents did the best they could. It's a daily blessing to tap into the energy of a childhood where I had no idea we were poor. I was allowed to believe I could be anything.

- I have the privilege of raising two wonderfully imperfect, average American kids that have the capacity to change the world, if they choose.

- My amazing husband has no idea how brilliant he is. Being married to him (and dating many frogs prior) has given me an appreciation of the essence of a true man.

- Having a business grants me the freedom to work to live, not vice versa.

- Many of my friends have grown up with me (some for more decades than I care to admit). Those friendships have remained ageless.

- White Pines Tuttie, Inky and Sarge, Benji, and every pug in between brought me pure joy while asking for nothing in return.

- A few favorite things: delicious food, a roof over my head, clothes on my back, physical and financial health, lazy summer days.

~ Lauren L. Darr

July 12

Being Nicer to Me

When I was growing up, a piece of life wisdom didn't come from the kitchen table, but instead was printed on an ordinary washcloth my Mom got for bath time. It said, "Be nice to me, I had a hard day." On it was a little girl, chin down, with a big flower serving as her umbrella and a butterfly floating near-by. Even though she was two-dimensional on terrycloth, my heart went out to her.

Nearly 40 years later, that message still sticks with me.

Many times I'm almost frantically monitoring my own thoughts for "stinking thinking" and even berating myself when a negative thought comes to mind while quickly muttering "cancel, cancel, cancel."

If those techniques work for you, great! But I think it's time to give myself a break.

It's okay to say to myself, "Be nice to me, I had a hard day."

Because hard days do come along. And, thankfully, they also leave.

On any day, what I'm now going to remember most is this: I'm doing the best I can.

With that thought, I think it's time to start being nicer to me.

~ Anonymous

July 13

A Thank-You Note

We don't know each other.

That was intentional. The rules.

Hopefully, you will read this and realize that you're the person for whom it's intended. If you wish, you can contact me. Whether or not you do, here is a thank-you note for your gift, twenty-two years later....

In mid-July 1988, a male in his late teens or early twenties was killed in an accident. He came from Pennsylvania. His family donated his organs, and you were a part of the decision to do so.

I know this because Shabtai Wishky, my husband, underwent a kidney transplant at Presbyterian University Hospital, in Pittsburgh, on July 14, 1988. You are a member of the donor family.

In Israel, where we live, it is difficult to obtain transplants. I am an American citizen. This entitled my husband to enter the U.S. and made him eligible for a transplant.

Since then, he has been living life to the fullest.

Tomorrow, July 14th is special for yet another reason. It is also my husband's birthday.

Thank you for giving him the greatest birthday present anyone could receive! Life!

My husband and I pray this kidney will sustain him always — and this thank-you note will bring you comfort and joy.

~ Tziporah Wishky

July 14

Gratitude:
The Key to a Joyful Life

"In ordinary life we hardly realize that we receive a great deal more than we give, and that it is only with gratitude that life becomes rich."

~ Dietrich Bonhoeffer

My life took a hard left turn in 1987 when I was diagnosed with undifferentiated connective tissue disease, which progressed to lupus. Today in remission, I look back on an amazing journey—a journey that opened new doors in my life for which I am grateful. Having earned a master's degree in holistic nutrition, it is rewarding to help others like I was helped. Thus, lupus gave me a new purpose in life.

Lupus taught me how much I took for granted in my life—how negative thoughts are limiting and how in a state of gratitude, one can't take anything or anyone in life for granted. You can't both feel gratitude and limitation in your life.

My journey taught me that how you think about difficult times determines whether they become opportunities or prison sentences. If you concentrate on what you have for which to feel gratitude, it lifts you up, as well as the people around you, and then the positive energy comes back to you. Most importantly, I learned that gratitude is a stepping stone to a richer, more joyful life.

~ Pam Murphy

Catalyst for Change

"There's no education like adversity."

~ Disraeli

You may classify the word no as a slammed door, but not me! I'm grateful for the many no's I received in response to my health questions. For decades, the medical community slammed their collective doors as I dragged myself from one appointment to the next.

At one point, my medical chart listed over thirty symptoms.

Clearly, I was sick, so how did the no's help? They provided the catalyst I needed.

When I heard:

No, there's nothing wrong with you—I sought new opinions.

No, your insurance won't approve that test—I sought alternatives.

No, that specialist hasn't been approved—I became my own team captain and coordinated my records and referrals.

No, we can't help you—I sought treatments that brought me success.

No, you won't get better; you'll get worse—I sought truths proving I could rebuild my health from chronic illness to chronic wellness.

I'm thankful for the opportunity to share my self-growth and self-education experiences in my book, *FibroWHYalgia*. Hearing from readers that I serve as a catalyst for change, helping them make healthy lifestyle choices, fills me with gratitude beyond measure!

~ *Susan E. Ingebretson*

July 16

My Mom

Porcelain skin, sapphire eyes, chestnut brown hair, a beautiful smile.

Birthed eight children, three who have died, five are alive, her love is so strong.

A cook and a baker, a Susie homemaker, a woman who loves her home.

A semi-pro gardener, a true nature lover, a laugh that is heard for miles.

Compassionate, kind, with a great sense of humor, and tells jokes galore.

Tough, yet so sensitive, strong yet so fragile, lots on her mind.

This is a woman I've known all my life, who I've watched through her struggles and pain. This is a woman I've grown to admire, and whose heart I have seen expand.

This is a woman I've grown to admire, someone I truly respect; whose love is just constant, and honest and pure, and whose thoughtfulness never does end.

With her great generosity, so many lives she touches upon every day, I wish that you knew her the way that I know her, because you would love her the same.

She was born Patricia Louise Baldwin, and she is my mother...

I am grateful for her every day! Thank you, Mom!

~ Kim M. Baldwin

July 17

Courage

I am grateful for John. He entered my life when I was almost 5 and has been a constant presence through the years, no matter how far apart we live.

When I was growing up, I loved to watch how easily John made friends wherever he went. He has survived two cancers. He went to college to get his doctorate degree so he could teach college students. John has lived in physical pain for years and never complained. He has had his share of grief and loss, has endured back and hip surgery, and still goes on.

Laughter and humor are his trademarks. Gentleness and celebration his spirit. He asks little and gives much.

Dancing wildly in his cap and gown after graduating with his doctorate degree.

Standing on top of the mountain, his head bald from chemo, doing his lizard imitation.

He makes me laugh, reminds me of what is important, and teaches me courage.

I love him. He loves me. I am proud to call him my hero and my brother.

~ Margaret A. Hicke

July 18

I Am Grateful for My Daughter Nicole

My daughter Nicole taught me more about life than many of my own life lessons.

Nicole was born on July 18, 1974. Because of complications with her birth she had cerebral palsy and was developmentally challenged, yet with the help of special education she graduated from high school.

Nicole persevered.

At age 13 we discovered she had muscular dystrophy, a type that shut her skeletal muscles down over time, and by her early 20s Nicole was a full quadriplegic. Only once did she ever say, "Why me?"

Nicole made the very best of her circumstances.

The last few years of her life she was on a ventilator to assist her breathing. She kept on keeping on, was always cheerful, and would go out of her way to help others and the caregivers who took care of her.

She cared more about others than about herself.

Nicole passed on December 10, 2007, yet she is always with me. At her memorial service attended by nearly eighty people, about one-third were family and friends; two-thirds were caregivers that had been touched by her spirit and love.

Nicole's gift to all was her love. I am grateful.

~ Dwight Artemas Holden

July 19

Journey to Gratitude

When I was 68, I found myself wanting to expand my horizons. So I participated in a program where four hundred people gathered to learn, test themselves physically, and sleep in tents near a glacier. It was unseasonably hot, and twelve-hour days tested our endurance.

I was one of the oldest participants, and I wasn't physically fit. But I went with the intention of doing my best. I was grateful that people recognized my determination, encouraged me, and helped me when needed. When I chose to meditate for the group instead of participating in one of the challenging experiences, I thought others would be angry with me. Instead, they told me that I was their hero because I did what was best for me while supporting them on their journey.

I was grateful for the caring, encouragement, and physical help my team gave me. When you think you are performing at your lowest level, you could actually be a role model and inspiration to others. This experience helped me take risks in my personal life and business.

I am grateful that I found my courage!

~ Diane Cunningham

July 20

MyMo

The perspective of a toddler: still learning the lay of the new land, diving into the language, and acclimating to the culture.

My sister and I had been babysitting little Matthew since he was days old. Because we often traded off in the middle of sitting with Matthew so one of us could finish homework or attend another event, Matthew became very familiar with my entire family. When he was almost 2 years old and his verbal skills were exploding, he walked right up to my mother and called her "Mommy." I quickly corrected him by saying, "No, Matthew, that's *my* mommy. Her name is Evelyn."

He scrunched his face as if to communicate, "Look, girlfriend, I've been hanging around here quite a bit. Every person who walks in the room calls her mommy. But if you've got another nickname for her, I'll run with it."

And then he repeated himself with a slight modification: he now referred to my mother as "MyMo-Mommy." He was absolutely right, and we all called her MyMo for many years to come.

~ Anonymous

July 21

A Lesson in Gratitude

Lessons learned in gratitude come when you least expect them. In unplanned moments. From a little boy, who was listening when I didn't realize it.

I have intentionally tried to teach my 3-year-old son, Thomas, to have a thankful heart, so I started singing songs of praise to him every morning when I entered his room. I wanted him to know that each day was a special gift from God — a new beginning.

One particular morning I woke up late. As I came downstairs to the living room, I heard the most delightful sound. It was Thomas. He was building with his Legos, singing to himself, "This is the day, this is the day, that the Lord has made. I will rejoice and be glad in it." Then he looked up and smiled at me. "Hi, Mom. You're awake. Do you want to play with me?"

My heart was filled with joy. His tender heart had been listening all along. This was his song now.

I wrapped my arms around him and smiled back. "Yes, Tom. I would love to play with you."

This little boy is my special gift. And I am filled with so much gratitude.

~ Cynthia Trygier

July 22

Self-Love Lessons from a Puppy

I am grateful that in 2002 a tiny, four-legged teacher bounced into my life. Chloe was my new yellow Labrador puppy, and she showed me what real self-love looked like.

The full-length mirror in my bedroom had always been my nemesis. Each pass by it triggered instant self-scrutiny. Like a frog I once saw on Animal Planet who flung out its tongue and snatched a bug so fast I couldn't see it happen until it had been replayed in slow motion, my mind flung out tiny lashes of judgment so fast I couldn't see how they diminished me.

"I look fat." "Bad hair day." "New wrinkles."

One day Chloe noticed herself in the mirror for the first time. Her reaction was simple: She paused, gave her little face a quick lick, right on the mirror, and walked on.

I was stunned. With one quick lick of her puppy tongue, Chloe had caused the frog tongue of my mind to be replayed in slow motion. For the first time, I saw how to stop rejecting myself.

Chloe's puppy mind had no self-rejection. She met herself with the same open-hearted love and acceptance she offered to everyone, unconditionally. Now I could, too.

~ Martia Nelson

July 23

The Memory of the Heart

"Gratitude is the memory of the heart."

~Jean Baptiste Massieu

Gratitude found its roots one meaningful night of my life when my daughter, who was 6 years old at the time, was experiencing severe pain due to a chronic illness and almost passed away in my arms.

Her suffering was so intense that I felt powerless in helping her get any relief, even though I had tried everything I knew. I was really desperate. That crucial night, I finally accepted, deep in my heart, to let her go, if it was the best thing for her.

I can tell you it was the hardest experience I had ever lived in my entire life, and still is, but as she woke up the next morning, I saw sparkles in her eyes that I had not seen for a very long time, and I knew that something beyond my understanding had happened during her sleep.

Since that night, her health has improved, and she is now a wonderful young woman, full of life and energy. Thank you, Mylene, for staying in our lives. You are a true blessing, and I will be forever grateful for your presence!

~ Sylvie Olivier

July 24

A Life Filled with Passion

You asked, "What are you most grateful for?" My answer is probably different from many others, because one of the things I am most grateful for is having a chronic illness.

Five years ago, I began to have problems that eventually led to quitting the corporate world. I searched for the reason why this happened and, as time went on, I received my answer.

My pancreatitis has allowed me to take charge of my life by working from home and watching my grandbaby whenever I want. It has allowed me to write my first book. And it has allowed me to travel, both personally and professionally.

My chronic illness made me look outside the box and find new ways of achieving success. It has allowed me to see the gifts I bring to this world and to be able to use them.

I am grateful for my chronic pancreatitis because it has made me a stronger woman. I start each day with excitement and passion because I am doing the work I love! Do I have down days? Absolutely! But I know those days don't define me, and neither does my illness. I choose a life filled with passion.

~ Vickie I. Turley

July 25

The Power of Choice

Nothing seems more satisfying than the hearty laugh of a baby or the smell of summer on my sheets, except maybe the sweet rewards of being able to make choices. With a fresh garden of choices, I can grow new perspectives and possibilities. These choices, large and small, will ultimately blossom into experiences today, tomorrow, and a year from now.

Many times I've experienced the impact of choices that weren't in alignment with where I wanted to go and who I desired to be. I used to think I had to settle and stay stuck in the resulting muck. I even conveniently blamed others for my circumstances. Along with discovering my role in arriving in places that I didn't want to be, taking responsibility, and realizing that I could make new choices, I have given myself my power back.

It is quite amazing that the six-letter word "choice" has the capacity to influence what I will have, do, and be. If the choice is empowering and nourishing, it moves me toward a bountiful outcome.

What I am most grateful for — what yields my deepest desires — is the power of choice.

~ Julie Anna Brady

July 26

Steeped in Gratitude

Each morning when I wake up, before getting out of bed, I pause and say "thank you" for another glorious day. I put on the kettle and go through my daily ritual of brewing a variety of loose leaf tea from around the world. My gratitude is heartfelt for my husband, family, and good health, and in knowing more of who I am. It's interesting how this in-depth knowledge has come about.

Like so many Americans, I have had personal challenges during the past two years. I have learned there truly is refining power to adversity. Never in my wildest dreams would I have imagined that I would be my personal happiest and best self in spite of the duress. I am grateful to learn that I am not defined by a job title or a company I work for. And for me, aligning with your true passions means bliss follows. And my bliss means tea and writing.

As I sip Darjeeling tea from the Himalayan Mountains and close my eyes, I am transported to the soaring heights of possibility. Today, one cup just won't do! So I put on the kettle again. I am steeped in gratitude for how truly blessed I am.

~ Gretchen Iler

My Little Angel

Having suffered much abuse in my early life, I had pretty much closed off my heart and decided that children were not for me.

But I was wrong.

In the wee hours of the morning, after exhausting all attempts of inducing labor, the doctors decided that, for my health and for the health of my unborn child, they needed to do a C-section.

That was how my darling son made his entrance into the world. A rather bumpy beginning for us both. But now, five years after his birth, words seem such inadequate vehicles to express the amount of love and gratitude I feel.

My little angel is a beautiful, loving spirit who has inspired much of my own healing and forgiveness—of myself and of my abusers. I've learned more about unconditional love than I even thought possible.

Each night when I tuck him in, we name the five things we appreciated most about the day. But I always have six, because every day my number-one appreciation is that I am gratefully enjoying my second chance at experiencing a happy childhood with the most amazing angel named Tyler, who I'm blessed to call my son.

~ Melinda Weese Anderson

July 28

The Comfort of Home

"We often take for granted the very things that most deserve our gratitude."

~ Cynthia Ozick

I sit in my kitchen in the hushed grayness of a rainy morning. Looking out the window, I focus on the peaceful feeling of the moment, hearing the drip of rain and the drops of coffee brewing in the pot. Suddenly, I hear a noise upstairs.

I sit still, tilting my head to try to hear more clearly. In a moment I realize that the noise is the sound of my daughter drawing in a deep, sleepy breath. I listen more closely and pick up the same sounds from my other children. Their breathing is soft and flows with a gentle, even rhythm. It is the breath of children who know they are safe and completely at home.

In this moment, I am so immensely grateful for the gift of these children and for the comfort of our home.

~ Kelli O'Brien Corasanti

July 29

The Importance of Friends

I've always immensely enjoyed the company of friends; connecting and sharing with others are very fulfilling to me.

After getting a divorce three years ago, I realized the true necessity of having good friends whom I could depend on in a variety of circumstances. As a single parent, I now believe wholeheartedly in the concept of it taking a village to raise a child. I also have come to realize the importance of allowing others to help me, which doesn't always feel comfortable, since I have always taken pride in being independent and taking care of all of my needs. Getting help from others, though, allows me to care for myself, which leads to me being at my best in all the areas of my life.

The ability to build and maintain friendships is such an important gift that I am now able to pass on to my daughter, so that she may cultivate nurturing friendships throughout her life.

~ Candace Smith

July 30

From Suicide to 'What a Ride!'

I am so very grateful that I have had ten birthdays since my attempted suicide in May 2001.

Surviving was a miracle, considering the three-hundred-plus pills that I ingested, which did no long-term damage. My doctor told me it was a miracle I survived; the amount I took was enough to kill an elephant. But somehow, I lived through it.

I made a decision to find out why I was spared, and realized that I was spared in order to make a difference. My journey had peaks and valleys since that day, but in the last two years I've begun to realize my ultimate potential to help others.

I've been blessed with being part of a speaker's club the last two years, and during that time led a local charity to have a "Walk for Water" for victims of the Haiti Earthquake that raised $17,000!

During this time, I set up a website to educate people on global water issues along with a podcast, and have very recently undertaken high-level training to become a motivational speaker, so I can influence many more.

So, every July 1st, I celebrate my birthday, my greatest gift, my life!

~ Tracy Allen Baker

July 31

Biggest Struggle...
or Biggest Triumph

L ife hands you many hurdles you must cross. It is inevitable. As the saying goes, "what doesn't kill you, makes you stronger." For me, having an eating disorder has been the biggest, yet the best, hurdle I have ever faced.

If I wasn't plagued with anorexia, I wouldn't be where I am today. It has been a long journey, but now I love my body. I appreciate its magnificence, and I honor it by giving it wholesome food, lots of movement, and stints of play.

My eating disorder has given me many gifts. It opened the door to find the love of my life, with whom I have the pleasure of sharing the most precious gift: our son. It allows me to share my purpose with the world each and every day by helping other women feel good about their bodies. And it enables me to see beauty in everything.

I will forever be grateful for the journey the Universe imposed on me, because without it I simply wouldn't be me.

~ Kimberly Riggins

August

*"There shall be eternal summer
in the grateful heart."*

~ Celia Thaxter

August 1

The Healing Power of Art

Ten years ago, I had a severe head injury and had to re-learn how to walk and talk. I am grateful for my art and my family for helping me recover from this trauma.

When I spoke after the head injury, it came out as babble. I fainted twenty times a day and couldn't stay awake after eating. Many hours a day I sat in a rocking chair, staring at the wall.

After two years of going to doctors, I decided to stay in my studio and work with clay. This allowed me quiet time and gave me a tool for expressing my innermost feelings. This was healing for my body and seemed to create new pathways in my brain. I began to feel more connected to life. Building figures and animals from my dreams caused a sort of magic to occur. My nervous system relaxed, and I could walk and talk and think again.

Thank you for the healing power of art to help me return to the land of the living.

~ Caroline Douglas

August 2

Gratitude in a Jar

I am filled to the brim with gratitude, that I have no shortage of hope nor happy within myself, and more than enough to share with each and every one of you.

Though, if I could wish for one thing, I'd wish to give you a "gratitude jar" filled with all the joy, love, and laughter I have.

It would be filled with all the brightest of shiny things, so you could see what I see in you. All the love you generously give to others, all the unbridled happiness you bring, and all the best parts of yourself — parts you don't keep just for yourself.

What I know in my heart to be true is that it's the beauty and wonder I see in you — that is your very soul shinning from within and because of you. I have no shortage, but unlimited gratitude filled to my brim. Gratitude: It's a circular thing. Now open your jar and dig in!

Namaste.

~ Linda P. Giangreco

Breath

My gratitude lies solely in one thing; this thing so simple, yet so powerful that it fills me each day. It is the essence of life, or rather, my life force.

In times of joy or grief, it can be difficult to catch. At other times, its slower, deeper pace draws in a calm steadiness. It is invisible at first glance, yet so visible in its endless manifestations.

Such simple niceties like a whispered "I love you" cease to exist without it. It is so clear in the forms and shapes that it takes, that it exhales upon me great beauty. It is what gives me the greatest means to express my gratitude for my many plentiful blessings.

When it escapes me, I am always assured that it will return. With it in my possession, I can create endless other reasons to be grateful. It is my substance — that which provides me with spirit and vitality. It reveals itself to me even through my deepest sleep. It is such a natural occurrence that I sometimes forget to thank it. Even now as I express my gratitude for it, I use it, for it is my breath.

~ Nicole Vetere

August 4

Time and Perspective

"I'm sorry. The cancer has metastasized into his liver, lungs, and muscles, and there are no treatment options." It was almost a year ago, and the day my life changed forever; my husband of twenty years and the father of my two children was embarking on a battle that didn't have any odds of victory.

A lot of emotions happen: anger, resentment, fear, and grief, to name a few. Anyone who has walked down this path can attest to the fact that gratitude is hard to find.

However, during the past eleven months, we have learned to shift our perspective and focus on how much we have to be grateful for. Every day we get to share together is a blessing.

We are never promised time. Most of us just take for granted the minutes, days, and years. We don't cherish the small stuff, and we spend way too much time worrying about things that in the long run really don't matter.

Time. At first we worried about how much time we have, and when it will run out. Perspective. We shifted it to gratitude for every second and cherish the gift.

~ Laura Lee Sparks

In Between

In between noise I enjoy the silence—and in between the quiet I enjoy many sounds.

In between the darkness I witness the stars and the moon—and in between the rising and setting sun I am warmed by its light.

In between stillness I find pleasure in movement—and in between motion I relish tranquility.

In between errands I love coming home—and in between the comfort of home I love being out.

In between people I appreciate solitude—and in between aloneness I am blessed with companionship.

In between fear I am filled with faith—and in between confidence I have something to strive for.

In between sorrows there's joy to be found—and in between successes there are lessons to be learned.

In between tomorrows I have my today—and in between moments I am creating my future.

Somewhere in between time—on what was and what wasn't my 34th birthday—your journey here ended and another one began.

Between the day you brought me into this world and the day you left this one behind, you filled me with love, hope, courage, and laughter.

Because this is so, I am grateful for all things in between.

~ Michelle Dimsey

August 6

Thoughts of Gratitude

I was at the fall Toastmasters contest and conference when the idea hit me: What better way to find out what gratitude is than to ask a bunch of public speakers. I interviewed many people, asking "What are you most grateful for?"

Here are their answers:

Gratitude is a natural state of being. The only thing that keeps you from indulging in gratitude is fear on some level.

~ Victor Jenkins

The fear of not having enough leads to the fear of losing everything, which leads to the fear of not being good enough.

Gratitude is a combination of humility and love. It's a grounding emotion.

~ Brian Sharp

Gratitude, when genuinely felt, is the ability to get out of the center of your universe and see others' contribution to that universe.

~ Ruth Schuwart

Gratitude motivates you and puts you back into perspective, honoring yourself and what surrounds you.

~ Carmen Carr

Gratitude is acknowledging that what you have is more than you could have, and more than some people have.

~ Lisa J Lehr

And my contribution is this:

Gratitude is the vibrations that shift the feeling of not good enough into the feeling of appreciation, which moves you into worthiness. You are good enough.

~ Jolen Punches

Why I Smile

"Gratitude is when memory is stored in the heart and not in the mind."

~ Lionel Hampton

I am standing at the grill on the covered porch my husband built for me because I kept whining that I wanted one. Behind me is my family, three adult sons, three girlfriends, and my husband of twenty-eight years. The radio is playing in the background, the sun is dancing on the pool water, and I am smiling inside and out.

Talk about noisy: The boys are trying to out-talk each other, the girls are laughing, and Mike is telling another story to anyone who will listen. This is the moment I realize I am the most blessed woman in the world.

Love and laughter with family and friends are the most precious of gifts. What more could I ask on a Sunday afternoon? I thank the Lord each day for blessing me with my family and their love and laughter.

~ *Donna Amos*

August 8

Perhaps

Perhaps gratitude is measured by age — the blessings of a long life or the innocence of youth. Last Thanksgiving my 3-year-old grandson announced he was most grateful for "Daddy's iPod." Perhaps gratitude is measured by events or special occasions in our lives — marriages and milestone anniversaries.

During a hurried lunch hour I rushed to the grocery store. Red lights are never convenient or considerate of our time schedule. While waiting in the line of cars for the change to green, a flock of birds flew down from a wire overhead. I watched as they landed in a sand pile along the side of the road, a few cars ahead of mine.

Oblivious to the waiting motorists, they frolicked and fluttered and sprayed sand into the air. Like children, they jumped in and out, in and out of their "sandbox." At one point they flew back onto the wire, then swooped back down to the sand and resumed their play. I couldn't help but smile at their contentment. Anxious to share the moment, I looked to the cars around me.

The drivers stared ahead.

Perhaps gratitude is not to be measured at all, but appreciated in moments as they come.

~ PC McCullough

The Red Chair

As I sit in my comfortable red chair listening to my client, who has suffered through challenges that seem so unbearable, I am amazed at how this person has become such a success.

How did the child within her overcome the obstacles that plagued her? The lonely tears she must have shed. Nevertheless, here before me sits this strong woman. She has taken the high road when it would have been so easy, almost natural, for her to follow the low road, where she would have created more problems for herself. Too, I think of the many people who have come before her. Amazing individuals, who in spite of tremendous hurdles and heartbreak have reached for the stars. They have not given up hope for a bright future.

I am in awe of the human spirit and its ability to triumph from adversity. I am so grateful for the wisdom, and strength, of the people who share their stories with me. I respect their courage to expose their vulnerabilities. I am also thankful for my red chair, where I have the opportunity to sit, to help, and to learn from the souls who come through my office.

~ Tamra Hughes

August 10

Perfect

I am grateful that each day is perfect. When it is sunny, it's a great day for a walk. Perfect. When it is rainy, it's a great day for a book. Perfect. The perfection in each day is always there for me to discover and experience. I am always on the lookout for the gem of perfection each day holds.

Just the other day I took a walk with my wife, experienced a beautiful day, and helped to raise money for a great cause. Three gems of perfection in a simple walk: my wife, a beautiful day, helping others.

Sometimes when I am feeling wimpy and weak, the perfection is harder to see. It is harder to seek. Yet when I simply take the time to look, there it is. I am grateful for the knowledge—the belief—that perfection is all around me and that gratitude is my best response to my world. I am grateful for this day. This perfect day.

~ Ron Shuster

Ask and You Shall Receive

I witnessed a miracle, and it changed my perspective forever. It was just an ordinary day, but I felt my determination become more focused, crystallized.

I sat in silence within the chapel, listening to the peaceful sound of the water flowing from the waterfall. They called it the perpetual adoration chapel. I went there every Thursday at 4 p.m. It was tranquil and most of the time peppered with the slow, respectful motion of others coming and going to enjoy the solace, too.

One day I noticed a quiet stream of traffic leading to a notebook placed at the back near the door. Individuals wrote in it before they left. My curiosity got the better of me, and I went to take a peek. Page after page of prayer requests. I must have stood there reading them for an hour. I, too, requested a miracle that day.

My daughter was born just three weeks later. Her name is Anastasia and, when I held her in my arms, I couldn't help but know for certain that miracles happen every day. We simply need to ask.

~ Crystal O'Connor

August 12

The Breath of Now

Some days I forget about gratitude. I get caught up in the minutiae of the "to dos" and the future "to dos" that I miss the golden moment of now and what is shiny, bright, and wonderful. So I take a breath and feel immense gratitude for the now. And for:

- My body and how it works perfectly almost every day even though I have used it well for almost fifty years.

- Being a woman in this time and this place. I have freedom and opportunity that women before me did not, and that those living in other global areas do not.

- The fact that I don't have children. A little controversial, I know, but being childless has given me the luxury of self-reflection and tending to myself in a way that being a mother never could have.

- My delicious relationships: my husband, my best friend, my circles of women, my family, my "goddess daughter" and other special kids, my teachers.

- And the rest: my bed, wine, books of all kind, public libraries, airplanes, crossword puzzles, iPhone apps, a great flow with money, pretty sparkly things, nature's beauty, dancing and music, spicy conversation, dogs, Oprah....

~ Catherine A. Bruns

August 13

What a Poopy Day!

It's been a poopy day, and I wouldn't have it any other way. Imagine one of those days when you are exhausted and over-burdened with stress from every direction. Your cat crawls onto your lap to snuggle, and that is when you feel it: poop. It is all over him and now it's all over you.

For some people, that would completely ruin their day. For me, it is reason to celebrate! You see, my seventeen-and-a-half-year-old cat has lymphoma. I have had him since he was 4 or 5 weeks old, and he is truly my baby. If he has poop on him, then that means his bowels are still functioning! It also means that I have been given another day to spend with my furry baby.

I am grateful for every minute that I have to spend with him, for each purring and snuggle session that we share, and for his fur that is everywhere. I am even grateful for those poopy days. In fact, I can't think of anything more wonderful than having another poopy day tomorrow!

~ Rhonda Chuyka

August 14

Crap

Yes, I do feel gratitude for all those wonderful things in my life, but believe it or not, I am now learning to be grateful for all the crap, too. Yes, the crap: the flat tires, broken hearts, burnt cookies, cancer, layoffs, and stubbed toes.

When you're grateful for the crap, it makes it easier to own the crap. And when you own the crap, you start to realize what a brilliant, genius creator you really are.

Some people call the crap "contrast." Some call it the "cloud with the silver lining." Without the crap, the great things in life would not feel so exhilarating.

Don't you see? Without the crap we wouldn't have such a fabulous experience.

~ Kim Beckett

Intimacy

I am in love — yes, in love. Even after more than fifteen years, I can still say that. Can you believe it?

Mind you, it hasn't always felt or been so great, but I am so grateful and blessed that now each time we're faced with challenges we still put it all on the table and show up for each other. And most importantly, we show up for ourselves now. Showing up for me means letting myself be vulnerable, open, and honest about what my needs and desires are, too, as well as hearing his. Being seen and heard at this level allows me to be open for intimacy.

So intimacy is the deeper place of gratitude for me. It's the place where I feel safe enough to look into his eyes, even though it may feel hard at first, and hold his gaze, and to let him see the depths of my soul and I his. It is this that leads to our deeper connection, and then I fall in love again.

~ *Teresa C. Lea*

August 16

Finding Riches

When I became all grown up, I felt I was supposed to be rich. Time has gone by, and the abundance of money has never come. I like to dress in a hat and fine clothes from the Goodwill store. I live in a split foyer house on a hill, drive an old Buick, and even have had an old, long, white Cadillac.

I am blessed with five children, eight grandchildren, a husband, and a kitty cat — the list goes on and on. One day my granddaughter Stephanie told me, "I'll bet you will have a lot of people at your funeral." I said, "What do you mean?" With her wide smile on her face and her blue eyes sparkling, she said, "You have a lot of friends."

It dawned on me really big this sixty-seventh year: I am rich beyond measure. Maybe, just perhaps, I was not supposed to be rich with money but rich with love and family and friends. Thank you, Father. Continue to show me Thy ways, oh Lord.

"Trust in the Lord with all thine heart; and lean not unto thine own understanding."

~ Proverbs 3:5 KJV

~ Annette Denton Livingston

Express Your Gratitude Through Giving

Gratitude is beyond a word. It's beyond a sentence. It's beyond a book. Nothing can really encapsulate everything there is to be grateful for. So, rather than listing all of the things I'm grateful for, I'll only encourage you (and me) to express it by giving to others each day as a thank you.

Give a smile. Stop when someone needs help. Send a thank-you card. Surprise someone anonymously and pay for his or her dinner, coffee, or toll. Compliment a stranger. Gift a CD with inspiring songs. Bake for a homeless family. Organize a food drive. Pray for someone who feels pain. Pick up garbage.

Show your gratitude for life and all of your blessings by giving!

~ Jeanie Barat

August 18

Young Wisdom

My business partner Joe and I were celebrating a milestone with our company. We decided to invite friends and family out to an upscale, locally owned and operated restaurant.

After work, I went with Joe back to his house so he could change, I could freshen up, and we could pick up his wife and 2-1/2 year old son. Patrick was extremely smart, very creative, and in the middle of being potty trained. Goal number one: a dry "pull-up" type toddler diaper. With all of us encouraging young Patrick, surely he would make a last-minute trip to the bathroom.

Joe's wife, knowing how Patrick liked to be part of a group, tried one last bit of persuasion, "Patrick, why don't you just try and go potty here at the house. That way you won't have to leave everybody at the table to go to the bathroom while we are at dinner."

Patrick's reply was irrefutable and put an end to the conversation: "But Mommy, that's what the diaper is for."

~ Anonymous

August 19

Grateful for the Queues

I recently took my young son to Disneyland. Watching him light up when he met Mickey, Tinkerbell, etc., and seeing the joy in his eyes as he danced to the music of the big parade was truly magical. But Mickey fanatics were abundant, and that meant only one thing: long lines!

Astonishingly to me, my son seemed to have more patience than I did at first. I watched him as he marveled at the "whole new world" around him. Despite his excitement as we stepped into each new wonderland of rides, he was clearly not waiting for anything.

Lines are a funny thing. You can always find people who are bored, people who are chronically impatient, and people who think they deserve to pass up everyone else. I imagine that those folks treat life pretty similarly.

Regardless of the line I must wait in, the schooling I must acquire, or the job I must take on my way to my dreams, it's important to consider that life is happening all around us. Always. There is no waiting for it to begin. Life is truly the greatest ride I have not ever had to wait for, and I am grateful for the queues.

~ Erin Tullius

August 20

Today's Experiences Become Tomorrow's Memories

As a father, I watched in amazement as you entered this world. As a dad, I've had the incomparable joy of seeing you grow before my eyes.

From the toddler with boundless energy and unquenchable fascination, to the boy who has now grown to be a fine young man, I'm truly blessed. It has been said that life in not measured by the breaths you take, but by the moments that take your breath away. There have been countless occasions when you have taken my breath away. From the day when you stood on the stage at kindergarten graduation proclaiming your aspiration to be "an engineer and a dad," to someone who in a few short years will be going to college, I am filled with precious memories. Thankfully, I've been able to share these days of your life with you, and while the days became months and have now turned to years, it's been a fantastic journey. This experience has been unlike any other and has exceeded my best expectations. As sweet as the memories are of yesterday, I look forward to the experiences of today, for they become the memories of tomorrow. And I'm grateful for them all.

~ Gary Horman

Gifts Attached

The summer from hell. It was only one of the descriptions I gave to my professional life in 2010, during what is usually my favorite time of year.

Oh sure, somewhere, hiding in the depths of my unconscious was a knowing that the universe had a reason for bringing such a difficult time into my life so close on the heels of the decision to end my marriage. I wasn't ready to call that summer a gift until about a month ago. This gift: an opportunity to be the architect of a new position to my workplace, one very much suited to my strengths and passions.

As a woman very close to her 60th birthday, I can easily say, as can most people my age, I have weathered numerous stress-filled periods in my life. None of them came even close to killing me, and each left me stronger, wiser, and with more self-confidence and appreciation for myself and my place in this world.

I am grateful for every trial, trouble, and challenge in my past and for the ones still around the bend in my future. They come with gifts attached.

~ Lois R. Arsenault

August 22

The Silver Lining

"Too many people miss the silver lining because they're expecting gold."

~ Maurice Setter

Recently, I coached a woman who wanted to change careers and find something more fulfilling. As the conversation progressed, she became less focused on what would fulfill her and more focused on what she didn't want. Each new idea that came up was quickly met with scorn; she'd already tried that one, the next couldn't possibly work, another didn't apply, and on and on she went.

As she continued, a picture flashed into my mind. I saw her standing in the middle of a large, circular room, surrounded by doors. With each new thought she so carelessly tossed aside, one of those doors would slam shut, echoing around the room like the doors of a cell, cutting off another possibility and locking her ever more tightly into the prison she was creating.

That conversation opened my eyes to the doors I'd slammed shut and unlocked a new appreciation for my life. Today, I am grateful for everything I do have—the little things I've taken for granted that truly make my life so fulfilling. Today, I appreciate the silver lining.

~ Beverly Simmons

August 23

A Mother's Love

What I am most grateful for — well, it's really a who. It's my mother. Yes, I know that sounds cliché, corny even. However, I am truly grateful for the intelligent, strong, and independent woman I am lucky to call my mom.

My parents divorced when I was in my teens. It was at a time when divorce was not as accepted as it is today. It was a hard time for all of us. She lost the support of our church and many close friends. But no matter how badly she felt, she persevered. I am the oldest and knew that she had to change her life because of us. She was raising three children on her own. Still to this day, her devotion to us is so remarkable.

Because of her example, I have become the strong, independent woman I am now. Looking back, if I was in her position, I'm not so sure if I could have done what she did. I credit her with so much and can never thank her or repay her for all the love, the experiences, the knowledge, and all that she had given up for us, for our family. Her giving is truly enduring selfless love.

~ Raissa Spatola

August 24

What a Paradox Is This Life — Thank Goodness!

As my beloved mother fades toward death my heart breaks open repeatedly: evidence of the depth of our capacity for love. We are love in the midst of the wonder of facing the eternal mystery of all existence.

This loss is unimaginable even as I know it is already true. I open more deeply to receive her more completely even as I know her within me: perfect, infinite beauty growing clearer with each moment that passes.

I am brought closer to the deep knowing, proven mathematically, that time and space are infinite and continuous — that we are connected to the past and the future and to that which is absent. Thus, we have nothing to fear and nothing to grieve: We are in the continuum of infinity even as we live.

May my heart grow lighter, my spirit wider, my mind deeper, my body easier. May I find oneness, delight in each moment, awe in the ultimate possibilities of the unknown. May I remember the power of my own light as it unites me with the universal light embracing us all. May we blossom in truth, beauty, and clarity here and now.

Breathing with you in the light, in gratitude, in love.

~ Stefany G. Burrowes

August 25

For You Today

"Twenty years from now you will be more disappointed by the things you didn't do than by the ones you did do. So throw off the bowlines. Sail away from the safe harbor, catch the trade winds in your sales. Explore. Dream. Discover."

~ Mark Twain

I encourage you: Be bold today in action and thought!

~ *Anonymous*

August 26

Life Lessons

I am endlessly grateful for being born into an amazing family. My parents, Lou and Marion Iovieno, fondly known as Mr. and Mrs. I, were an incredible couple, devoted to family, devoted to society, and, more importantly, devoted to each other. Married for sixty-nine years before Lou died at 94, they taught me an incredible lesson: The best gift you can give your children is to love your own life. It gives your children permission to love their lives.

My mother was an incredible role model for women of all ages. She knew how to blend being a sweet, nurturing lady with being a resilient woman. She was bright and strong, creative and wise, and never afraid to be exactly who she was born to be. From my earliest memories of lessons she gave me, I especially cherish her brand of leadership training: "Angela, be the engine, not the caboose."

She gave me power and wings to fly! She died at 97, and, although I miss her terribly, I am immensely grateful for being raised by a woman who knew that powerful life lessons can be learned over a cup of coffee.

~ Angela I. Schutz

Opportunity Given and Taken

For years I dreamed of going to New Zealand. It always seemed that when I had the time I didn't have the funds, and when I had the money I couldn't get away for that long. Then I was handed the opportunity: I was being laid off and I had a nest egg. There was absolutely no reason I couldn't go.

People told me it wasn't safe to travel alone and that I was foolish not to line up a new job first. My inner voice kept telling me, "Go!"

I am so grateful I listened to my soul and took advantage of this rare opportunity!

The dream of visiting New Zealand grew to a four-month odyssey that included diving on the Great Barrier Reef and exploring Bali, Fiji, and French Polynesia. I had incredible experiences and met wonderful people of all ages and cultures. I rekindled my love of sculpting as I learned to carve jade. It truly was the experience of a lifetime — for it will stay with me forever.

This trip reminded me that I can do anything that I desire. I am now self-employed and have dropped over 125 pounds, two more things I'd dreamed of doing! I am grateful for opportunities given and taken.

~ Laurie Tossy

August 28

Earth School

I am a spiritual being. And I've been looking for the rule book about how the Universe works since I was a little girl.

Hollyhurst Cottage Inn became "by accident" and after a relationship painfully broke up, when I really started my search for how I fit into it all. It was nothing short of magical.

In my deepest overwhelming, I made a friend who taught me to meditate for answers. The relationship had been a lesson.

The adventure I went on! People and things came to me, at just the right time in just the right way. I couldn't have imagined! It was exhilarating.

But I always had that nagging feeling: "I don't understand how I'm doing this. I won't be able to sustain it." Of course, whatever you believe, you're right.

I re-created chaos with another wonderful teacher, even though the "little voice" said, "Don't go there. No, no...." I didn't listen. Same lesson. Been there, done that.

And then, finally, I understood! I attract by what I allow, what I believe, and the feeling! Now, I'm consciously co-creating joy and wellness, grateful for the teachers and lessons that brought me here.

~ Alice Rosalie Touchette

Stationery, Envelopes, and Stamps

"To send a letter is a good way to go somewhere without moving anything but your heart."

~ Phyllis Theroux

I am grateful for stationery, envelopes, and stamps.

Although we live in a world of electronic communication, nothing remains as personal as a handwritten letter. It is the first piece of mail opened and is often kept in a special place to savor again and again. My story is no exception.

Last month, I reread the letters my parents and grandparents wrote to me during my first year of college. In these letters, they expressed words of praise and love, recalled memories of my childhood, and shared details of their day-to-day lives. Each letter is special because of the individual advice that stemmed from their unique life experiences. Their encouraging words warmed the heart of an 18-year-old college freshman, and, over twenty years later, brought tears of joy to a 39-year-old mother of two.

Following in their footsteps, I now write letters whenever someone comes to mind. I may never know the impact of my words, but I am certain that the power to encourage someone else is possible with only stationery, envelopes, and stamps.

~ Kelly F. Zawistowski

August 30

The Rainbow Connection

The question "What am I grateful for?" has been giving me writer's block — not because I couldn't think of any blessings in my life, but because I am so grateful for everything in my life: the good and the bad.

The good is amazing! My beautiful daughter, supportive family and friends, purposeful work that speaks to me — all of these blessings fill my life with joy. Even everyday pleasures thrill me: the changing of the seasons, the smell of freshly baked bread, the blue sky, the beach.

The strange thing is that I am just as thankful for the "bad" in my life. A serious health crisis in my twenties that became chronic, starting over after leaving a relationship, financial struggles — all of these challenges are making me stronger, more persistent, and more passionate about helping others. Because of my struggles, I believe that I am a better person, a better mother, and a better coach/intuitive than I would have been without them.

I am a big fan of rainbows, and I know that they don't exist without the storms. If I didn't have the bad, I wouldn't have the amazing, and for that I am grateful.

~ Jenny Bryans

Things I Am Grateful For...

Chocolate

The ocean

My yellow Lab, Maggie May

Terry, my amazing husband of thirty-one years

Caribbean islands

Wine country

Laughing until I cry

Being a twenty-year breast cancer survivor

Italian food

God

Eye candy, especially surfers and soccer players

Roses

Angels

Incredible friends

Freedom

My awesome son, Chris, who is working for a non-profit and lives way too far away (in Tanzania)!

My beautiful daughter, Lindsey, who lights up every room

Writing poetry

Kindness

Christmas

Open minds

My country

Bill and Maggie, my fantastic parents

Peace

Snorkeling

Cicero's Pizza in Cupertino, California

Books

Raindrops

Massage

The Beatles

Stars

Walking on white grains of powdery sand

Truth

Tiramisu

Candles

Sleep

~ Mary Armstrong Hines

September

"Nothing contributes so much to tranquilizing the mind as a steady purpose—a point on which the soul may fix its intellectual eye."

~ Mary Wollstonecraft Shelley

September 1

How Lucky Am I?

As I walk toward the room, a certain feeling overwhelms me: nervous excitement. It's not the first time I've felt this way. I open the door and see a sea of little desks. Soon the bell will ring and I will get to meet my new charges.

I have knowledge and experience I want to share. How wonderful is it to have a room full of faces wanting to hear it? How many people get to passionately teach their wisdom to so many? We are a perfect match.

Shy looks greet me. A second bell rings, and the day commences. I take my place at the front of the room. Soon the teaching begins.

I learn how fast one girl can tie her shoes. I'm taught how to whistle and told "funny" jokes that I've "never heard before." I hear why Rover passed away and that, even though he's gone, a happy memory will always bring him back to his boy's heart.

Daily I discover many wondrous things and am loved just for being me. I am grateful for all that my students have taught me. How lucky am I?

~ Monika Huppertz

September 2

Gifts, Guides and Insights

I express gratitude for the gift of life and contributing to the evolution of humanity. Within this experience I am grateful for:

- The gift of duality, fumbling in the darkness as to appreciate the light.
- The gift of inner strength, by trudging through life's tribulations and prevailing.
- The gift of unconditional self-acceptance, by appreciating all of my imperfections, including my body.
- The eyes of my child, for here I see the extension of my soul.
- My guides and navigators, those who walk along side me and those who carry me.
- My clients and students, for inspiring me to live my purpose and passion.
- Those who condemned me, for teaching me self-worth and confidence in having to defend myself.
- My teachers, including every mentor, supporter, or manipulator for helping identify the lessons I am here to master.
- The insight and wisdom to recognize the gifts in all of life's situations.
- The language of love for being the unity that connects us all.
- This magnificent planet, which houses the experience of this grand journey.
- And for you, the reader. Your presence allows me to express my joy.

~ Susan Mann

September 3

Bumbling into My Heart

At 49 I had a life of luxury, especially the luxury of time — a fulfilling business, freedom to travel, and hours to write and refine a poem. On a day like today I could gaze out a window in total peace as leaves drift to earth against a backdrop of blue sky, orange and gold.

At 50 I gave all that up to become a mother. Who knew how much time it takes to replace outgrown shoes and clothes, pack lunches, set up play dates, and sports, help with homework, exclaim over triumphs, organize parties, negotiate limits? With all that and "tween" moodiness, what I am most grateful for is that I did not pass up my daughter's gifts:

1. She has made me grow in ways that travel, journaling, poetry, and career could not. I used to be able to leave any distressing family gathering, job, or mate. Now I stay and stumble through each challenge.

2. Watching life bloom all over again with experienced eyes is more rich than the discretionary income she absorbs.

3. I was a perfect mother until I had a child. She taught me patience with my own and others' flaws.

My quest to have and be "the best" could never match the joy of connecting my bumbling heart to her heart.

~ Maggie Anderson

September 4

On Children

I am grateful I was able to spend so much time with my son, Shannon, and my daughter, Molly, while they were growing up.

We had time to talk, time to read, time to be in nature, and, of course, time to run from one activity to another.

There were frustrating times, which seem insignificant now. Shannon and Molly are in college, where they are independent, intelligent, talented, loving people happily pursuing their dreams.

As Kahil Gibran wrote in "On Children":

> *"You may give them your love but not your thoughts,*
> *For they have their own thoughts.*
> *You may house their bodies but not their souls,*
> *For their souls dwell in the house of tomorrow,*
> *Which you cannot visit, not even in your dreams.*
> *You may strive to be like them*
> *But seek not to make them like you.*
> *For life goes not backward nor tarries with yesterday..."*

What I'm grateful for is the feeling I have when I receive a text that ends with "Love you Mom!"

~ *Patricia McKinney-Lins*

September 5

Loss Is Gain

It was on September 5th that I found out my baby died. Nothing prepares you for that kind of pain, and nothing can take it away. Grief is the unwanted guest that you fear will set up permanent residence in your life. The journey of grieving is a long one and can feel impossible to move through; it's the hardest thing we'll ever do.

There have been many losses in my life: my unborn baby, my mom, dad, and sister. Loss comes in many ways, not just in the death of our loved ones. There's loss of a marriage, job, health, mobility, finances, youth, dreams, etc.

This path, which I never would have chosen, has led me to a deep fulfillment that I never would have known. It is the intense pain of loss that leads to the true understanding of the preciousness of life and to cherish every moment. It's the darkest hours of suffering that allow you to truly celebrate the beauty of a hope-filled new day. And further, gives you the ability to be that hope to someone else. God has given us these gifts so that we can have life more abundantly.

And, for that, I am truly grateful.

~ Maureen Day

September 6

The Magic of Energy

As I watched the morning sun glistening on the beautiful yellow fall leaves, I found myself sighing deeply in gratitude for the beauty all around me! The evening before, my husband, Richard, and I attended an event, "The Answer is You," with Michael Bernard Beckwith and his wife, Ricki, from Agape International Spiritual Center in Los Angeles. What a gift! Michael's energy was as crisp and clear as that fall morning. He offered a powerful and profound message.

During the talk, Michael led the audience in a spiritual visioning process. He asked that we stand up. As I stood, pain seared trough my right heel. It was so intense that I had to balance on my left leg and foot to avoid pressure on my right side. I focused on the moment and the spiritual energy sweeping through the audience. As a wave of energy engulfed me, I allowed it to move through from my head to my feet. In amazing grace, all pain immediately released. I was able to easily stand on both feet, and I have been pain-free since. I celebrate in thanksgiving for this miraculous gift, and I continue to be grateful every day. Thank you, God!

~ Trisha LoveJoy

September 7

Mother Nature's Gifts

I am grateful for the sun and the moon, the stars, the wind, the rain, the snow, and all the gifts of Mother Nature.

My heart feels joy in all the celebrations of our Mother's seasons.

Spring fills my blood with a quickening beat of newness as her buds bursts forth from bare limbs. Furry babes, conceived in wintertime, now breathe sweet innocence into the world.

Summer warms my soul with her lush breezes and her long days. The long-legged foals have gained strength and now play with reckless abandon.

Fall wraps me up in her festive embrace. The glorious Harvest Moon dances and sings of abundance. The Beasts of the Land have heard her call to prepare for the lean times ahead.

Winter, so peaceful and still, blankets herself around me and all her creations, as I dream my beautiful dreams, which will be born anew in springtime.

All of Mother Nature's cycles heal and renew my grateful Spirit.

~ Susane D. Schuler

September 8

My Take On It

"God grant me the serenity
to accept the things I cannot change;
courage to change the things I can;
and wisdom to know the difference."

> ~ Reinhold Niebuhr, from "The Serenity Prayer"

Ever want to throttle someone? (But didn't.)

Or save someone? (But couldn't.)

Or thought "if only…" but then shook yourself back to the here and now?

It's "The Serenity Prayer" at work.

We cannot change other people, but we can change our reaction to them. Accept them for who they are—and who they are not.

We can always choose differently—for ourselves.

And wisdom? Well, wisdom comes. Sometimes slow and steady like a tortoise and sometimes as powerful as a lightning bolt. (Along with promises never to forget again.)

I'm grateful to be given choices and the freedom to make them. For the serenity and peace I feel when I remember. And for the chance to make the right choices for me…again and again.

~ Anonymous

September 9

Oh Heck,
Did I Really Do That?

"A great life has at least one 'oh heck, did I really do that?' moment that blesses you with a lifetime of smiles and fond memories."

~ Jeanne Huber Morr

Skydiving is something that I always wanted to do. On a visit to my daughter in San Diego, my chance arose. Arriving at the facility, I asked if they had any more flights for a first-time dive, to which they said yes, in ten minutes. "Put me on!" was my response.

An "oh heck" moment is one that truly defines you, and shows what you are made of and are possible of achieving. Whether it is jumping from an airplane, watching magnificent nature up close, or even a friend being a mirror to remind you who you are. These moments are a fantastic blessing, and I am very grateful for the many "oh heck" moments in my life. These moments are made even better when they are shared with others that you love.

"A friend is someone that reminds you to see who you really are. A true friend inspires you to believe and achieve all that is possible."

~ Jeanne Huber Morr

September 10

Gratitude Demands an Action or a Response

Gratitude is appreciating and valuing what have been given to us. I believe it is not real gratitude if it is not shared or if you don't act or respond to it.

About two decades ago, I was chosen to represent my country at an international youth forum in Europe. It was my first time to travel overseas, and I was very grateful to God for giving me a unique and special opportunity. While I was on the plane, and literally on cloud nine, I was so thankful and so happy for this wonderful gift that I could not help but share this joy with my dad. I wrote my first and only letter to him, thanking him for all the wonderful things he has done for me and for our family. This moment made me experience real joy in gratitude.

My husband also has a way of responding in gratitude. When he got an opportunity to partner with another firm with a possibility of doubling his income, he was so grateful and happy that he quickly doubled his weekly contribution to our local church.

Gratitude cannot be contained "within." It has to be shared "with-out."

~ Roslyn Rajasingham

September 11

Veteran's Day Gratitude

I am grateful my body was able to survive the war in Vietnam. I am grateful I have been able to survive the war in my head and my heart for over forty years.

I am grateful that my life has not ended tragically as way too many of the lives of my brother and sister veterans have.

I am grateful that I was able to find solace and hope by embracing the blessings of a Higher Power.

I am grateful that I was able to raise my consciousness to the point of releasing the self-hatred, the alcohol and drug abuse, and the medication that was slowly becoming my demise.

I am grateful that relearning how to give and accept love and forgiveness has made my life worthwhile once again.

I am grateful that I am now grateful to still be alive.

I am grateful that I now know that PTSD (post-traumatic stress disorder) does not have to be forever.

And I am grateful that, by the grace of our Creator, I am now able to help other veterans release the demons of their wars so that they may also find their way home.

~ Miguel Gabriel Vazquez

September 12

The Ultimate Flyer

I held him as he took his last breath. Surely my last breath would follow. John and I had inhaled life's sweet fragrance together for twenty-six years. But John passed, and I stayed. Numb, but barely breathing. That first Christmas I ordered a handmade Ultimate Flyer sled made out of golden birch planks with willow hand-carved rails. Our initials, JBM and LTM, were emblazoned on Flyer's body.

Flyer rested in a closet, motionless, waiting like me to feel something — anything. Time passed. I imagined Flyer, awash with the seasons, gathering life's breath, collecting dew as daffodils grew between its knotty spine, at water's edge soaking up salty brine while sandpipers danced on its back, drifting ashore to settle under an apple tree circled by kids with gooey s'mores in their hands singing "I won't climb your apple tree, if you won't be good to me."

And then it came: snow. Glorious snow. The Ultimate Flyer flew, and I took my first new breath since John's passing. With it came my life's calling. I founded a charitable organization called Kids Play For Good, inspired by John, my mom, and Flyer, for which I will be forever grateful.

~ Lynn Morrell

September 13

Public Education

I fell in love my first day of school. My teacher wore swishy dresses, wrote on the chalk board, and played the piano. School provided friends for me, a late-in-life baby with much older siblings. I loved reading. I tolerated math, but I struggled with handwriting. Somehow my 6-year-old fingers couldn't make those lines stay on the tracks of penmanship paper. Still, I fell in love with public education.

My love affair with public education continues until this day. I am so grateful for caring teachers. I am grateful for a process open to all students. I am grateful for our education system standing as a cornerstone of democracy.

~ Margaret G. Holmes

September 14

This Too Shall Pass

"This too shall pass." It's a phrase repeated through the ages, from Sufi poets to presidents.

This saying has gotten me through a great deal of heartache. I've remembered it when in the throes of grief from parents and grandparents dying—times when I thought my sorrow knew no end. If that's where you are now, believe this to be true: The grief eventually lessens while the sweet memories remain.

"This too shall pass" also helped when a boy broke my heart. In the moments after the dramatic conversation that brought everything crashing down, I literally felt a heavy, heavy sadness settle in my chest. I wondered if I'd ever be the same again. I am and I'm not. I think this might be what other poets refer to as "sweet sorrow."

"This too shall pass" is also a reminder to see, really truly see, the good that is around right now. Count your blessings on both fingers and toes. Realize that in this very moment, the one where you're reading and focusing on these very words, all is right in your world. Don't let another moment pass without remembering to...

Feel it! Savor it! Claim it!

~ Anonymous

September 15

Grateful for the Faith

"Limitations live only in our minds. But if we use our imaginations, our possibilities become limitless."

~ Jamie Paolinetti

The year, 2010, has been one of great change for me and has been a result of many years of growth and learning. I am grateful to have had a family that encouraged me to reach high and believe in myself, and provided me the education and opportunities that paved the way to my current success.

I am indebted to the many people who came into my life to open my eyes to the world's limitless possibilities, have led by action, demonstrated courage, and had the generosity to share their gifts to empower others.

I am most thankful for my family and friends who have supported and encouraged me to break free of stability, act creatively, and leap into new opportunities.

Thank you for having faith in my talents and giving me the freedom to step into another life to follow the path of a dream.

~ Danielle Chonody

September 16

Yachts in Monte Carlo

I'm grateful for…money. There, I've said it. I'm brave enough to admit it. To be clear, I'm not talking excessive wealth, but rather the achievement of financial stability. I can now afford more than life's essentials, like a place to live, food on my table, and a winter coat. Many good things have come into my life, now that I no longer struggle:

1. My husband and I get to fight about real things when we are not worried about money.
2. It's fun to treat friends to lunch or a glass of champagne.
3. Money brings safety and security, so I can focus on self-fulfillment.
4. I can donate to causes that are important to me.
5. Sleep comes easier.
6. I can pay my bills, so I can work on changing the world.
7. Money bought me a formal education.
8. It will buy my children an education.
9. While I don't have a yacht docked in Monte Carlo, I've traveled there and seen the yachts.
10. The ability to buy makes me want for less.

Bonus: Having money reminds me that things do not bring me fulfillment; people and experiences do that for me.

~ Lorin Kierklewski Mask

September 17

'Someday' Is Now

I am grateful that I learned that "someday" is now.

I had a wake-up call in 2006 that I would not wish upon anyone, yet it changed my life in powerful and positive ways. I learned through example. Two of my favorite people died much sooner than expected. They got sick. Their "someday" — retirement or when they achieved that mystical "something" — never happened. "Someday" plans were not realized.

It taught me to live life now. Don't wait! I examined my life. I noticed where I was settling. I took time to think: What do I want out of life? What is important to me? I discovered what brings me happiness and what makes me miserable.

Inspired to make changes, I created a plan. I chose action. I found my unique path, one that had risks but intuitively felt right. I took a chance even though it was a bit scary. It is the best decision I ever made. After leaving a job I was where I was miserable, I found one I love. While traveling the world, I fell in love and married the most amazing man. It is amazing what happened in four years. I am grateful I realized that "someday" is now. I love the life I live.

Now it's your turn!

~ Laura M. Fischer

September 18

Room for Cream

I'm grateful for my barista, Ashley, and our talks about Harry Potter theme parks or how to make the best Bloody Mary at home (much more fun than spending a lot of money at a bar).

One workday in particular, I needed an escape. I was ready to shut down my computer, exit the building, and keep walking until I found a perfect patch of grass. Removing my shoes, I'd wiggle my toes and toss the cell phone out of earshot. After entertaining that luscious fantasy for a few, I decided instead to get some coffee.

There was Ashley, training a new guy. After my order, the cash register tape needed changing. My curiosity kicked in, and I watched the elaborate process. Take this part out, unroll, tear, and unstick. The new guy couldn't get the paper to go, so my barista kindly took over.

To me, she murmured with a smile, "Your drip is free today." My face lit up; it was perfect. I offered to tip, and she said to catch her tomorrow afternoon. I've been practicing my skills of receiving kindness; giving is more comfortable for me. Thanks, Ashley, practice perfect.

~ *Linda Eaves*

September 19

Grateful for Cat Wisdom

Hippolyte Taine said, "I have studied many philosophers and many cats. The wisdom of cats is infinitely superior." From firsthand experience, I have to agree.

Liza and Frank taught me that being open-minded allows you to discover new loves. I went from being a dog person to being a cat person.

Belle was abandoned at two weeks old. Tending to her needs on her time schedule reminded me of the benefits of taking time to "stop and smell the kittens."

Mitz showed me how to love her on her terms, and that give and take is necessary to nurture any relationship.

My mother passed away just before Xena came along. Even though Xena was the runt, she was also a fighter, and this gave me courage as well as comfort through my grief.

Gabrielle adopted me. She reminds me with her hilarious antics at unexpected moments that life isn't all about work, and that you should do something fun every a day.

From my successes to my most sorrowful moments, my cats have been the constant through it all. I'm truly grateful for the wisdom they've provided and the unconditional love they've given me.

~ Joyce Layman

September 20

My Amazing Life — A Love Story

My life changed the moment I met him. We met when our lives were at a crossroad. We were searching for answers. Oh boy, the road is a bumpy one! We challenge each other while we grow into the people we knew we were meant to be.

As we went through our journey of self-discovery, an opportunity to spend six days with Bob Proctor, a teacher from the movie *The Secret*, appeared.

Initially, I thought, it would be nice, but.... And then the unbelievable happened: He asked me to go with him!

Bob taught us that it is our paradigms that hold us where we don't want to be. He also taught us that we are the makers of our destiny, and that by changing our paradigms we can create any future we like.

It was a truly magical time that changed our lives forever. Slowly, a day at a time, our lives are changing for the better. Now, we face each new day full of excitement and joy.

I am very grateful I share this journey with a man who shows great courage, love, and kindness.

~ Cathy Morrissey

September 21

A Brother's Smile

My inspiration to live with a grateful heart in all things great and small is my special-needs brother. Larry suffered birth trauma during a breech delivery. He cannot walk or talk, and is completely dependent on others for his total care. Doctors said he wouldn't survive passed the age of 15. However, today, at 57, he is still with us.

His smile when I walk through the door for a visit is all it takes to send gratitude kisses up to heaven for the blessing I see in his eyes. To me, his life's purpose is simply to remind those closest to him to be grateful for things in life like being able to walk and talk, and having good health.

I love my life and, thanks to my brother, I take nothing for granted. My life is not fancy or full of frills, but it is rich and full with people who love and give unconditionally. The family chosen to spend a lifetime with me speaks positive things into my life.

Especially my dear brother, Larry, who, with his beautiful smile, motivates and inspires me to be my best.

~ Carol A. Pena

September 22

Where Determination Comes From

"Every blade of grass has its angel that bends over it and whispers, 'Grow, grow.'"

~ The Talmud

I'm grateful for what drives me forward.

This invisible miracle worker, who, mixed with the perfect amounts of compassion and determination, says, "That didn't work? Try again!" or "Well, you learned something. Give it another shot!"

My angel is sure to whisper "Good job!" after a sweet success, yet it shows its true strength when times are tough. The insistence that I can overcome and do it drives me along faster and farther—stretching me to achieve far more than I ever imagined.

I'm grateful for the part of me that doesn't give up and instead looks for a way to persevere and thrive!

~ Anonymous

September 23

Two Little Words

"If you mess up, 'fess up."

~ Unknown

I'm grateful for learning to say "I'm sorry."

There were times where I would "fight for my right" to no end. Eyes blazing, voice loud, chest tight, I'd insist—all "proud and loud." Or I'd put my energy into creating a stony silence worthy of the Ice Age. It was the principle of the matter!

Sometimes others would cave in. That didn't feel good. And the situation continued to be above our heads, like a big black cloud.

Other times we'd part ways—friendships fractured, perhaps never to be repaired.

But sometimes, many of those times, I was wrong. And somewhere along the way I learned to say "I'm sorry."

Oh, the freedom it gives me! A moment of discomfort (in getting over my own ego) can lead to a whole new world of happiness and understanding. I'm so grateful for the times I take a deep breath, admit where I was wrong and say those magic two little words.

~ Anonymous

September 24

Grateful for the Beauty of Two Becoming One

When I was in my early twenties I had a modern art poster on the wall inscribed with the words "Let there be such oneness between us, that when one cries, the other tastes salt." At that time it was a beautiful and quite romantic notion. This quote by an unknown author now has a deep and powerful meaning to me because I am seeing these words in action each day as my parents serve and care for one another in myriad ways. Their example is a shining beacon of what love and marriage can be: beautiful, sacrificial, and enduring. I am grateful for my parents and for the example they have provided day in and day out to our family. They have established a cornerstone in the foundation of our lives that grows more significant with each passing day.

As I write this, my parents have been married for sixty-four years. They are not in good health. Yet the tenderness between them is an inspiration to us all. There is a wink, a smile, a touch, a shared memory, and, yes, the taste of salt when the tears fall. I am grateful for the oneness between them.

~ Beverly Beckerdite Dracos

September 25

Yes, My Dear, That's All There Is

Two days that changed my life forever: September 24th and 25th. It was on September 24th that I was in labor, delivering my baby, VBAC, but during delivery my uterus ruptured. I was rushed to surgery for an emergency C-section and put to sleep. I awoke later to learn that my beautiful baby boy, William, would probably not live long. I was not able to see him or hold him until the next day, right before he passed away.

Shortly after this I had a dream I will never forget. In my dream I was following three elderly women around, it was as if we were all floating. I was behind them and couldn't see their faces, but I could see what they were watching.

They were viewing different moments of their lives, and thoroughly enjoying recounting all these memories. Then I said out loud, "Is that all there is?" and one of the women turned to me. There was a bright light all around her. She was glowing and, with a beautiful, warm smile, she said, "Yes, my dear, that's all there is." I took that to understand what really matters in life: all the moments we create with our loved ones.

I am truly grateful for my son in heaven who reminds me every day to be grateful for all the moments I have here with family and friends, because that's all that really matters.

~ Di Ana Ford

September 26

Releasing Desires with Gratitude

While sitting on the beach one evening in 1998, I breathed in the yummy ocean air with a heart full of gratitude.

It was one of those big-picture moments as I reflected on my childhood and all that had transpired since then.

I grew up feeling close to God and knowing He was with me, loving and cheering me on and helping me co-create a happy life.

Although I loved children and had wanted to be a mom, at 32, I was at peace with releasing this and said, "We've come so far, God. Thank you. I love you and my life, and I feel complete. It's okay, God, if I don't have children."

God may have been smiling, knowingly, for on September 26, 2000, David Michael ("beloved," "child of God") was born.

Being his momma is the best part of my blessed life, and every day I hug him in God's sunshine and thank God for him.

His beautiful eyes, his heart, how he still shares everything with me ("Momma, watch this!"), the way he sings love songs to me and texts me "Love you, Momma," and the way he treats others and makes me laugh — I am so grateful.

~ Kathy Bowes

September 27

Sunshine in My Heart

If it wasn't for the past, I wouldn't be in the present. If it wasn't for the many challenges, I wouldn't have perceived lessons. If it wasn't for the lessons, I wouldn't have learned. If it wasn't for illness, I wouldn't know health. If it wasn't for attachment and loss, I wouldn't have realized everything is impermanent, except that divine spark.

Thank you for showing me this spark and allowing me to know all as divine and knowing. If it wasn't for the clouds and dust we would not all know this. (So I guess I am grateful for housework!)

I am grateful for the fear, anger, jealousy, guilt, and sadness that surface, because in knowing the shadow I can know truth. I can connect with love, compassion, courage, peace, and contentment. I am grateful that I can assist others to do this same process because we are all created in God's image. Our truth is divinity. I am grateful for each day, which begins with the sun rising and shining in my window, and reflecting in my heart. I am grateful for sharing my heart and for knowing that you, too, can know the sunshine in your heart.

~ *Fiona Om Shanti*

September 28

What I *Can* Do

My life is an adventure, and my blessings are many! I'm grateful to be able to recognize that I am the creator of my own world and that perfection is not a requirement. I can trade my old beliefs for new ones, choosing a different path that reveals my personal growth and how far I've come. I can learn from my challenging situations, rise above, and share them to help others overcome theirs. I can love my family deeply and be a source of love and comfort for them. I can marvel at the amazing people the Universe/GOD/Spirit has placed on my path, at the perfect time, to assist me in my journey — amazing people I now call friends and some even family. I can delight in recognizing that there are no coincidences and that we are constantly receiving confirmation from the Universe. I can set my mind to something spectacular, and see the resources and people start manifesting instantly! I can choose to be inspiration through example. I can be in awe, as I watch my life magically unfold like the grand adventure it is.

I'm extremely grateful for all the things I can do and more!

~ Denice Rivera

September 29

Survival Gratitude

September 29th started like any other day, except, after I called her name throughout the house, my wife didn't answer. I found her lying on the floor in the downstairs laundry room. After rushing to her side, I realized she was not breathing. I called 911 and immediately started CPR.

She never regained consciousness, and I was left with my two young sons to forge ahead in life as a widower. The pain is something that will be with me forever, but what saved me in the long run was my belief in gratitude—survival gratitude.

The thought of trying to raise my two young sons, and to survive the trauma of losing my wife, was only made possible by my belief in gratitude. I started to write in a gratitude journal, and each day encouraged me to focus on all that was good in my life in spite of this horrific event.

The human spirit can survive, but it helps to have tools to assist in the process. They say that time heals, and it does, but gratitude can truly propel you to a life of renewed happiness and joy.

~ David George Brooke

September 30

For the Love of Socks

"One can never have enough socks."

           ~Albus Dumbledore

The answer is always the same when anyone asks what I want for my birthday—SOCKS!
I have a deep and profound appreciation for them.

It's not uncommon for me to go through three or four pairs in a day.

I keep spare socks in my glove box and in my trunk—because you never know when you might have a sock emergency.

If you put on a new pair in the middle of the day it's like getting an afternoon foot rub.

They are the best guilt-free pick-me up ever created.

They're not fattening. They don't raise your blood pressure. They're relatively inexpensive.

They might be addictive—but I don't care.

I will wear my socks until they are well worn but in a perfect world I would never wear the same pair twice—because the feeling of a brand new pair of socks on a pair of tired feet cannot be matched.

Socks—you are simply splendid.

My feet appreciate you tremendously.

~ Anonymous

October

"God gave you a gift of 86,400 seconds today. Have you used one to say 'thank you?'"

~William A. Ward

October 1

Seasons of Grace

My grandpa died this year. As it does for so many people, losing a family member caused me to reflect. I didn't know him as well as I wish I had, but I've benefited most from his legacy of faith and unconditional love — things money can't buy. My family's belief in me (long before I believed in myself) has been a critical part of my success.

This year has been challenging: I lost my job and, as of this writing, still don't have another. My engagement ended in a breakup instead of a wedding. But I've also been blessed with some incredible opportunities. I realized a long-held dream with the publication of my first book, and I was able to connect with an incredible mentor (who appeared just as I lost my job) and start a new business with "found" money I didn't even know I had.

The future is still very uncertain right now, but I'm excited by the limitless possibilities. The ancient book of Ecclesiastes says "To everything there is a season…" All seasons are seasons of grace. As I write this in the month of November, I'm overwhelmed with gratitude this Thanksgiving season.

~ Michelle Nightengale

October 2

Warm Tears and Sloppy Kisses

Above my fireplace hangs a picture of my children and their families. Each time I see this picture a joyful feeling runs from my toes to the top of my head, where it explodes into a shout of pure gratitude.

My family bantered about which picture to choose for me — "not that one; my eyes are closed"; "no, no, I look dorky in that one"; etc. Little do they know, when I look at that picture, I see baby faces! All those babies I held tenderly, their heads tucked under my chin, their breath on my face. I see their precious smiles and frowns, their beautiful eyes. Never enough!

I hear their sighs, their coos, their gurgles, their cries and screams, their laughter. Never enough!

I feel their tiny hands curled around my finger, sloppy kisses all over my face, warm tears from their hurts and joys. Never enough.

When I look at that picture, I don't see the adults approaching wisdom age, the young adults, the teens, the kids. I see their precious baby faces and feel their sloppy kisses. Warm tears run down my face. My tears. Joy. I am grateful.

~ Margaret A. Hicke

Depression vs. Mourning

I am extremely grateful for understanding the difference between depression and mourning, and, if I start to get depressed, how to bring myself back to life. Let me back up and explain.

I was mildly depressed half of my life but didn't realize it. I guess that I partly learned it from my mother, who suffered from depression in my childhood.

I didn't understand, or know how to accept, that there are lots of things to mourn — small and large — in our daily lives (e.g., having an argument with someone and feeling misunderstood, or dissatisfaction with parts of our life but not knowing how to change them).

Our "spirit" needs to mourn — it's a healthy part of being able to heal and move on — but as a culture, we have forgotten how to mourn, so we end up being depressed instead.

I have since learned that I, and we all, have deep inner values that are always trying to guide us toward "aliveness." Identifying their messages is a huge gift! The clients that I support, like I do, now know how to move toward a life of "aliveness" and meaning. And I am so grateful for that!

What are you grateful for?

~ Rachel Monde

October 4

A Laugh a Day Keeps the Bugs Away

Did someone say gratitude? I am grateful for laughter. I am without a doubt a goofball and love to laugh.

My wife, Teresa, and I recently attended a costume party on Halloween night. To no one's surprise, I decided to be a clown. I enjoyed tooting my big, red nose and pulling on my oversized colorful necktie as much as the kids (and my wife) did.

Laughter is contagious and fun. One of my fondest memories in my childhood includes creating "theatrical" plays where I entertained the audiences with laughter. In one performance entitled "The Haunted Tea Room," I portrayed a character named Horace Witherspoon, a bugologist. The setting presented the perfect environment for bug collecting. The audience focused on me as I scurried about the stage racing down rare insects. The laughs were abundant and joyful.

I am a child at heart and enjoy a precious moment of laughter. I laugh each day at work. It helps my day and reduces work stress. To me, laughter is the path to happiness and togetherness. Laughter brightens your day, strengthens your emotions, and creates a positive energy your family and friends will appreciate and love.

Laughter is one of the best gifts of life.

~ Brad C. Castleman

The Precious Gift

Why is standing in line a half hour at Disneyland more fun than standing in line at the post office? Because our *expectations* create our *attitude*. (If you think about it, kids get just as cranky in line at Disneyland as at the post office. They only know the experience and not the expectation.)

But what if we left expectations behind and appreciated each experience for what it is?

I sit here on this October evening in deep gratitude, enjoying the open windows, the covers thrown back, and the sound of insects outside, knowing winter is on the horizon and knowing these unseasonably warm days are urgently numbered. This makes the experience as precious as gold! Like my days on the planet, give or take twenty or thirty years.

They are all quick as lightening, they are all numbered, and they are all precious. To be in that preciousness—to take it in fully—that is the gift. I close my eyes; I take a deep breath; I fill with appreciation for everything just as it is right now. There is no future moment for which we all pine. There are only continuous moments, each unique and precious, waiting for our attention and gratitude to bring them to life.

~ *Wendy Mackowski*

October 6

Your Lottery Winnings

Two decades ago, I heard a quote that has stayed with me to this day: "To be born a woman in America is like winning the lottery."

The speaker added, "A woman born in America has been afforded opportunities that women born in other countries only dream about, fight for, and endure hardships to pursue." For this, I'm eternally grateful.

American women haven't always had these opportunities. The suffrage movement of the 1920s was fraught with many of the same struggles as the civil rights movement. In the same way that the protagonist in the movie *Saving Private Ryan* felt he had to "earn this," I feel a sense of obligation to make the most of my lottery winnings.

Each day, I thank God that I have the right to vote and to choose whom to marry, and the choice to attend college, to work, to pursue a full-time career, and to raise a family, or any combination of the above.

As the mother of a 14-year-old "lottery winner," I endeavor daily to pass along this sense of duty to the next generation.

What are you doing with your lottery winnings? Make the most of them. Make them count.

~ Kris Lozano

October 7

Full Heart
Susan M. Secord's Gratitude List

Angels   Aunts

Birds • Books • Boys   Brothers • Cats • Chocolate

Cousins • Dad • Dogs • Earth • Faith • Family • Flowers

Food • Freedom • Friends • Girls • Godchildren • Guides

Horses • Husbands • I AM • Jewels • Kisses • LOVE • Lovers

Mom • Money • Moon • Music • Nephews • Nieces

Om • Peace • Quotes • Rain • Roses • Sisters

Sleep • Smiles • Snow • Spirit • Stars • Sun

Telephones • U • Uncles • Vacations

Wings • Wonder • www.

Xs • Y?

Zzzzzzs

~ Susan M. Secord

October 8

Grateful for Life's Road Trip

A hit song from the past has compared life to a highway. I am so grateful for that highway. With the fast pace of our road trip, life can become a blur.

Our life's highway bends and straightens; it climbs and descends. As we drive it, we don't always take time to savor the people and experiences in our lives. I find someone hurting and lacking. I am grateful I can help them. I meet someone inspiring. I am grateful they have touched my life. I meet someone fun and give thanks for the joy and laughter they have brought to me. I know someone suffering from a serious illness. I am grateful for the lessons they are teaching me. I am grateful for my health.

I am so grateful for those special people in my life, both friends and family. They make life rich and full. They make my road trip memorable and worthwhile. I am grateful for traditions, and travels, and quiet days at home.

I really am grateful for life's road trip. I plan to turn off the cruise control on a regular basis, so I can fully experience the trip.

~ Susan Brownell

October 9

L.I.F.E.: Life Is for Everyone

I was hospitalized for an emotional breakdown in 2004. During that experience, I discovered I had never coped with the murder of my sister Nicole Brown Simpson.

One day, during my in-patient stay, I was sitting on the edge of my bed looking out at a panoramic view from La Jolla to San Diego, Laguna Beach to Palos Verdes. And I could not see the beauty in anything. I asked God, "What is so beautiful about this? I don't see anything beautiful here." At that very moment, a little hummingbird flew in front of my window. Immediately, I saw the waves crashing and the dog playing in the back yard below me. I finally saw the beauty that I had known all my life.

I am grateful for my hospitalization, because the life skills I learned made me a stronger person. They got me through to now. With the support of my mom, dad, friends, boyfriend, Sean, and Christ, I was able to stay above water. I found the beauty around me and share a smile with someone every day.

Be grateful to be alive! Amen!

~ Tanya Brown

October 10

God's Gift

In all her beauty she talks to me. I feel God's invisible language speak through her every move. She guides me, surprises me, delights me, and supplies me. I love her morning glory and evening grace. Her moods have four seasons, and are forever changing, yet as dependable as time.

Every day I am thankful for her. Even though she feeds my soul, she can be a commanding teacher.

Her name is nature, and in all her power and magnificence she has touched my soul like a lover, taught me wisdom like an old sage, and colored my life with the richest palette.

We forget that she has ears to hear and feelings to feel, and that she is just as alive as us. So sometimes she needs to reminds us and wake us up.

My favorite part of our relationship is how she lets me know with a breeze by my side, or a shooting star in the sky, that my son, who died, is still by my side.

Heaven can be right here, she says — no dividing line. Just look for the beauty; the wonders abound; open your eyes they can be found.

~ Louise Rouse

October 11

Learning from Hardships

What am I grateful for?

What I am going to say that may seem counter-intuitive: I am grateful for what I learned from the hardships in my life.

When I was 18, my father passed away. I married my first wife, Brenda, when I was 21. We had two beautiful daughters before she was diagnosed, at 28, with cancer that killed her slowly for the next ten years. Both of these terrible events left an indelible mark on me, but both have helped me to grow tremendously.

They helped me to leave the safety and comfort of a successful corporate job and start as an entrepreneur in the coaching industry. It is only by experiencing and overcoming adversity that we recognize our own sense of worth and our sense of who we are — that we understand our own strengths.

My work as a career coach brings me into daily contact with people at a crossroads in their own life and career. My own life history has given me unique insights into what it takes to confront those life-changing questions, and to help others answer those questions with confidence and courage.

~ Bert Goos

October 12

Magic Numbers

Twenty-five years ago today, I walked down the aisle and, before family and friends, committed to love and honor one man.

9,131 days later, there have been moments – some filled with frustration and confusion, but many more filled with wonder, joy, and quiet bliss.

We have shared our few losses and celebrated our countless victories.

There have been eighteen moves around the U.S. We have enjoyed the company of seven dogs and two cats.

We have welcomed three amazing sons.

We have prepared him and sent him off to one war and welcomed him home again.

We have each lost one parent to cancer.

We have nursed each other back to health through four surgeries, three labors and deliveries, and far too many sprains and pains.

We have owned eighteen cars, six homes, four snowmobiles, and ridiculous amounts of sports equipment.

While we weigh more, move slower, and wear bi-focal glasses, there is only one *us*, and for this I am eternally grateful.

~ Mrs. Carolyn E. Stys,
wife of Mark V. Stys

October 13

World Mind

Today I salute the thirty-three Chilean coal miners who were buried under 2,500 feet of earth for sixty-nine terrifying days in 2010. No miner had ever been found alive after five days in a mine, but the thirty-three Chilean miners were discovered alive after seventeen days! Every country in the world rallied behind the miners in non-stop prayer and collaboration.

Beneath: "Group survival" was chosen against all odds.

Above: It was not likely that thirty-three miners were about to manifest a huge global event.

They endured ninety-plus degrees temperatures all the time. It was always hot, smelly, and dark. No sunshine. No light. Lots of health risks.

They shared food every two days without killing each other or giving up. Some were diabetics. Some had heart disease. One was terrified of ghosts and the dark. The oldest was retiring and celebrating his last day in the mine.

Once found, they stayed the course mentally and spiritually another two long months.

It must have sounded like Grand Central Station in heaven with the whole globe praying in a multitude of languages and religions for these courageous Chileans. I appreciate everyone who prayed for them.

~ Timi Gleason

October 14

How to Attract Great Things to You

"A grateful mind is a great mind which eventually attracts to itself great things."

– Plato

What a wonderful place to be — grateful for all that you have and all that comes your way. Everything happens for a reason, whether it seems good or bad at the time. When things happen to us, we need to stop and wonder, "What can I learn from this?"

Maybe I was stuck in traffic for my own safety, the loss of my cell phone wasn't an accident, or when a loved one died too young, I was changed and made stronger.

Every day, we may experience pain, love, anger, joy, frustration, and happiness. Take each event for what it is. Cancel any negative thoughts, and think hard to find the lesson in each event. Sometimes it may take time to find the good, but don't give up.

A higher power is always with us. We must be comforted and renewed by this truth. It is no accident that you have this book and are reading this page today.

Never forget to be grateful for all you have and all that happens to you. Tell the universe every day: "Thank you, thank you, thank you!" And so it is.

~ *Gail Mettler Swain*

October 15

A Lost Phone Number

Shortly after moving to New York, I was given the phone number of a medical clinic that was interested in my training as a physician assistant, with a background in alternative medicine. I was not looking for a job, but called and scheduled an interview. On the the day of the interview, I decided to cancel. I found the address, but no phone number. Reluctantly, I went to the interview.

Career-wise, that was the best decision I ever made.

I was hired that day by one of the early pioneers of the complementary/integrative medicine movement, Dr. Robert C. Atkins. Though best known for the Atkins Diet, he was a magnet for leaders in this field of medicine. He was passionate about his work and expected no less from his staff. Working with him was never boring.

With his guidance, my role expanded from physician assistant to writer, lecturer, and researcher, among other things. These skills I have since used to help start Medicine 369, an integrative medical practice with another Atkins' alum.

I am grateful I lost that phone number. Had I canceled, I would have missed working with my mentor and friend, Dr. Robert C. Atkins.

~ Karen Paris

October 16

October Sun

Today I am hiking alone, on a newly discovered trail, high above the I-70 corridor. Two thousand feet below me, the cars and trucks rumble their traveling songs, a soft bass that drifts high above them, up to where the trees stop growing, and the clear blue heavens meet this golden Earth. The angle of the October sun sparkles from a creek as it gurgles its way down a worn mountain path, tread for a million years — a path unlike the one I walk today.

Usually, I hike with the love of my life, but today he is making his way home from Philadelphia, far above the air that I now breathe. This day, I am thinking of how lucky I am to live this life — how thankful I am for every day spent on this Earth.

Each day holds its own beauty, but today the warmth of that beauty fills the air with a joyousness that catches my breath, and a soft smile saunters across my face.

The choices of a thousand ancestors have brought me here today. All the gratitude in the universe is not enough to thank them for drawing me to this place.

~ Dana R. Fletcher

October 17

Gratitude Is My Birthright

On the day before I was born, my mother boarded a bus to go into the city to purchase tickets for a Marian Anderson concert. The driver drove off precipitously as my mom stepped from the bus. She was thrown to the sidewalk thirty-one weeks pregnant.

Early on October 17th, a very premature baby was born. There were no specialists, nor special equipment to take care of babies born too soon. The baby struggled and appeared to be losing the battle. At my mother's discharge, my parents were given the choice of leaving me at the hospital to die or taking me home. They decided to take me home. My dad hardly moved from the rocking chair where he sat for several months, praying and anointing my forehead and the soles of my feet, day and night, hardly sleeping or eating. His faith was that I was born to live.

At six months of age, the pictures of me resemble those of the happy, healthy "Gerber baby."

When my mom died, I discovered on a certificate dated October 17th — miscarriage!

I was born to live a life of gratitude. And I do!

Thank you Lord, Daddy, and Mamma.

~ Marion Smith-Waison

October 18

Explore. Dream. Discover.

"Twenty years from now you will be more disappointed by the things that you didn't do than by the ones you did do. So throw off the bowlines. Sail away from the safe harbor. Catch the trade winds in your sails. Explore. Dream. Discover."

~ Mark Twain

I am eternally grateful to my parents, who always encouraged me to experience life to its fullest and to love learning. I know they think the world of me.

I am grateful that I successfully completed an Ironman Triathlon, a grueling, fourteen-hour effort of which I'm very proud.

I am grateful for being a late-life mom to my three children. Their arrival changed the course of my life. I discovered a way to share myself with the world that is much more personally satisfying, something I didn't feel in my corporate science career.

I am grateful for the enthusiasm, energy, and passion that I bring to everything I do.

I am grateful for the great friendships in my life. You know who you are.

I am grateful for my own wonderful company. I treasure my quiet moments with myself, thinking, imagining, daydreaming, planning.

~ Andrea Cinnamond

October 19

Who's in the Musical?

Every autumn for the past eight years, anxious and excited students at Mira Mesa High School in San Diego audition for the spring musical.

The audition is one of many steps leading up to opening night, and the students are part of a larger group who make the production a collaboration of both school and community.

As the director, I am grateful for them all.

Sarah directs the choreography in a beautifully professional manner.

Our musical directors, Mary, Cindy, Bob, Julie, and Jeanne lead the student orchestra and vocalists.

Jodie, our accomplished accompanist, brings magic to the piano.

Roxy designs and sews the most exquisite costumes, while her husband, Craig, is frequently on hand with a video camera.

JoAnn stations herself in the lobby collecting tickets.

Colleague and friend Art works late into the night printing tickets and programs.

Mark and Jennifer lend talent to sound and concessions.

Sandy, the passionate art teacher, researches authentic costuming and scenic designs.

The Pacific Coast Theatre Company provides technical expertise.

Finally I'm thankful for my parents, family, and friends, who support me as the production rolls along—sometimes by sitting right beside me, while other times from miles and miles away.

~ Daniel Kriley

October 20

Big Piles of Leaves

I've always been fascinated by leaves, especially those from maple trees. From their first appearance after winter snows where they looked like green mist enveloping the tops of trees to their furling forth and completely covering the branches. Towards summer's end it was the release little "helicopters" of seeds onto the grassy floor and dirt roads.

But it's fall, glorious fall, when maple tree leaves take center stage. Raked up into big piles for jumping in. Swirling around in the wind and providing the staging as I pretend I was in The Wizard of Oz shouting "Auntie Em! Auntie Em!" while Mom smiles and laughs with me from the front porch.

They became a finger-painting palette for Mother Nature, who produced gold and burgundy-colored leaves along with ones that had several colors on one paper thin, five-pointed star. Carefully collected and pressed between wax paper into books, they remain reminders of the beauty and uniqueness of each person in this world.

I'm grateful for the beauty of nature, especially the seasons of maple tree leaves.

~ Anonymous

October 21

Reflections on My Brothers
In appreciation of you both!

"After a girl is grown, her little brothers—now her protectors—seem like big brothers."

~Astrid Alauda

"To the outside world we all grow old. But not to brothers and sisters. We know each other as we always were. We know each other's hearts. We share private family jokes. We remember family feuds and secrets, family griefs and joys. We live outside the touch of time."

~Clara Ortega

"Sibling relationships—and 80 percent of Americans have at least one—outlast marriages, survive the death of parents, resurface after quarrels that would sink any friendship. They flourish in a thousand incarnations of closeness and distance, warmth, loyalty and distrust."
~Erica E. Goode, "The Secret World of Siblings," U.S. News & World Report, 10 January 1994

"A sibling may be the keeper of one's identity, the only person with the keys to one's unfettered, more fundamental self."

~Marian Sandmaier

"There's no other love like the love for a brother. There's no other love like the love from a brother."

~Astrid Alauda

"Siblings—the definition that comprises love, strife, competition and forever friends."

~Byron Pulsifer

~ *Anonymous*

October 22

In Appreciation
of Friendship

"There are big ships and small ships. But the best ship of all is friendship."

~Author Unknown

"The best kind of friend is the one you could sit on a porch with, never saying a word, and walk away feeling like that was the best conversation you've had."

~Author Unknown

"If you're alone, I'll be your shadow. If you want to cry, I'll be your shoulder. If you want a hug, I'll be your pillow. If you need to be happy, I'll be your smile. But anytime you need a friend, I'll just be me."

~Author Unknown

"A friend accepts us as we are yet helps us to be what we should."

~Author Unknown

Piglet sidled up to Pooh from behind.
"Pooh!" he whispered.
"Yes, Piglet?"
"Nothing," said Piglet, taking Pooh's paw.
"I just wanted to be sure of you."

~A.A. Milne

To each of you who are willing to ride the bus with me when the limo breaks down—I love you.

~ Anonymous

October 23

The Princess and the 'Pee'

I'm thankful our cat "went" all over our bed and ruined the mattress. This mattress was a fifteen-year-old hand-me-down and was supposed to have been a temporary solution six years ago. As I stood in our beautiful apartment with my nostrils burning from the stench, I said to my husband, while looking at the rancid yellow and gold floral-print mattress, "Well, I guess we finally have a reason to get a new one."

Then I thought, "But we just can't afford a new mattress right now."

Immediately it struck me that I had repeated that exact same statement for the past six years. I decided right then to change my beliefs about my financial situation.

Instead of taking out credit, I wanted to manifest the money, and I believed I could through my coaching business. In two short weeks, I had a brand new, never-been-slept-on, extra-firm white mattress (plus waterproof cover) and had let go of my limiting beliefs for good. Since that day, I have lived a more abundant life and never uttered words of lack again.

I am forever grateful for the signs from the Universe, even if sometimes they really stink.

~ Tracy Tobler

October 24

Love Letter

Being able to appreciate the gift of gratitude is intrinsically gratifying. The act of being grateful is such a powerful way to bring about a feeling of peace and happiness, sometimes when we need it the most.

Looking back at my life's journey of personal development, I notice that when I struggled, my entire focus was on what was wrong, which blinded me from seeing any hope.

One day, along this journey, I "found" gratitude. I learned that, no matter what I am experiencing, there is something to be authentically grateful for. And focusing on it, rather than only on any negatives, can help remind me about what really matters in the big picture of life. For me, this brings me back to a place where I am proud to be me, which ultimately helps me to achieve my life mission: to coach, inspire, and contribute to people leading great lives!

I truly love my life and am extremely grateful for everyone who has helped me along my path, especially my incredibly supportive husband, our beautiful children, our loving families, my amazing tribe of friends, and my incredible clients. I have learned so much from each of you!

Namaste.

~ Kim Stahler Zilliox

October 25

The Not-So-Obvious

When I think of what I am grateful for, the list is honestly endless. There are so many obvious things: my husband, our daughter, my family, the roof over my head, my health. And maybe some not-so-obvious things like failures, bumps in the road, and challenges.

I've had the ability over the past several years to actually take these seemingly negative, challenging situations and turn them into something positive — things to be abundantly grateful for — and I have to tell you: It's liberating!

The ability to look upon these situations with deep gratitude has given me the opportunity to see nothing as a failure, and nothing as a challenge. There is a positive lesson to be grateful for in all of it. I am meant to learn something, meant to be challenged, and meant to have the experience.

Gratitude is a fullness of life. The ability to see gratitude in everything — whether good or bad — is freeing. It brings the whole process of gratitude full circle, allowing us to learn and be full of gratitude in ways we never thought possible.

~ Deanna Collins

October 26

Best Day Ever

Every morning before I get out of bed I am grateful for being welcomed into the day. With my head still tucked under the pillow, I can feel the eager anticipation from four eyes waiting. My dogs, Duke and Murphy, lie patiently, waiting to see if miracle upon miracles I will again make this their best day ever. With their tails wagging, how can I not once again get dressed in my slightly tight walking shorts and my too-old walking shoes, put on their leashes, and step out my front door to greet the day? The best day ever!

~ *Laurie D. Dupar*

October 27

Second Chances

"Don't get discouraged; it is often the last key in the bunch that opens the lock."

~ Unknown

I'm grateful for being able to have a "life do-over." After following what I thought everyone else wanted me to do and being professionally and financially successful as a chemical engineer, I became very ill and one hundred pounds overweight. At 32 years old, I left my job, my "identity" and my lifestyle, and the marriage to who I believed was the "love of my life" eventually ended. The subsequent years of healing led me to go back to school and gave me a second chance at life.

I now have the privilege to help others lose weight, heal digestive and reproductive disorders, overcome sleep problems, and gain more energy and vitality in their daily lives.

As I work with others I am reminded daily of the many generous friends, family, and mentors in my life who have shared their wisdom so I can be a better person, a better practitioner, a better friend, a better family member, and a better caretaker of myself as a human being. I'm grateful I was blessed with the gifted blend of curiosity and faith to take calculated risks for a life well lived. I'm grateful to be alive and to be able to "pay it forward."

~ Stephanie J. Solaris

October 28

The Tragedy Blinked

The phone rang about 7 p.m. After the ravages of diabetes left me in kidney failure and I spent more than a year in the humiliating pain of dialysis, there was a donor that was a match.

The donor's lifestyle issues forced us to think long and hard about whether this was the right donor and the right match. A long conversation with a close friend, a nurse, put our minds more at ease.

We were on the road in less than twenty minutes after accepting the offer. In Pittsburgh by midnight and in surgery by 3 a.m., I left dialysis, fluid restrictions, critically low red blood cell counts, and daily nausea behind.

The family of that 32-year-old man had stared down their tragedy. The tragedy blinked.

I will forever be grateful to them for their decision to let their son save several lives, including mine. Their second sacrifice let me return to the things and people I love stronger, more vital, and prepared to carry on. From that humbling gratitude to them comes this request: Please make sure your donor card is signed and your family knows your wishes.

~ Edd Sturdevant

October 29

Quest for the Perfect Pen

"The Pen is mightier than the sword"

~Baron Edward Bulwer-Lytton

So true...
Some girls like shopping for clothes and shoes.
Me? I like pens.

All kinds of pens. (Mechanical pencils are good too!)

I hope whoever thought up that little pen testing station in office supply stores was properly compensated because that was brilliant. (It's like getting to try on the shoes or test drive the car before you purchase.) And there are so many things to consider when selecting a pen...

- The weight...
- The grip...
- The color...
- Ballpoint...rollerball...gel...
- Soft and comforting click vs. hollow and metallic...
- Fine, extra fine, medium points...
- To refill or not to refill...
- The balance point...

A pen allows me to share my thoughts with the world. There are more expedient ways to do it now—with the advent of computers and such.

But the satisfaction of putting a fine pen to crisp paper can never be compared to a word processor. Words written with my favorite pen of the week reveal components of my personality that a perfectly type-written page can never convey.

Though I enjoy trying on all kinds of pens—I hope I never find the perfect one—I enjoy the quest too much.

~ *Anonymous*

October 30

Metamorphosis

"It's not that some people have willpower and some don't. It's that some people are ready to change and others are not."

~ James Gordon

There is nothing about the appearance of a caterpillar to suggest the beautiful butterfly that will one day emerge.

The dragonfly, while in its water nymph stage, looks like an unattractive little alien creature.

Technology has come a long way with 3D sonograms but the in-vitro pictures of yesteryear gave us no indication our kids would resemble normal, attractive people some day.

The dictionary defines metamorphosis as a profound change in form from one stage to the next or any complete change in appearance, character or circumstances.

Some changes are an inevitable part of the process of life even though there is nothing wrong with being a caterpillar, or a nymph or a fetus.

We don't have to do anything to make some changes happen.

Nature takes care of itself that way.

Other transformations require our participation.

Inner consciousness shows up in our exterior world.

Paying attention to our thoughts and learning to direct them can cause intentional metamorphosis so we can change on purpose. But we don't have to.

How cool is that?

~ Anonymous

October 31

My Mother-in-Law's Porch

I exit the car. I see you for the first time. You're standing on your mother's porch.

In an instant the Universe reveals to me the secret order hidden in what appears to be the chaos of life—by sucking all the wind from my body.

I knew then you were meant for me, but we both had business to finish.

It took seven years.

For many since then you have been mine—to have and to hold.

But I believe I was yours the moment we collided.

So I remind you again that…

By the life that courses within my blood

And the love that resides within my heart

I take you to my hand, my heart, and my spirit

To be my chosen one

To desire and be desired by you without sin or shame

For none can exist in the purity of my love for you

I promise to love you wholly and completely without restraint

In sickness and in health, in plenty and in poverty

In life and beyond

Where we will meet, remember and love again.

It's not my porch. It's not a fancy porch. It's just the best porch I've ever laid eyes on.

~ Michelle Dimsey

November

*"Hem your blessings with thankfulness
so they don't unravel."*

~ author unknown

November 1

In Heartfelt Gratitude for Family Caregivers During National Family Caregivers Month

Each day I marvel at the generosity of so many caring people. No matter their lot in life, there are those who are always caregivers. They give their time, money, and heart. They embrace those who are hurting, both physically and emotionally. They administer medications and clean up messes only someone with love in their heart could. They hold hands. They comfort. They are present when most would turn away.

I am so grateful for family caregivers. I know their pain. I want to ease their burden. I think of the love they must have to do what they do. I think of the exhaustion and sacrifices they endure. They truly practice the Golden Rule. Wouldn't this world be a far better place if we all did so, regardless of our calling in life?

We all are caregivers in some capacity. Let's make it count. Caregiving may be hard to bear at the time, but you will be rewarded with some unexpected sweet memories and an unspeakable peace knowing that you did the right thing. You will also know that someone was grateful—very, very grateful.

~ Susan Brownell

November 2

Unconditional Love

When I was going through my child-bearing years, I felt as if I had a black cloud over my head. I was pregnant —and then not—so many times that my obstetrician and I both lost count. All I ever wanted in life was to have children. From my earliest memories as a child myself, I loved children and dreamed of the day I would have my own.

My earliest jobs in life were all about the care of children. I even went into teaching, and over the years taught children from preschool, to elementary special ed, middle school, and lastly undergraduates.

It was incredulous that someone so in love with children couldn't find the recipe for having a child! But then, in 1976, the stars and moons were finally in alignment, and I gave birth to Peter.

What am I grateful for? A son who is rock solid, who gets me like no one else, who is incredibly talented and endlessly funny, who has the ability to push my buttons and tease me mercilessly. And I take it with a smirk and a laugh! I am grateful for the unconditional love of my child.

~ Angela I. Schutz

November 3

Grateful for My Family

It took me a long time to learn about gratitude. I spent most of my younger years angry with my life and those in it. I had an unconventional childhood at best. I felt like I was suffering because of my family's issues. I wanted to replace them. I certainly was not grateful for them.

Fast forward fifteen years, and I am more grateful now for my family than I ever was. Maybe it is because I am a mother now and I see how hard some decisions can be. Or maybe it just took me growing up to realize that seeing my family struggles taught me so much and that I am wiser because of them.

My grandmother taught me strength. My grandfather taught me that it is never too late to change. My aunt taught me unconditional acceptance. My sister taught me about self-sacrifice. My brother showed me survival. My father showed me that it is okay to stand alone and withdraw from unhealthy situations. Lastly, my mother has taught me forgiveness, compassion, and, most of all, empathy.

Everything I have learned has made me a better, stronger mother. I am so grateful for my family.

~ Deanna E. McAdams

November 4

I Am Grateful for My Skin

I am grateful for my skin, the frontier where I venture into the world and the world crosses into me, hundreds of touch receptors and responders attentive, watching and waiting for the next true move.

Bare feet pressing down on cool sand.

Cashmere sweater cascading over head, pouring down arms and shoulders.

Pima t-shirt slips on, second skin, breathing in, breathing out.

Flowing pressure of spring-fed water on Walden Pond as I stretch out my right arm to take the first stroke.

Amorous contours of my lover's body, longing, listening as we spoon.

Lap time, my daughter's womanly figure still seeking the intimacy of infancy, forever a baby in my arms.

Deep stretch reaching from skin down to bones, cooling down after my workout, reuniting life and limb.

Bubbly jets in the hot tub, final finish.

Luscious softness of my mattress, sheets, and down covers, a queenly bed to cradle achy joints and surrender body and mind to deep slumber.

Melding with the Being in the Body when I massage my clients.

Kissing my own fingertips hello.

~ Dawn AV Marie Jordan

November 5

Gracious Donor, Grateful Lives

A life donation, a donation for life. He was a young, strong, and seemingly indestructible. A 21-year-old athlete with the heart of a champion, two strong kidneys, and a clean liver.

It happened fast — suddenly. Only God can explain: brain aneurysm, life ends, his journey on Earth over. A tragic ending for one young life, but a ray of hope and new beginnings for four lives. The young man who departed had an organ donor card.

Within days his heart was transplanted to a middle-aged doctor, one kidney to a twenty-something policeman, the other kidney to a high school teacher, and his liver to a fifty-something artist. Four lives saved, by a kind, selfless act of one person. The doctor continued to heal the sick, the policeman able to protect fellow citizens, the teacher able to impart knowledge to youth, and the artist to create beauty for many eyes to see.

At a "Gratitude Gathering" for transplant survivors one year later, all four grateful lives sat together in a circle holding hands: the doctor, the policeman, the teacher, and the artist. Each person spoke with one grateful voice — an "organ voice." The organs of a gracious donor were talking, in a whisper, in a smooth symphonic meter: I lived, I loved, I gave, so others can live, and love, and give.

~ Lawrence J. Indiviglia

November 6

In a Grace-Filled World

Grace is defined as the free and unmerited love of God. It can neither be earned nor spurned. It simply is.

Perhaps gratitude at its finest is an act of grace — something freely and oh-so-generously given.

If our gratitude didn't have to be earned, how free would we be with it?

If we didn't insist that others thank and reward us, what unexpected gifts might have room to show up?

What if we all chose to live gracefully?

In a grace-filled world, it is possible to
- love deeply,
- forgive easily,
- trust completely,
- and be free from resentment and regret.

Thank you, God, for all of it. Thank you for every minute of every day of my life, even the parts that I made you wrong for. I was a jerk. You loved me anyway. Thank you. For the graceful and the grouchy, the caring and the contemptuous, the brilliant and the boring, the warrior and the pacifist — for all people — I am grateful. I am more than a little in awe of your Creation. Like you, I promise not to give up on us. Ever. Amen.

Thank you for Your Grace.

"Grace finds beauty in everything."

~ Bono (U2)

~ *Maureen A. Charles*

November 7

Eleanor P.

When people ask where I got my sense of humor, I reply: my mom.

We shared that "dry one liner" approach to life that also ringed of a "simple practicality." A few examples:

When I was five and saw a public service announcement on TV encouraging "non-resident aliens" to go to the post office and register, I wondered aloud to Mom if aliens from other planets would do it, too. "I certainly hope so," she replied in an even tone.

Another time I got home from school and mom described a harried day that included a bag of dry Friskies spilling all over the pantry floor. Her solution: "I sent the cats in for a picnic."

My birth wasn't easy, and when I was a teenager a relative let it slip that Mom and Dad were advised not to have any more kids after me.

I asked Mom, "Then why did you have Teresa?"

Without missing a beat, she replied, "So you'd have someone to play with."

I'm grateful for my mom, Eleanor Pearl Oldenski Kozik, and the humor and love she brought me (along with my sister!).

~ Donna Kozik

November 8

A Passion for Teaching and Coaching

I love teaching and coaching. I am so grateful for this passion and gift! But it wasn't always like this.

When I was a child, I used to gather all of my friends together, organize them, and teach them new games to play. But as a young adult, I didn't know how to transition to being anything other than an employee. The leader and teacher in me wouldn't stay quiet, though, and occasionally I would "get in trouble" for stepping "beyond my position."

It wasn't until 2004, when I discovered what I now professionally call Speaking Peace, Hearing Peace, that I realized I had finally found the medium that I am passionate about. It was hard to step out, though; I wish that I had had the support I needed back then. Eventually, I started to see that the gifts I have to offer are, actually, greatly appreciated — and I am celebrating that!

Today, my clients range from people wanting not only personal support, but also a trainer and leadership support. Because of my clients, and allowing myself to trust my passions and gifts, my life is full of meaning and "aliveness" — and I am immensely grateful!

What are you grateful for?

~ Rachel Monde

November 9

O.D.A.A.T.
(One Day at a Time)!

It's age-old advice: Take one day at a time. For Heather, whom I met during college, O.D.A.A.T. was more than a cliché; it was a mantra.

At first, we all wondered why the cute, skinny girl with the wicked sense of humor coughed incessantly. Born in the 1970s with cystic fibrosis, each birthday was a milestone.

Heather knew she would not live forever. In fact, none of us will, but we ignore that reality in our own lives. Heather dealt with it on her own terms: head up, O.D.A.A.T.!

She lived every day to the maximum with her family, husband, and pets, a creative career, and a love of travel. If she wanted to do something risky, like get a tattoo, she would laugh and say, "What? Is it going to kill me?"

Heather celebrated her favorite holiday, Halloween, and then passed away on the first of November, All Saints' Day — perfectly fitting for her.

Heather's greatest gift to her friends was teaching them to live every day to the fullest, with enthusiasm and no regrets. For that I am grateful.

~ Melisse L. Campbell

November 10

Our Full Potential

Each of us was put on this earth for one simple reason: to marvel at how Tom Selleck still finds meaningful work. But we were also put here to realize our full potential as human beings. Each of us has an innate ability to do magnificent things in life using our unique passion, skills, experiences, energy, and — with any luck — an iPhone. We can pursue our true potential through a process of self-examination and personal development. Or we can go to Target and buy an espresso machine, which is also kind of a nice perk.

For those choosing a path of personal development, there have never been more opportunities to learn, to connect, and to grow. An entire community of Positive Psychology researchers has been unraveling the nature of human achievement and happiness. Beyond the social sciences, other nerds have brought us more than microwaveable burritos and crumple zones. We now have the Internet, which lets us connect with friends and colleagues, share our aspirations, work together to achieve our goals, and watch videos of babies sleeping.

I'm grateful that we live in a time where it's never been more possible — or more important — to live to our full potential.

~ Matthew Poepsel

November 11

A Reason, a Season, or a Lifetime

A reason, a season, or a lifetime. This is in gratitude to those that enter our lives for a "reason."

Call it coincidence, destiny, fate, or chance, some people enter our lives to lead us or open our eyes to a new path. When we are receptive and open to these chance encounters, our lives can be forever changed — a casual acquaintance who introduces you to someone who reshapes your destiny, or that person at the dog park or sitting beside you on the plane who talks about a program, class, or activity that sparks something in you and plants a seed of interest or awareness.

When I look at the surprising and exciting path that is my life I can trace each major shift or change back to a person who, though I wasn't aware of it at the time, appeared by chance to illuminate my new path. Most of these people were in my life for only minutes, hours, or weeks, but their impact was profound. It's my wish to enter others' lives for a "reason"—to shine that light — because in a single moment of awareness lives can collide and change forever.

~ Rachel Bellack

November 12

Hurrah for My Birthday!

I'm extremely grateful that I'm another year older!

I don't understand the taboo about a woman telling her age. What's that all about? Seriously, you have two choices: get another year older, or die! What else is there?

I faced that reality over twenty-four years ago. The day before my thirty-fifth birthday, I was told I had breast cancer. I didn't know how many more birthdays I would have. Would I see my young kids grow up? Would my high-school sweetheart husband and I grow old together? Who knew?

There is nothing like a life-threatening illness to get your attention! And it puts things in a whole new perspective.

With the love and support of family and friends, I faced the surgery, the chemo, and the fear. I found out just how strong I could be, and I saw just how silly it is to dread another birthday.

For my part, I celebrate and cherish each birthday, so I can tell the world: "Here I am! I just squeezed the juice out of another great year! I'm ready for more!" I am alive and extremely grateful to be able to welcome another birthday.

~ Gail Patterson

November 13

Opportunities for Growth

I couldn't perform a recall on the words that sprinted thoughtlessly from my lips, or my actions that followed, but I found myself wishing I could. Well, at least initially. My daughter, in her carefree five year-old way, had dismissed my repetitive pleas to get into the car. She was busy with her determined ascent up the incline her older brother had effortlessly conquered. Her sheer willfulness triumphed, but, before I turned around, she made use of the muddy slope as a personal slide.

I angrily scolded her for ruining her new pants and firmly planted her in the back seat. My husband gave me one of those looks that he is used to receiving from me. I apologized to him for the judgment he must experience each time I choose to give that look. I apologized to my daughter for overlooking her joy in achieving her climb, my rush to go nowhere, and my poor choice of reaction. She apologized for not thinking about her pants.

What I am grateful for are the opportunities that were presented through this experience and ones like it. Through honesty and forgiveness, mistakes were transformed into growth.

No regrets, no judgments. Just priceless.

~ Julie Anna Brady

November 14

Changing My Perspective

"Our environment, the world in which we live and work, is a mirror of our attitudes and expectations."

~ Earl Nightingale

When I think about gratitude, I think about how changing my perspective changed my life. Ten years ago, I was at a crossroads. I had been chasing "happiness" for years, expecting it to come through a new relationship or the next great job, but it continued to elude me. I was unhappy personally and professionally, and I was sure there were others to blame.

Feeling stuck and lacking direction, I began reading and reflecting. The more I read about others' success and happiness, the more I considered where I was and what had gotten me there. In doing so, I had a life-changing realization: I had never truly "owned" my life. Blaming my unhappiness on things outside of me — people, jobs, bad luck — kept me from taking responsibility for my past, which ultimately kept me from believing that I had control over my future.

This empowered me to expect more of myself and my life, giving me the confidence to found my own business, which, coincidentally, helps others find their own paths to success.

It all starts with a change in perspective.

~ Theresa Valade

November 15

Our Wedding Story

I am grateful for taking a leap of faith.

After I struggled with wedding preparations for months, my sister, Donna Kozik, and my friend Tara Maras offered to plan us a surprise Las Vegas wedding. Sounds crazy, but it was a wonderful decision! Brad and I provided a wedding date and a budget. After that, we gave up all responsibility to Tara and Donna. The result: Best. Wedding. Weekend. Ever!

We had a meet and greet at the Monte Carlo, a bridal luncheon at the Bellagio, a service at the Little Chapel of the West, a gondola ride, a dinner reception at the Venetian, and a champagne toast complete with cake, a bridal dance, and a special rendition of the "Maria." We spent the evening traveling the Vegas strip in our wedding finery, enjoying the sights and the cheers from tourists. Every day for months after, we looked at our wedding pictures while listening to "Con Te Partiro," our favorite Bellagio fountain song.

My face still lights up with pure joy whenever I share our wedding story, and I am so thankful to Tara and Donna for giving us an amazing experience. It makes our anniversary, November 15th, extraordinarily special.

~ Teresa A. Castleman

November 16

Resiliency

As a child of 9, I lost my mother to an insidious brain cancer known as glioblastomas. Mom defied her medical prognosis of a few months by living a full life with her family for several more years. Resiliency.

After Mom's death, my sister and I went to live with an aunt and uncle. Unbeknownst to my family, our uncle suffered from severe mental illness. We who had lost our mother put on a big façade and smiled during the day, but endured psychotic rants at night from an uncle who threatened his family into silence. Two decades later, my aunt made a choice herself and, after years of marriage, divorced my uncle. Resiliency.

Tragedy struck again with the deaths of our oldest sister, Mary, at 43 to cancer, and of our brother Mark to suicide at 47.

Today I am a clinical health psychologist. I help others move through adversity, pain, and illness to health and well-being. Without fail, those of us who come through the other side of this journey can say that we have embraced life, felt true love and loss, and have grown into who we are supposed to be. Thank you, resiliency!

~ Dr. Leslie A. Loubier

November 17

Still Sweet Sorrow

This morning I pause, breathing in the crispness of autumn. The trees still preen their yellows and reds, oblivious to the lateness of the season. As I survey the vista, my eyes come to rest on a slender steeple, its tiny cross cutting sparkling slivers of silver into the clear, blue sky. Stillness. I can't believe it's been a year. She fills my heart, reminding me of everything I value. Carly.

Exuding excitement at the promise of each new day. Eyes sparkling with anticipatory delight. Happy howls. Joyful jigs. Smart, vibrant, fun, and funny. Authentic. Empathic. Giving and forgiving. Connection, comfort, compassion. Elegant lover of people, and lover of life.

In psychotherapy, people sometimes weep. Carly searches their faces, and understands in an instant. Soulful eyes convey her tender message: "Don't worry. I'm here. Everything will be all right." The distressed return Carly's gaze. They start to slowly stroke her, calming and comforting them both.

Love and compassion will do that.

In the end, when there was no more light and laughter in her eyes, it was our turn to comfort Carly. Holding, stroking, soothing: "Carly's such a good girl. We love you so much. Don't worry, Carly-Girl. We're here. Everything will be all right."

~ Melanie Wilson

November 18

Give Thanks for Adversity

"Gratitude can turn a negative into a positive. Find a way to be thankful for your troubles and they can become your blessings."

~ author unknown

I'd had lots of experience with adversity by the time my mother was diagnosed with cancer.

And after getting past the fear and anger, I gave thanks and asked the Universe what the lesson for me is. I heard: "Go live your life with passion!" Five months later I quit my secure job in social services. My mom was in remission when I took up teaching and traveled to Asia with my two sons. I had the most amazing time of my life! The icing on the cake was meeting the man who is now my life partner.

I am grateful that I have the ability to recognize the gifts in adversity. As I say thank you, I open myself to experiencing miracles.

~ Lorna Blake

November 19

The Sunset Years

I'm grateful to be in my "sunset years," although I never liked that term. Perhaps it's because of what I heard from parents and other elders, lamenting that they were in their sunset years. I had the idea that this meant old!

I love sunsets, especially the brilliant ones I often witnessed in New Mexico while growing up, so it makes sense that there has to be some beauty to the term.

If we look at the last third of our lives as the sunset years, we can be grateful for the brilliant colors in our life and for the peacefulness that sunset brings.

So it is with us in the sunset years. And maybe that's where the term comes from. It's the calm, peaceful knowing that we can finally choose our way of life, whether it be with great energy, color, and excitement, or with quiet dignity and wisdom—or both.

To me, the gift of being over 60 (other than the senior discounts, of course) is that we are fortunate to have lived this long and can create a whole new life with more freedom and a greater sense of self.

Tonight, watch the sunset.

~ Dolores Hagen

November 20

Like Any Other Day

The day started like any other: Friday, January 9, 2009. I had no idea the next few days and weeks would be unlike any I had known before.

After work, I told my husband, Eddie, I wasn't feeling well. We both assumed I was run down and just needed to rest. Still not feeling well, I took the kids shopping the next day. I didn't want to let them down.

The next thing I knew, I was at the brink of death. At first I was told I had a viral infection, then tracheitis, then a chest infection… and I was getting worse.

I lived in bed, rapidly lost weight, and looked ghastly. My temperature rose, and my breathing worsened. I was hospitalized, and the chaplain offered me Holy Communion. I thought, "Am I going to die?"

I feared the worst. And then I thought about the kids.

I was determined to stay alive and to get better. The driving force within me would not allow me to give up. I asked God to double my years; I declared that my days be outnumbered. And, over five months, I made a slow but full recovery.

Thank God. This is what I'm grateful for: I am alive to see this day.

~ Evelyn Samrian Pindura

November 21

Every Wrinkle Tells a Story!

I love my wrinkles. I am grateful for getting older.

You read it right. On July 4, 2001, I was diagnosed with advanced-stage metastatic breast cancer and told to get my "affairs in order." The doctors said I would not survive long. I was 45.

That night I cried and I prayed. At one point I heard "I'm not going to let anything bad happen to you." I thought someone had broken into my house, but nobody was there. And I realized that I had just heard God, and the truth in that statement settled into me. God loved me, and the worst that could happen to me would be that I would leave this world and go on to the next. Until then, every day was mine to glory in and use to be a better person. My whole attitude changed to a strong, powerful, joyful one.

I found targeted low-dose chemotherapy and combined it with a holistic healing platform, and after nine years, I am still "thriving while surviving." I established the Best Answer for Cancer Foundation to help cancer patients experience cancer as a non-event.

Every day is a gift; every wrinkle tells a story of love and laughter.

~ Annie Brandt

November 22

Light Behind the Clouds

I express my gratitude for the existence of choices and, more importantly, for the awareness of having a choice.

See, I never understood the deeper meaning of the "having a choice" phenomenon until a couple of years ago when I lost someone.

Now, it's hard enough to lose something, as we all go into a mini grieving process when we lose items like our keys or the ring that has been in the family for generations. But losing someone — this is a different ball game all together.

You can only begin to imagine the emotions that poured over me at the time. It was hard. However, in the midst of feeling overwhelming grief and sadness, I had that split-second experience where I clearly saw the two ways this can head: one of being selfishly depressed and diving into the dark place of entertaining thoughts of self-pity and sadness (slippery slope, been there, done that… never sure how hard the rock bottom is), or consciously focusing on the memories of the most beautiful and satisfying moments we had had together. I chose the second one.

I chose the light behind the clouds.

I have never looked back since.

~ *Rumyana Grueva Nenova*

November 23

Serving Others Has Served Me the Best

"Gratitude opens a crack in consciousness that lets grace in."

~ Harry Palmer

Most people go through life without any groundbreaking, mind-boggling, or life-saving phenomenon. So have I. No dramatic episode or success happened, but hundreds of small miracles over a lifetime are what I am grateful for.

But true success as an occupational therapist gave me the most to be grateful for. It provided me with the platform to live out my life purpose with creative passion. To serve physically and mentally challenged people, by bringing relief to their suffering, giving them hope, empowering them to realize their own strength and beauty, thus improving their quality of life and a way to peaceful living.

It has helped me to realize my own strength and provided me with opportunities to learn and grow. It has enriched my life tenfold.

Serving others has served me the best.

Setbacks, losses, oppositions, and pain. I have dealt with them all by understanding the true nature of the challenge, accepting what is, and surrendering to the Higher Power, with a thought that everything works out in its own time and for my highest good.

My Prayer:
>Think through me,
>Speak through me,
>Act through me,
>Love through me.
>So Thank You, God!

~ Armaity Hathidaru

November 24

Blessings of the Wonderful People in My Life

I am grateful for my true friends who accept me for who I am (the good and the bad) and who make me laugh. I work shifts including weekends and family is far away; therefore, I'm so grateful for a couple friends who have offered standing invitations to celebrate the holidays like Thanksgiving, Christmas, and Easter. All I have to do is ask if I can come for dinner and what to bring. As well as sharing laughter, I also love to share hugs, as I'm an affectionate person.

My dearest friends have also been there for me in many other situations, and I for them, as true friendship works both ways. I consider my true friends as family.

I'm thankful for the family and friends who attended my fiftieth birthday party at my favorite restaurant and made it special. My sister and niece made beautiful handmade cards, which I will cherish forever.

I'm thankful for certain people I work with who share the same sense of humor and make me laugh.

I appreciate my coach, who helps me move forward on my goals when I'm stuck.

My life has been truly blessed by all the wonderful people in it.

~ Avery Thurman

November 25

Robert Lee

At eighteen months you were so proud of yourself. There is a memory of your surprising me with your first steps, holding your little chest out and laughing infectiously as you trotted past me. It was as if you had been practicing in secret.

Three years old, you called me to observe a bug on the windowpane. I felt awe at your wonderment, then shock as you flattened it with your small hand. Again we laughed.

Six years old at the theater came the heart-stopping moment of silence: Bambi's mother was killed. You could have heard a pin drop, it was so quiet. You yelled out, "You won't find her. She's dead!" The whole audience laughed.

Twenty-three now, you phoned and asked me if I was happy; yes, I was! Your reply: "If you are happy, Mum, then I am happy." Two weeks later you were gone. I miss you, Lee, yet I am grateful that you chose me for those experiences and memories. I am grateful for you teaching me to accept life in every moment, to be happy, and to laugh out loud — a lot. I am eternally grateful.

~ Jyothi

November 26

My Beautiful Mother

When I think of the many blessings I have in my life, they are all a result of one woman — the woman who gave me life: my beautiful mother, Donna Brady.

I know the sacrifices she made for us kids, always going without to ensure that we had the best.

The hundreds of miles she would drive, taking my sister and me to baseball games, never once complaining and never missing a game after working a long day. My mom always made time for us and made our home open to all our friends, treating them like her own.

There is not a person that has known my mom who has not loved her smile, her warm spirit, and her giving heart. She is a woman you will never forget.

She did not judge me for the mistakes I made along the way, but allowed me to learn and to grow, while being supportive and encouraging. She is always there when I need a shoulder to lean on, a loving hug, or someone to listen.

I will be forever grateful to my mom, my role model — the woman who gave me the best example to follow.

~ Susan Brady

November 27

The Path to Gratitude

Many clients come to me suffering from what I like to call "overwhelm." They feel overwhelmed with serious issues such as job pressures, child-rearing, or relationship difficulties. One strategy I use is to help them rediscover pleasure.

One of the first casualties of overwhelm is our ability to appreciate the many pleasures we experience every day: the warm, comforting feeling of the bed when we awaken in the morning, the relaxing feel of hot water caressing our skin as we step into the shower, or the invigorating aroma of coffee brewing. Relaxing at the beach, feeling the caress of a mate, or hugging a child.

Overwhelm inures us to these experiences, both great and small, and thus deprives us of the awareness of why we face each day with such resolve and equanimity. We must retrain ourselves to notice pleasure, to welcome it, to savor it. We must re-sensitize ourselves to the pleasures that greet us from the moment of our waking to our falling off to sleep at night.

If we open ourselves to the plenitude of pleasure in our lives, we open ourselves to experience joy. And when joy is in our lives, we feel gratitude.

~ Robert A.K. Ross

November 28

Bunny

My mother, Bunny, has a history of being overwhelmingly talkative, especially in the car. She reads every sign with dramatic expression ("Open late!"; "Jim's Tire and Tread!") and points out things that only a nurse with forty-seven years in the profession could notice. ("That guy looks like he's on booze, pills, and God knows what else!") She'd drive me nuts with her incessant observations.

Then cancer struck.

Chemotherapy depleted her spirit and squelched all verbal commentaries about the world around her. For the first time, she was silent. Ultimately chemo ended, but her depression didn't. Her body was tired, her spirit exhausted, and her voice weak.

Shortly after, she sat in the car looking out as we drove through town. A shapely woman with an extremely generous backside walked down the street, chatting on a cell phone.

Suddenly, my mom lifted her head straight, craned her neck to follow the woman's pace, and then proclaimed, "Now that's what I call junk in the trunk!" My mom was back! My talkative, non-stop chattering, amazing mom was back. She was alive, she was alert, and I never wanted her to stop talking!

I learned to love my mom exactly as she is and to appreciate every moment with her. For that gift, I am eternally grateful.

~ Nancy Marmolejo

November 29

Let Go and Let God

I used to manage departments of engineers developing computer software in the Silicon Valley. In 1995, I became a "stay-at-home" mom for our then-12-year-old son. One day we were folding laundry when I grumbled.

"This is crazy. I had important jobs, now all I do are these!"

He listened as I recounted my glorious days. Then he asked, "Mom, so how long did you work?"

"Nineteen years!"

"And how long have you stayed home?"

"Three months."

We burst into laughter—and grew closer!

One thing led to another. By 2003, I became a licensed marriage and family therapist. I am grateful for helping people, especially parents of American-born Chinese. I am thrilled doing what I enjoy: speaking, writing, counseling, coaching, and mentoring. I am grateful for my husband of thirty-five years, our adult son, his wife, and their baby—our precious granddaughter! I appreciate people God places in my life. I am most grateful to Jesus Christ, who has turned my life, relationships, and career around.

"For I know the plans I have for you," declares the Lord, "plans to prosper you and not to harm you, plans to give you hope and a future" (Jeremiah 29:11).

~ Winnis Chiang

November 30

Mac and Mel

Some people are night owls. I am not. I don't like being awake when everyone else is already sleeping. I am not afraid of the dark, but rather the uneasiness I feel when I'm alone with an imagination that is difficult to power off when the sun goes down and the sky grows dark. Eight years ago routine blood work came back positive for HIV. As I dealt with the shock of the life-changing news the nights became unbearable. I lay awake suffering from one anxiety attack after another as I obsessed over my own mortality.

A month later that all changed when I brought home two, tiny, wide-eyed black Chihuahua puppies. I named this brother-and-sister duo Mac and Mel. There has only been a handful of nights since then that I have not had these two furry little creatures curled up beside me, keeping me company and chasing away my uncertainties.

I am healthy. I am content. I am positive about the future. I am thankful that two graying, scruffy dogs have given me so much comfort and peace all these years and that the nights are no longer quite so dark and scary.

~ Daniel Kriley

December

"As each day comes to us refreshed and anew,
so does my gratitude renew itself daily.
The breaking of the sun over the horizon is my
grateful heart dawning upon a blessed world."

~ Terri Guillemets

December 1

"The Greatest Artist of All"

"Life is a great big canvas and you should throw all the paint on it you can."

~ Danny Kaye

This quote defines the courage it took to unveil my true colors. Today I thank God for the gift He gave me to become my own paintbrush, from which I was able to create on the outside what I had been hiding inside.

Two decades ago I was over one hundred pounds heavier than I am now. But what I saw on my life-canvas was a much slimmer and healthier me. Soon I began to "paint" a picture of my ideal self. I made that canvas a living, breathing work of art, *me*. Twenty years later I've still managed to keep off that weight, attesting to the power of the greatest Artist of all guiding me here. I am eternally grateful to God for all the colors on my life's palette that gave me a lighter, more joyful self inspired by:

Faith: to guide me.

Delight: in exercising.

Patience: in the journey.

Joy: in reaching my goal.

Appreciation: for my family.

Gratitude: in helping others achieve their weight-loss goals.

Double Gratitude: I can slide into my jeans without a struggle! Yes!

~ Christine Jones

December 2

Moments Are Treasures

"I fill my treasure chest, by celebrating moments."
~ Wilhelmien van Nieuwenhuizen

It is almost Christmas, and my home will be filled with loved ones and dear ones, those who make me laugh, and those who have brought new meanings to friendship in my life.

As I paged through a "toys for Christmas" catalog, I came across a golden treasure chest, filled with the most beautiful jewel stones: rubies, emeralds, sapphires, amethysts, and diamonds. The ideal present for little Ryan the pirate!

Although I am now a grown-up, the joy and pleasure of celebrations have not changed. In fact, they have become the treasures that fill my chest. My parents celebrated birthdays, Mother's Day and Father's Day, Easter, and Christmas in special ways, to make each occasion as memorable as they could.

Today I continue with these beautiful traditions, but, you see, through the years I have learned to add new ones, by celebrating new beginnings and small victories, and making you feel special just because I care. I am grateful for all the special moments that I gather throughout each year, and they sparkle in my chest of memories.

~ Wilhelmien van Nieuwenhuizen

December 3

Laughter Is
the Best Medicine

My sense of humor has gotten me through many a dark time in my life. Hearing my diagnosis of late stage III breast cancer only fueled my desire to seek all manner of laughter opportunities.

My daughters made me laugh and brought grandchildren. Daughter Allison gave birth to my first grandchild, Sienna, and two years later, Scarlett; April gave birth to Lucia and then, two years later, Seamus Flynn.

I have discovered that laughter lightens the stress and boosts the immune system. Immediately after hearing my diagnosis I went in for a radical modified mastectomy to save my life, and then seven years later I opted to have a second prophylactic mastectomy on the remaining breast. It was then I decided to throw myself a "BOOB Voyage" party! "Tit Bits" and beverages, as well as my "breast friends" made for a hilarious event! I set the tone for this party by looking at life one laugh at a time.

I know now I have been blessed to have laughter in my life as my best medicine. Between my sense of humor and the laughter around me, it is a gift that has kept me on the planet!

~ Teena Ferris Miller

December 4

Yippee for TV

This isn't politically correct to say, but I'm admitting it anyway: I'm grateful for TV.

Now is a time that a many of my Facebook friends don't mention TV, say they don't watch TV, or (gasp!) claim they don't even own a TV.

Not the case with me. When I was 4, Big Bird and Mr. Rogers were more popular in our house than my parents.

While perched in the living room window watching for the bus, I listened to the first 10 minutes of *The Today Show* with Tom Brokaw and Jane Pauley, a habit that continues to this day with Matt and Meredith. (We're on a first name basis now.)

When I was a teenager I'd stay up late on Friday nights to see latest in the newest TV phenomenon: music videos.

I bought and hooked up the family's first VCR and showed my dad, much to his disbelief, how you could watch one show while recording another.

Now, of course, with DVRs and hi-def, I'm in heaven: *The Amazing Race, Top Chef, Project Runway, Big Brother, Grey's Anatomy*—I'm grateful for the entertainment and the escape.

I say yippee for TV!

~ *Donna Kozik*

Gratitude is Loving What You Do by Being Who You Are

"Gratitude is being grateful for all the small things that lead up to all the big things."

~ Deb Farrell

When I think of gratitude, an overwhelming amount of thoughts and feelings come forth for which I am grateful. It's such a wonderful feeling to celebrate being grateful for all the "little" things that build up to the "big" thing. I used to be grateful for only the big things; up until I found the joy in celebrating all the little gifts I'd been given along the journey to receiving the big ones.

I have been blessed to embark upon my third career and being over fifty at that! How fun is that? I am so grateful to have chosen to take the time to engage in a 3-year process to find my true purpose & passion. I had met and built so many incredibly wonderful relationships with so many magnificent people throughout my journey, I couldn't begin to tell you how richly rewarding the experience has been!

Living life serving in my purpose by helping people "discover who they are so they can do what they love to do" rewards me with such a feeling of joy! I am truly blessed.

~ Deb Farrell

December 6

Nick

I didn't know what pure love was…until I held you in my arms.
More powerful than anyone I'd ever known,
An old soul, I saw the wisdom of the ages
When I looked into your eyes.

And I said, "I know you…from before."

All you have to do is BE
And my strength surges.
My determination is unwavering.

Nothing and no one can ever come between us.

And on the day we met I was awed, little one,
And amazed
And oh! So determined
To give you the best life I possibly could.

Gladly and wholeheartedly
Frightened I may not be up to the task
Of the most important commitment I'd made in my life till then…

I accepted.

What did I do to deserve such a precious child
So wonderful in every way?
Whatever it was I am so grateful you came into my life, my dear son.
And though it amazes me that it's possible…
I love you more each day.

~ Chrissy Caeliss

December 7

Beauty from Ashes

I write for a vintage magazine, and once in a while I interview someone who enjoys making art out of trash. The collector will pick up used items, realize what wasted potential treasures they really are, and create art worth selling.

When I think of the pride and passion they have for their art, I am moved to tears by how passionate God must feel when we go to Him with broken lives feeling thrown away and used.

I'm so grateful that no matter what we've done in our past and no matter how we've been rejected by others, God still chooses to use the wreckage of our lives to create beauty from ashes.

Like the artist I wrote about recently who creates sayings out of old license plates and street signs, God takes pride in the new creation He forms out of our pain.

This year, I'm grateful I can look at the Christmas season through different eyes, all because I have a relationship with a God who chose to do this for me.

~ Nicole Bissett

December 8

On Being a Rule-Changer

I am enormously grateful for my parents and the role models they have been for me.

My father had a college degree in mathematics, but in the 1950s, the career choices for an African-American man were limited. He chose to become a postman and work in a blue-collar job because it paid more and had better benefits than any white-collar job he could get at the time. He and my mother, who was a schoolteacher, raised four children. Three of us went on to college and graduated without any debt due to the sacrifices that they made.

Because of my parents, I know that there is unlimited opportunity to succeed all around us. I believe that our success or failure is a result of our attitudes and our choices. We can either complain about circumstances we can't control, or we can change the rules by making a decision to be successful.

This approach has served me well throughout a successful corporate career and has given me the edge to succeed as a business owner.

I encourage you to be flexible and open to opportunities, even if they don't fit the established or traditional path.

~ Linda Griffin

December 9

Yes, I'm Grateful
for Middle Age

I wasn't exactly relishing the thought of middle age, but I have to admit that the reflective wisdom it has brought me is actually both settling and gratifying.

Past decisions, experiences, and tough, sometimes negative, events are now used as solid reference points to plan for the future and are recognized as just part of the journey onward in life.

I realize now, that the (then) devastating exam results that held me back a year, led me to a different college, the successful career I now have, and lifelong friends, and enabled me to move to the USA.

The relationships that ended in tears and disaster were what ultimately led me to be free to meet my husband.

The births of my son and daughter, though very different experiences, have made me stronger, more confident, and more determined, and have shown me that I can achieve what I want to achieve if I set my mind to it.

But I think overall, that I am most grateful to my parents, who, in their middle age, were always there for me.

Sometimes it takes time to be truly grateful, and middle age is a good time to reflect on that.

~ Sheila Kamp

December 10

A Vehicle to Awaken Compassion

I am a survivor of intense physical, emotional, and sexual childhood abuse, commencing at age 3 and continuing for years. I would never wish this experience on anyone, but am grateful it happened to me.

First, it became my vehicle for awakening compassion — in me, for me, and for others. It sensitized me to suffering, and helped me realize it wasn't okay to hurt myself, or others, with my wounds.

Second, it provided the painful raw material that drove me to cultivate forgiveness. The only way to avoid being consumed by hate and self-pity was to reach for forgiveness. The only way to live in the moment, rather than being trapped in rage over the past or fear of the future, was to reach for forgiveness. I forgave so that I could be whole (i.e., nothing broken, nothing missing).

Awakening compassion and cultivating forgiveness created a perfect fit to work with the suffering. Today that's what I do. I am a hospice and palliative care clinician who is honored to reduce the pain and other symptoms of the dying, to empower the grieving, and to provide emotional and spiritual support to both. I'm so grateful.

~ Jay Westbrook

December 11

Imperfection

I am grateful for the ability to be imperfect. I know this sounds a bit strange, but trying to be perfect in an imperfect world created huge amounts of insecurities and anxiety for me. So, I decided to flip the script and go for imperfection.

Instead of wishing away my belly stretch marks, I now appreciate the support each mark contributed to the birth of my three healthy and wonderful children.

Instead of beating myself up for being "moody" from time to time, I now appreciate my unique personality and how I can better relate to the wonder of fall, the survival of winter, the beauty of spring, and the playfulness of summer.

And my imperfect life serves as a reminder to never take life for granted, that sometimes I must crawl before I can walk, and that faith is so much stronger than will.

Long story short, embracing my imperfections has made me, well, just perfect!

~ Shirley Ann Brown

December 12

Life Time

I'm grateful for time. It's the most valuable asset I have. Every day I get to decide how I'll spend the minutes that make up my moments.

What do I most love about time? It's allowed me to experience life in all its many textures—with all its twists and turns. It has given me the opportunity to remember the good times and to forgive and forget the bad.

I've spent it with my friends, laughing, dreaming, and sharing life's experiences for hours on end. I've tapped into its very essence when I've entered "the zone," fully immersed in something that resonates with my being. It's given me the chance to dream and think—to introspect, to retrospect, and, yes, to prospect into the future!

Whether I'm working in my business or enjoying my many interests, time is a gift that has brought new people and opportunities into my life. I'm grateful when others share their life time with me and honored when I can do the same in return.

While time has added years to my age, for every year it adds, it gifts to me more understanding, patience, and wisdom. Truly, this is the time of my life!

~ Tara Kachaturoff

December 13

Socks: My Feral Kitty

"Until one has loved an animal, a part of one's soul remains unawakened."

~ Anatole France

The little black kitty comes running whenever she hears me come outside in the early morning or late evening to bring her food. I have been coming out with food for her twice a day for ten months. She has not always been there, but if she is close by, she runs to within three feet of me hissing and spitting as I sit and quietly talk to her.

Last week she got close enough to briefly put her nose to my toe. Yesterday she only quietly meowed as I sat and talked softly. This morning she rubbed against my back as I sat near her food and then she let me carefully touch her paw. I think we are both realizing the absolute magic of these moments as we finally begin to cement our friendship with trust.

~ Melinda Coker

December 14

The Opportunity

December 14th will forever hold a special place in my body, mind, and spirit. On that date I was given the ultimate opportunity to actually save the life of someone I love.

A few weeks before, my only sister, Patti, suddenly experienced sharp pains in her lower abdomen. A severe infection had specifically targeted her kidneys. Visiting her in the hospital, I couldn't find Patti among a huge army of machinery that was now functioning as her kidneys. Eventually, these treatments were repeated three times a week.

The prognosis for a cure was dim. The next step was kidney transplantation. The wait for a new kidney, though, would be many years. I stepped in as a willing volunteer and went to the hospital for tests to determine if I was a suitable candidate. The results showed I was a near-perfect match. On December 14th the surgery was performed. Ever since, Patti has been healthy, happy, and living a busy, normal life with her family.

Now, on this day, I reflect on the miracle of having the chance to participate in my sister's life and well-being in such a profound, meaningful way. That was the opportunity of a lifetime.

~ Roberta Roberts Mittman

December 15

The Blessing of Friends

Recently I broke my ankle. While not a big deal for some, I did it while out of town alone. I was rushed to the nearest hospital, and informed that it was smashed and I needed immediate surgery. I was operated on the next day and then spent two weeks in a skilled nursing facility, until I could safely be transported home (where I live alone). I knew no one in the area. Calls from friends kept my spirits high.

I arrived home in a wheelchair, and I was greeted by two of my friends. They rearranged my furniture to make my home accessible. For the next few months, I could not shop for groceries, pick up my mail, or get out of the house without help. I didn't even have to ask. Friends asked what they could do, took me shopping, cleaned my house, and ran my errands. Some called to ask if I wanted a ride to church. They made what could have been a very lonely, difficult time a blessed time. I am so grateful for my friends.

~ Greer Tavel

December 16

Let it Shine!

"Lord, make me aware of the needs of those around me, and let me be moved with compassion to meet those needs" was the recent prayer of my heart.

I am grateful today that I can now see the needs of a lonely, old neighbor, who has lost her mobility. Every morning, before going to work, I visit my neighbor's home and make care of the many tasks she would not otherwise be able to accomplish. I prepare meals, clean house, and run errands, thus making life a little more comfortable.

Sometimes we do not realize the difference we can make in the lives of others when we do small favors for them. Did you let your light shine today? When we demonstrate our love and care with kind gestures that touch and improve the lives of others, we let our light shine. May God be glorified in our good deeds!

Thank you, Lord, for giving me a heart of compassion and a discerning eye.

~ Avenelle M. Warde

December 17

Persistence

In honor of those who will never give up—even if they want to!
"The most essential factor is persistence - the determination never to allow your energy or enthusiasm to be dampened by the discouragement that must inevitably come."

~ James Whitcomb Riley

"Persistence is to the character of man as carbon is to steel."

~ Napoleon Hill

"I am overwhelmed by the grace and persistence of my people."

~ Maya Angelou

"No great achievement is possible without persistent work."

~ Bertrand Russell

"Do not be afraid of making mistakes, for there is no other way of learning how to live!"

~ Alfred Adler

~ Anonymous

December 18

The Secret Language of Sisters

The secret language of sisters comes with its own lexicon—one that needs no words.

A subtle gesture, a raised eyebrow, or the utterance of a single word reveals the message and more often than not results in uncontrollable laughter.

I love the contagious, spontaneous, outrageous kind of laughter borne of the inside joke only sisters can share. I even love the "ugly face" laughter: rolling tears, squinty-eyes, and splotchy face.

Laughter so irrepressible, it consumes all audible sounds—leaving a gaping mouth and shaking shoulders as the only evidence of the shared amusement.

It is not pretty, this full-out expression of hilarity, but it's the most beautiful thing one could ever experience. I'm grateful for every crazy adventure, every foolish escapade, and every "it-was-a-good-idea-at-the-time" antic my sister and I have lived through and laughed about later.

I'm grateful for the secret language of sisters.

I'm so very grateful for my sister, Christine; she never stops making me laugh.

Thanks, Sis!

~ Allie Casey

December 19

Recipe for Gratitude

Sift 3 tablespoons of INSIGHT together with 2 cups of COURAGE, add a pinch or two of INTELLECT, and set aside.

Take 8 ounces of FEELING and blend into INSIGHT and COURAGE until smooth, exuberant bubbles form on the surface. Lightly fold in the froth from much LOVE.

Crack six large, free-range SENSES one by one into the mix and continue to gently blend.

Finally, add a generous splash of RISK-TAKING and diced STAMINA.

Set aside for one hour in a warm soul before pouring into a body.

For the best result, continue to add LOVE and froth often.

Icing: Combine all achievable DREAMS, simple WANTS, and the juice of one NEED. Spread generously. Before serving, lightly dust all sides with CHEEKINESS.

Large portions of gratitude recommended daily.

Contains minimal calories and no superficial additives.

~ Jennie Richter

December 20

Remembering and Dancing

I'm grateful for the Internet, YouTube, and websites that let you download one song at a time!

When I search for the top one hundred songs popular in a year of junior high or high school and create a playlist of the songs I listened to most, all the memories come rushing back, and the junior high juices start to flow again. In addition to all the great songs that have been remixed in recent years, there were the ones that remain treasures of their time. Who could ever forget:

Leif Garrett — "I Was Made for Dancin'"

Knack — "My Sharona"

Andy Gibb — "An Everlasting Love"

Nicolette Larson — "Lotta Love"

Shaun Cassidy — "Hey Deanie"

SOS Band — "Take Your Time (Do It Right)"

Kiss — "I Was Made for Lovin' You"

Who feels like dancing?

~ Anonymous

December 21

The Light in Darkness

I had recently moved to New Hampshire, where the practice of gratitude found me.

Winter nights in this beautiful region of lakes and mountains can be quite dark—and dark can be scary. But I was looking for reasons to be grateful.

The full moon creates a magical effect with snow in this rural area of few streetlights. Those nights everything simply glows. While darkness remains, it is infused with silver light. The shadows of leafless trees reach toward the ridge above our house like hands reaching toward the heavens.

Then for two winters a local farmer has created stars and trees from birch branches to which he attached tiny lights of many colors. He mounted them on his garden stand next to the road. It seems that he never remembers to turn off these lights! So when I am driving home on this winding road from a late meeting or choir practice, I am delighted again and again by this tapestry of light and color, a never-darkened surprise each time I reach the top of the hill. It is a gift to all who pass by.

Like gratitude, it is a gift to me.

~ *Edith Jaconsky-Hamersma*

December 22

Positivity and Life

I am grateful for being alive and given the chance to celebrate another birthday.

I choose to be positive and know that I have everything I need.

Sometimes we think "what is there to be grateful for?" So many people are suffering today. Jobs are lost, homes are going into foreclosed, and people are starving. Many people are suffering.

Though I can't make their lives easier, I can live in gratitude for having a roof over my head, food in my cupboards, and clothes in my closet. I am healthy (a five-year breast cancer survivor). I have two loving sons, a daughter-in-law, grandson, brother, sister, and their families to love.

We never know when our time will be up on this earth. Each day is a gift from God to cherish. Sometimes we need to be reminded of this. Focus on God, glorify Him, and He will meet our needs.

~ Linda A. Distler

December 23

A Child's Power of Love Heals!

Four months of a wracking cough kept me in bed. The doctors found no remedy! I could not work. Money was running short. What was I to do?

Christmas came, and my son and his wife invited me to spend it with them. I lay in front of the blazing fire in their living room and the coughing persisted.

My 2-year-old grandson came running up to me, hugging and kissing me. Then he ran away. He is a loving child, and he continued to repeat the procedure of hugs and kisses until the coughing stopped. My cough was healed within hours and didn't return.

Over the years, I studied the miracle of energy healing. However, it was not until that wonderful Christmas season that I realized that it was the love of a small child that performed what the medical profession could not!

My gratitude knows no bounds for my grandchild and the lesson he taught me about the power of love and healing. It has served me well and increased my happiness ever since.

I am truly grateful!

~ Doreen Baran

December 24

Attitude of Abundance

This year has been one of much reflection. Not only did it include a milestone birthday, but also the hardest challenges and greatest gifts of my life.

How did I steer though such challenges? By acknowledging my blessings. This simple action took me on a journey of self-reflection and growth. Here is what I found.

I am grateful for the following blessings in my life:

* God—For my faith and conviction

* Family—For their love and support, and for sharing in this journey

* Friends—For listening and never judging

* My dog—For teaching me to smile and laugh at the silly things in life!

* Coaches—For inspiring me and making me grateful for doing what I do

* Each new day—Every day is a gift offering new hope and new adventures!

* Health—Nurture it!

* Unconditional love—There is no greater feeling. Give it, receive it!

* Small gestures—A smile or simple "hello" can brighten someone's day.

* Smile file—For reminding me of all the special things in my life

Jump-start each day with excitement and passion by reviewing your own daily abundance list, and watch what you appreciate in your life and your career grow!

~ Gina Marie Crittenden

December 25

Grateful for Being a Christmas Baby

Since I was a young child and into my adulthood, when hearing of my birth date, people would share their condolences with me, as I was born on Christmas Day. People often assume that I miss out on celebrating my birthday, but they are so wrong! I was born on a day of celebration, and my birthday has always been something my family celebrates along with the Christmas holiday.

My mom likes to say that my birth was her best Christmas present, ever! From a very young age, both my mom and my dad made a point to recognize my birthday during the holiday season. A birthday party with my childhood friends was always held weeks prior to Christmas. This was followed by my special family birthday celebration at a fancy restaurant on Christmas Eve. Then on Christmas Day, following our big turkey dinner, we would celebrate my birthday with a birthday cake with candles, and I would then open my birthday presents.

As an added bonus, thanks to being a Christmas baby, I was named "Cristy," rather than some other names my parents were considering.

Thanks Mom and Dad for always making my birthday special!

~ Cristy Hayden

December 26

Tradition to Cherish

L ove is the foundation of our family, and I'm grateful for our "family fund" that allows us to share it with each other during the holidays!

Thanks to parents and grandparents modeling strong family values, we contribute into our family fund ($5–10 a month, or divide airfare equally among the adults), which allows us to be together for Christmas Eve without the burden of undue costs for any one family.

We're four generations and thirty-six members strong, and have wonderful memories from this tradition, including our family football game (ZUGU Bowl), Christmas shows, snowball fights, cousins' theme parties, Texas Hold 'Em Tournaments, Dallas–Fort Worth excursions, blowout New Year's Eve parties, and great Italian food! We help each other with patience (usually), love, humor, and grace.

We've learned that through life's ups and downs that the fastest path to a positive state is to be grateful!

Our family fund is a tradition to cherish because it brings us together as one and helps us be thankful by remembering what love is, as we honor our parents and the memory of our Nani and Papa's present gift on Christmas Eve and reopen it with delight each year!

~ Corine Wofford

December 27

Answered Prayers

It was that day in early January, January 1, when our prayers were answered.

The day my son was born, a bundle of joy, the present of a long wait and many prayers.

Each year, we will celebrate the ending of a year, welcoming a new year and, most importantly, my son's birthday. It is indeed a triple auspicious celebration.

Each passing year, I am grateful for the opportunity to be able to celebrate all three of these events and seeing my son growing into manhood.

My son. He will be my joy, my pride, and my life.

Nothing can change it.

~ Mok Tuck Sung

December 28

"Can't" Ain't in the Book!

The one person who truly impacted my life, as well as everyone he met, would be my stepfather, Raymond Singletary, the most phenomenal teacher I've ever encountered, who died three years ago at the age of 101.

Oftentimes when I was a child, he would give me assignments beyond my capabilities or physical strength. One day I just flat-out said, "I can't do it, Daddy Rainy!" He got real close to my ear and yelled, "Can't ain't in the book!"

He said, "You'll encounter situations in life that cannot be found in any book or in another person, and you'll have to dig deep inside of yourself to pull up what's needed for the hour."

It riveted down into my bones, as he said it with great force.

That was fifty-three years ago, and I've made it a way of life, along with other equally valuable principles he took the time to instill in me.

But, this past winter, I found myself without heat in my home for twenty-three long days and began to give up the desire to even live, as the excruciating cold seem to overpower me. At that moment, the words he implanted in my being seemingly sprang up out of my cold bones loud and clear, which gave me the courage to go on. That's why I'm so grateful for the teachings of Daddy Rainy and for my faith in the mercy and grace of God.

So, remember: Can't ain't in the book! Do pass it on — especially to your children.

~ Leila Glenn

December 29

December Nights III

When darkness exceeds daylight and winter settles in, I am reminded of darker times in my life, when my heart was broken and Light was scarce. I remember that gratitude was sometimes the only thing that kept me going, acknowledging that in fact I had much to be grateful for despite the pain of the times we were in. On a dark December night, I wrote the following:

I want to open myself to the place where the Light will guide me again — out of the confines of sorrow and darkness.

I want to follow that Light, and not second-guess love that is showered on me, because love is not something one merits like a scouting badge. Rather, it is freely given by the other. Such love does not drown, but rather floats us to the surface when we are drowning.

Love cannot be kept hidden, and shrivels beyond recognition in cold, embittered hearts.

Love is colorless, odorless, and oftentimes invisible to the naked eye, but if we look beyond façades and reach into our hearts, the directions to love are clear:

Open here. Spread freely. Give thanks.

~ Joy Leccese

December 30

The Pillar of My Life

The pillar of my life is my wife.

It is on this day that we got married.

She has stood by me through all the challenges in my life, always there for me and giving me strength to carry on, caring for me during my darkest moments, and holding my hands and never letting go.

Given a choice in the next life, I will marry her again.

~ Mok Tuck Sung

December 31

How I Became Dave, The Gratitude Guy

I had a dream one night, like no other I had before. I was being led by a strange-looking circular figure that kept saying "Great, Good, and Grow." Then another thing bumped into me, saying "Call me T, and follow me." It led me to a big umbrella tree where I witnessed a miracle. Slowly, one by one, letters appeared that revealed: G-R-A-T-I-T-U-D-E D-A-V-E. I could not stop smiling and my cheeks started to hurt. I realized I was now ready to show up in the world as "Dave, The Gratitude Guy."

This story exemplifies how I became The Gratitude Guy. The letters represent what is now a part of my grateful heart that started to expand when I completed a nine-day gratitude training course, and broke down my ego wall.

All my thoughts of what I could not do turned into beliefs of what I could do, as Dave, The Gratitude Guy was born. When I started this attitude of gratitude, I understood that, by being who I am, I will attract more of what I truly want in my life. I want to share these feelings of love and gratitude with as many people as possible. Together, we can produce enough positive energy to create amazing changes on our planet for generations to come.

~ Dave Block

About the Authors

Sandra Ahten is a diet coach for the "I know what to do; I just don't do it" crowd. Receive her free "5 Things You Must Know Before Starting Any Diet" report at ReasonableDiet.com/five.

Donna Amos is a business startup expert. She believes the greatest gift is encouragement and strives to inspire others to go for their dreams. Learn more at InfinitePossibilitiesCoaching.com.

Maggie Anderson is a communications professional and a coach who helps experts stand out so they attract more ideal clients and opportunities. Learn more at MaggieAnderson.com.

Melinda Weese Anderson is an author, personal excellence coach, and EFT practitioner who guides individuals to the life of their dreams. Contact Melinda at LiveInTheMoment.ca.

Anonymous lives everywhere and thoroughly enjoys bringing touches of gratitude to your daily life.

Lois R. Arsenault is an eldercare professional committed to helping elders live enjoyable, fulfilling lives every day of their lives.

Deborah Avery, a successful leadership and executive coach in New York City, teaches individuals and groups to use coaching skills in developing cohesive teams. Find her at NYExecutiveCoaching.com.

Tracy Allen Baker is a passionate advocate of global clean water access. Follow his passion and podcasts at WaterTweeter.com and weRwater.com.

Elisabeth Balcarczyk is an authentic communication and leadership coach living in Germany and working with clients internationally. You can find her at BodyMindSoulCoaching.weebly.com.

Kim Marie Baldwin is a freelance writer, book lover, and world traveler, as well as an award-winning massage therapist based in Palm Springs, Calif.

Doreen Baran, a full-time Toronto Realtor and team leader, writes a dynamite newsletter for 1,000 readers, volunteers for three charities, and turned 84 last August! Find her at DoreenBaran.com.

Jeanie Barat is a spiritual guide and life coach who helps you create a breakthrough! Find out more and get your free Monday Morning Meditation at JeanieBarat.com.

Robyn Beazley is an enthusiasm expert from Alberta, Canada. Her works as an author, speaker, life coach, and blogger inspire positivity. Connect at RobynBeazley.com.

Kim Beckett, a Montessori preschool teacher, gardens, sews, and is excited about energy healing. Read more of her writing at ZeroPointAwakening.com.

Michelle Beitzel helps people find success: involving a flashlight, dark corners, inner barriers, strategies, and "blow your mind" kind of stuff. Get your flashlight at TheSoulStrategist.com.

Rachel Bellack is a business and leadership coach and the managing director at Michigan Actors Studio. Contact her at MichiganActorsStudio.com or AspireCoachingGroup.com.

Jeremy Bennett can help you tune into yourself and your intuition, so you can pursue your calling with confidence! Find him at PurposeWithoutFail.com.

Nicole Bissett resides in La Mesa, CA with her 15-year-old son, Eddie. Her works are regularly published in several magazines. She can be reached at Nicole.bissett@att.net.

Lorna Blake helps clients create the relationships they've always dreamed of. You can reach her at LornaBlake.com.

Dave "The Gratitude Guy" Block, provides an awakening to individuals and businesses about the benefits of choosing gratitude and its powerful vibration. Reach Dave at facebook.com/DaveTheGratitudeGuy.

Jan Blount brings "Gratitude to Life" at GratitudeAndCompany.com.

Carol Boston, a health and wellness coach to Christian women, uses a biblical and natural/holistic approach to wellness. You can find her at AbundantLifeCoaching.us.

Kathy Bowes, MSW, loves to help others break free of their overeating cycle so they can live happier, more joyous, and freer lives. Find her at KathyBowesOnline.com.

Julie Anna Brady is an agent of change, blossoming author, sizzling speaker, organically sexy entrepreneur, fun-loving mother, friend, and collaborator. Join the movement at TheBigRipple.com.

Susan Brady is a speaker, coach, and mentor to women in the direct sales industry. You can reach her at TheCornerCoach.com or by e-mailing TheCornerCoach@gmail.com.

Jeff Brandes is a certified strength and conditioning specialist and fitness motivation expert. You can reach him at MakingEveryRepCount.com.

Jodi Brandon is a writer/editor based in suburban Philadelphia. You can find her on Facebook and Twitter, or at JodiBrandon.com and BrandonEditorial.com.

Annie Brandt is a nine-year cancer survivor and helps patients make cancer a "non-event." She is founder of Best Answer for Cancer Foundation. Learn more at BestAnswerForCancer.org.

Doug Brennecke is a San Diego, Calif., mortgage originator who listens to his clients, educates them, and tells them the truth. Reach him at DougBrennecke.com.

Marsha Lee Bressack takes great joy in helping others experience more success and happiness. You can reach her at CoachMarshaLee.com and HealingGriefOnline.com.

David George Brooke specializes in coaching people to cope and manage the stresses of life by applying an attitude of gratitude. Reach him at TheBrooker.com.

Shirley Brown counsels women and is "empowerment-focused" with a private practice in Newark, Del. She can be reached at facebook.com/ShirleyBrown.Havende.

Susan Brownell is a passionate care-giver to Cancer Caregivers. Her caring support helps care-givers when they need help most. Visit her award-winning website at SanctuaryForCancerCaregivers.com.

Catherine Bruns can be found at YourWiseVoice.com, where her sassy and truth-telling approach illustrates how to transform your life by tuning in to your inner GPS.

Jenny Bryans is one of Bob Proctor's LifeSuccess consultants and an intuitive coach. You can find her at JennyBryans.LifeSuccess Consultants.com.

Tom Buford is a musician, skydiver, author, and info product "geek" showing people how to profit with what's in their heads. Find him at TomBufordMarketing.com.

Louise-Annette Burgess is a brand-new mom, loving wife, daughter, sister, and friend. She is a founding member and chair of The Whiteside Theatre Foundation.

Stefany G. Burrowes, PCC, coaches creatives, entrepreneurs, and small business owners to deepen their clarity, confidence, and joy in all aspects of their lives. Find her at SensationalWisdom.com.

LaVerne Byrd lives outside of Washington, D.C., and enjoys reading, volunteer work, and traveling. Follow her at twitter.com/LaVerneByrd.

Linda Elaine Cain resides in Southern California, and is a sought-after event manager who, with her diamond team, makes any event sparkle! You can reach Linda at mceonsite.com.

Melisse Campbell is an artist and purveyor of antiques who photographs, paints, writes, and designs. Her work has been featured in national publications. Find out more at MelisseCampbell.com.

Liana Carbón, Ph.D., is a certified Shamanic practitioner in energy medicine and luminous healing, a teacher, and a spiritual director who can be reached at ShamanicWisdom.com.

Annette Carpien lives in Allentown, Pennsylvania.

Allie Casey still shares laughter with her sister, Christine Kolenda, and the two of them help women reinvent their lives. Find out how at ReinventionIntervention.com.

Brad Castleman lives in New Haven, Ind., with his wife, Teresa, and their wonderful pets. Brad enjoys sports and taking care of the local wildlife.

Teresa A. Castleman is happily married to Brad C. Castleman. Teresa loves cats, golfing, and reality television. She can be reached at facebook.com/Teresa.Castleman.

Eileen Chadnick, PCC, ABC, is principal of Big Cheese Coaching in Toronto. She helps people work and live with more meaning, success, and authenticity. See her at Bigcheese-Coaching.com.

Maureen Charles, a writer, editor, and instructional designer at wellwrittenwordshop.com, shares her adventures raising an Afghan Muslim teenager in an interfaith household at RaisingShakib.blogspot.com.

Winnis Chiang helps Mandarin- and Cantonese-speaking parents get along with, enjoy, and influence their American-born children. You can reach her at ParentingABC.com.

Danielle Chonody is passionate about teaching and mentoring others to start and grow their own pet business. Visit her blog at WorkingWithPets.com.

Christine Marie and Julie are mother/daughter radio co-hosts and certified Law of Attraction coaches. Find out more at ChristineMarieAndJulie.com.

Rhonda Chuyka teaches high school chemistry and jazzercise in West Virginia. She was Teacher of the Year in 2009 and lives to inspire others.

Laynita Cichy is an empowerment strategist who assists women in designing profound transformations in wellness, life, career, and business. You can find her at LaynitaCichy.com.

Andrea Cinnamond is a Boston-based online business manager and online business coach. You can reach her at WomenRockTheInternet.com.

Rev. Stephanie Clarke is a metaphysical teacher, writer, and spiritual counselor out of Africa and currently based in the UK. Contact her at MinistryOfLight.org.

Heather Clarke-Peckerman is a leadership development consultant specializing in emotional intelligence. She is based out of New Jersey and can be reached at HCPconsulting.com.

Marlene Clay helps parents have a harmonious divorce and successfully co-parent so their families can heal and thrive. Check her out at DivorcedHappilyEverAfter.com.

Louise Cohen, a life/professional success coach, wants to journey with you to find your "treasures within" for a life of accomplishment and joy. Check out PositiveAttitudeCoaching.com.

Melinda Coker is a Tyler, Texas-based author, health coach, photographer, and animal lover. You can reach her at DietCancerConnection.com.

Linda Cole, certified Law of Attraction counselor in Santa Fe, N.M., coaches/supports clients via phone/Skype. Contact HeartOfYurMatter@aol.com.

Margie Cole lives in Ontario, New York.

Deanna Collins is a life coach and gratitude advocate empowering women to live inspired through gratitude and the power of positive possibility. Find out more at TheGratitudeCircle.net.

Kelli O'Brien Corasanti teaches, motivates, supports, and inspires people to achieve their goals. You can reach her at FindingMyWayBackToMe.com.

Sandi Cornez lives in Portland, Oregon.

Elizabeth H. Cottrell ("RiverwoodWriter") is the Heartspoken Connections Expert at Heartspoken.com: Reflections, Resources, and Gifts to strengthen essential life connections that propel happiness and success.

Gina Crittenden is a career coach, speaker, and trainer who transforms clients' career and business challenges into professional and personal successes. Find her at ElevateUCoaching.com.

Barbara L. Cummings is a sassy-yet-classy, shoe-addicted Baby Boomer who inspires people to "get their laugh back" at BarbaraLCummings.com.

Diane Cunningham is a traveling life and dream coach who specializes in Baby Boomers and up. Find her at AmazingLifeAfter60.com.

Heidi Danos is the proud mother of twins, wife to her swell husband Pete, and entrepreneur extraordinaire. Find Heidi at MoraJunction.com.

Lauren Darr creates visionary marketing from her headquarters in Greens Fork, Ind., where she lives with her children, macaw, pug, and husband. Find her at LaurenOriginals.com.

Donna J. Davis is a consultant, author, and speaker. Visit DJDCommunications.com to rediscover your Joy. Happier souls have healthier bodies.

Deb Dawson-Dunn is an award-winning coach and speaker who helps women who are feeling stuck move forward with joy! Visit Deb at GetItDunn.ca.

Maureen Day offers comfort to empty-armed moms and honors their babies in heaven with handmade gifts from a network of volunteers. Learn more at HeavenBorn.com.

Robert Day is managing partner of Merchant Relief Council, a firm dedicated to helping businesses reduce their merchant processing fees. Find out more at MerchantReliefCouncil.org.

Ronda Del Boccio, aka "The Story Lady," number-one best-selling author of *The Peace Seed*, invites you to connect with anyone through story-telling with your free gift at ProfitableStorytelling.com.

Jerome DeShazo lives in Phoenix, Arizona.

Michelle Dimsey is a student of the universe and believes in the order hidden beneath the chaos. She works for the one and only Donna Kozik.

Linda Distler is a five-year breast cancer survivor who reinvented herself and became the Travel Pet Sitter. You can reach her at TravelingHouseSitter.wordpress.com.

Caroline Douglas is a clay sculptor in Boulder, Colo. and teaches classes on how to transform one's life through art. Find her at CarolineDouglas.com.

Beverly Dracos specializes in business communications and relationship marketing. You can connect with her at GenuineCommunications.com.

Dana Dunn is a certified life/business coach, business strategist, and speaker/trainer. She specializes in helping entrepreneurs create visibility to effectively market their businesses online. Contact her at DanaDunn.com.

Laurie Dupar is an ADHD life coach living near Sacramento Calif. and changing the world — beginning with herself! You can reach her at ChangeOfFocus.com.

Michelle Dupar is a student at Granite Bay High School in Granite Bay, Calif., with a passion for writing.

Linda Eaves is a Seattle area–based footed-pajama spokesmodel who loves magic, all things purple, and snickerdoodle cookies. Find her at LindaEaves.com.

Tricia Ebert is a Los Angeles Realtor who is devoted to educating people about the benefits of eating a plant-based diet. Find her at TheDangerousTruth.com.

Julie M. Edge lives in Mission Hills, Kansas.

Marian Edvardsen lives in Norwalk, Connecticut.

Louise Egan, LouiseEganDesign, and LouiseEganDesign.com maintain a studio in Irvine, Calif. Louise does visual branding graphic design, featuring a life-purpose assessment as a primary tool to business brand development.

Regina Eustace is an animal communicator and coach. She lives in Chilliwack, British Columbia. She can be reached at reustace98@gmail.com.

Suzanne Evans has a passion for teaching "helping-preneurs" to help more people, make more money, and enjoy more freedom. You can reach her at HelpMorePeople.com.

Annie Ferrigno is an active Lightworker, respectful gardener, and lover of life offering Reiki and other alternative therapies at FindingFocus.webs.com in Henniker, N.H.

Laura M. Fischer is a transitions coach and author who helps people to "Stop Surviving and Start Living." You can find her at ConnectWithLaura.com.

Michele Flamer is a sales director, major optimist, and lover of all things outdoors and food related! She loves blogging, ultra-running, and helping others succeed. You can find her at twitter.com/salesguru33.

Carol Lynn Fletcher is a writer, intuitive, graphic designer, and virtual assistant in the San Francisco Bay Area. You can reach her at FletcherBiz.com.

Dana Fletcher shows CAM providers how to plan and execute clinical research strategies to integrate complementary therapies into healthcare. You can reach her at EvaCRO.com.

Di Ana Ford is a wife, mom, and entrepreneur enjoying the sweet life. You can find her at SweetsInTheCityChicago.com.

Kristy Dunn Fox, Ph.D., MBA, integrates spirituality and holistic life coaching to help women thrive during all phases of motherhood. Visit KDFox.com to learn more.

JJ Frederickson, CFCC, is Today'sTMJ4 life coaching expert on Milwaukee's NBC affiliate. JJ the Life Coach is a coach and trainer with the Fearless Living Institute.

Kristine A. Friend lives in Hampton, New Jersey.

Carol Gailey, licensed spiritual healer, facilitates healing and wholeness using tuning forks aligned to the ancient Solfeggio frequencies. You can find her at facebook.com/carol.gailey528.

Alice R. Galassi lives in Madison, Wis.

Joseph Garcia lives with the love of his life, Dina Rocha, in San Diego, Calif. You can contact him at joeyjam12@gmail.com.

Liliana Garcia coaches people on how to heal their lives using art. Find her at YouCanHealYourLifeWithArt.com.

Tamara Gerlach brings light, spirituality, creativity, and experience to teach, mentor, and coach thousands of people to create their freedom and cultivate their radiance. Find her at TamaraGerlach.com.

Linda P. Giangreco lives in Hailey, Idaho.

Barb Girson, direct-selling expert, sales coach, speaker, and trainer, helps companies, teams, and entrepreneurs gain confidence, get into action, and grow sales. Reach Barb at MySalesTactics.com.

Timi Gleason, master coach and author, specializes in creating heart-based strategic plans for conscious companies. View her business books about strategic thinking on Amazon.com. Contact her at ExecutiveGoals.com.

Leila Glenn is a recognized neighborhood advocate with a passion for the youth and homeless, who's embarking upon her first book, *I Fired A Gordy!*

Bert Goos, psychologist and career coach from Holland, helps professionals discover their unique personal brand. Reach him at OnlineTalentManager.com.

River Grace is an angel-lover, gem angel designer, and aspiring author. While she is gracefully flowing through life, you can reach her at Gem-Angels.com.

Dr. Karen L. Gray, retired anesthesiologist, devoted mom, church singer, and entrepreneur, resides in Parkland, Fla., with two big kids and two big dogs.

Linda Griffin believes that every small business owner should be a star in the eyes of his or her customers. You can reach her at GrassRootsMarketingSystems.com.

Melissa Groom is the host and producer of *Toddlers To Teens: Parent TV Show* and proud mother to three children. Find out more at ToddlersToTeens.tv.

Dr. Mark Guariglia is the founder of FibroCare Center located in Point Pleasant, N.J. He can be reached at FibroCareCenter.com.

Dolores Hagen is a life coach who believes that mature women are truly sensational, and full of beauty and wisdom. She can be found at SixtyAndSensational.com.

Kim Halsey, author of *The Fast-Track Addiction Recovery System*™, offers twice the recovery in half the time at a fraction of the cost. See RecoveryToday.org.

Peggy Lee Hanson offers guidance to thinkers of "there's gotta be something better than this" who experience life-changing situations. You can reach Peggy at MyDreamArchitect.com.

Allegra Harrington of Norwalk, Conn., creates "Sculpture to Wear" and is at work on her first book.

Steve Harsh, pastor, teacher, writer, and life coach in Columbus, Ohio, uses drama and narrative to show truth too big for facts. Contact Steve at LivingWholly.com.

Amelia Hartfelder-Johnson, as a "petpreneur," empowers other animal lovers to live their passion for pets. You can reach her at YourPetsView.com.

Joan Hathaway-Sheldon now lives in Washington State and gives thanks to the people of Flagstaff, Arizona, Northern Arizona University, and Pine Forest Charter School. Contact her at JKHSheldon@live.com.

Armaity Hathidaru lives in British Columbia, Canada.

Cristy Hayden is a creative non-fiction writer, certified professional résumé writer, and career coach from Calgary, Alberta. You can reach her at CalgaryCris@gmail.com.

Patty Hedrick, RN, BSN, BA, CRRN, CCM, CLCP, is a nurse consultant, entrepreneur, speaker, coach, and author who helps and supports nurses. You can reach her at NurseCoachAlliance.com.

Michelle Heinselman specializes in self-image coaching and uses vision mapping techniques to transform lives and reinforce self-worth in her clients. Find her at Sincerely-YoursCoaching.com.

Victoria Herocten lives in Wexford, Ireland, and teaches individuals how to use the language of success. You can find her at TheWinnersLanguage.com.

Margaret A. Hicke listens to stories, relieves stress, and encourages personal growth for kids, parents, families, and friends. She is a therapist. Find her at MargeHicke.com.

Mary Hines works in the San Francisco Bay Area as a teacher and social worker. She loves to write, travel, laugh, and enjoy life. E-mail her at maryh11@att.net.

D. Artemas Holden is a client retention coach, an avid reader, and Nicole's father. His website is ProactiveEmotionalMarketing.com. "Your clients are someone else's prospects, if you don't stay in touch."

Gillian Holland lives in the United Kingdom.

Margaret G. Holmes is a speaker, author, and teacher who presented for the Volunteer Council of Texas Youth Commission and Texas Association of School Boards. Contact her at mholmes535@att.net.

Gary Horman lives in Morris Township, New Jersey.

Darlene Janke Horwath is a retired RN turned passion consultant and romance-enhancement specialist, speaker, trainer, and author. She is passionate about passion. Curious? Check out ThePartyLady.com.

Cherry Hsu helps people and animals feel healthier and happier easily. She also provides intuitive guidance to clarify direction in life. Reach her at EmbraceLite.com.

Tamra Hughes, MA, LPC, enjoys working with individuals, couples, and families as a licensed professional counselor in Denver, Colo. Find her at THcounseling.com.

Monika Huppertz asks "Are you ready to remove obstacles and leave your restrictive life behind? Step towards your success with purpose and passion!" Find her at LivingYourTruth.me.

Gretchen Iler is a certified tea sommelier and author promoting enjoyment, health, and wellness options for the daily tea lifestyle. Reach her at TeaSafari.com.

Lawrence J. Indiviglia lives in San Diego, California.

Sue Ingebretson is a writer and speaker dedicated to encouraging healing in others. Find out more about her book, *FibroWHYalgia*, and her blog at RebuildingWellness.com.

Julie Isaac is an award-winning author who helps people unleash their writing genius and S.H.I.N.E. online. You can reach her at WritingSpirit.com.

Edith Jaconsky-Hamersma is also grateful for having discovered the labyrinth and mindfulness practice. She runs workshops on both. Reach her at hamersmae@yahoo.com.

Millie Sunday Jett is a trainer, speaker, manager, and emotional freedom and healing facilitator based in Detroit, Mich. Find her at facebook.com/millie.jett or linkedin.com/in/milliesundayjett2cu.

Merrilee Johnson is the proud mother of three, a passionate author, and an entrepreneur promoting women's success through empowerment. Find her at MerrileeJohnson.com.

Christine Jones mentors bodywork professionals in taking their business to the next level. You can find her at twitter.com/MentorChristine.

Dawn Jordan helps people venture into the world that begins at the skin and goes in. Learn the lost art of talking to your body. E-mail Dawn at BodyWisdomDJo@gmail.com.

Joythi is a hypnotherapist, counselor, and budding author. Her passion is about bringing more joy and light into the lives of all she encounters. Jyothi lives in Alberta, Canada.

Tara Kachaturoff is an online business manager and host of Michigan Entrepreneur TV. A native of Southern California, she currently resides in Birmingham, Mich. Find her at twitter.com/TaraKachaturoff.

Louise Morganti Kaelin supports others in getting off the treadmill and onto the up escalator! Find her (and your best self) at TouchPointCoaching.com.

Sheila Kamp lives with her husband and two children in San Jose, Calif. She is an occupational therapist/certified hand therapist.

Jolina Karen: Healer. Teacher. Entrepreneur. Contact her at JolinaKaren.com.

Arnina Kashtan, Israeli facilitator, writer, and performer, supports liberation from guilt, fear, and anger through deep empathy and laughter. Want your authentic self? Great relationships? Go to facebook.com/Arnina.Kashtan.

Jutta Kastner lives in Ireland. Learn more about this visionary who's interested in autism, specially abled/gifted children and individuals, the Universe, fun, and life at JuttaKastner.com.

Lillian Kennedy lives in Boulder, Colo. Her artwork and teaching schedule can be found at LillianKennedy.com. For free online art lessons, visit WeeklyArtLesson.com.

Joyce Kenyon lives in Beverly Hills, California.

Kelly Kim lives with her family in San Francisco. For more gratitude tips from Kelly, visit kellykim.com.

Phyllis A. Klein-Buonocore lives in Stockton, California.

Jill Korn works with her husband, Joey, in the personal development field, helping people realize their unlimited potential. They can be reached at Remember.org/abe.

Donna Kozik lives in San Diego where she shows people how to Write a Book in a Weekend(TM). Find her at WriteWithDonna. com.

Daniel J. Kriley is a high school theatre and arts management instructor living in Southern California. Find him at facebook. com/daniel.kriley.

Yardena Krongold mentors Spanish-speaking managers and directors to become irresistible and get more from their careers. You can reach her at GerentesBrillantes.com.

Willie LaBonne will open your mind to access your creative power to live your life by design rather than by default. You can find her at WilliesWisdom.com.

Judy A. LaCroix lives in Sunnyvale, California.

Dr. Susan Lange, OMD, L.Ac, shares the wonderfully inspirational, healing, funny letter sent by her mother after she died at MeridianHolisticHealth.com/jane.html.

Leona M. La Perriere lives in Greensboro, North Carolina.

Melissa Anne Lawson supports others in making transformational changes in their lives through enlightened leadership and inspirational coaching. You can reach her at MelissaAnneLawson.com.

Joyce Layman is a keynote speaker and author who helps others connect the dots between their thoughts and results. You can reach her at joycelayman.com.

Teresa C. Lea shows people how to heal, reclaim their lives, and step into a place of personal power. You can reach her InTouchInLife.com.

Joy Leccese of Coaching Constructs LLC can be found at Better YOUniversity.net. Email her at JoyL@betteryouuniversity.net. Better You, Better Living, Better Life. Joy Leccese lives in Rochester, New York.

Gwen L. Lepard is a holistic health practitioner, dancer, beader, writer, reader, and positive lifestyle facilitator grateful to be here. Find her at ConsciousRejuvenation.com.

Meredith Liepelt mentors business owners to increase their reach, visibility, and impact through authentic self-promotion. Tweet with her today at twitter.com/meredithliepelt.

Annette Denton Livingston, a terminal illness survivor, shares her new book, *Living Wellness Today: One Woman's Search for Healing.* Contact her at LivingWellnessToday.com.

Bernée E. Long is head coach of the BE (Beginning Entrepreneurs) Team and founder of The Stepmom's Club. You can contact her at facebook.com/bernee.long.

Dr. Leslie Loubier, Psy.D., is a licensed clinical psychologist. Dr. Loubier helps others reach their highest potential through health, wellness, and successful coaching. Contact her at BestLifeYet.net.

Trisha LoveJoy is a certified professional success coach and small business consultant who inspires and empowers clients to live their dreams. Contact her at Trisha@TheLovejoysCompanies.com.

Peg Roach Loyd is an award-winning singer, songwriter, and composer of original songs in Irish and Irish-American styles. For song samples visit CellaDawnMusic.com.

Kris Lozano is pursuing her lifelong calling to write, with support from her dear husband and two teenagers. Follow her journey at MamaLlamaJr.blogspot.com and facebook.com/ NotKristaKristyOrKristenItsJustKris.

Wendy Mackowski, author of "Bluebirds' Song," inspires you to rise above your "pigeon fears" and soar in harmony with your "Authentic Bluebird Spirit!" See BluebirdsSong.com.

Lorraine Maita, MD, can help you look and feel healthier; prevent or reverse some degenerative diseases; and enable you to age gracefully and healthfully at HowToLiveYounger.com.

Deanna Mandichak is a physical therapist and health coach focusing on holistic health, prevention, and children's health. Contact her at HealthCoachingSuccess.com.

Susan Mann is a Toronto-based holistic energy practitioner and teacher who works with local and international clients. Visit her at HeadToHeal.ca for more information.

Tara Maras lives in fabulous Las Vegas, Nev. You won't find her in the casinos, but you will find her at facebook.com/taramaras.

Nancy Marmolejo is a high-achieving, mega creative and soul driven entrepreneur. Founder of VivaVisibility.com and fueled by spicy food.

Christine E. Marquette, RD, LD, ACSM, is a vegetarian, registered and licensed dietitian, running coach, and certified health fitness specialist. Find her at MarquetteNutrition.com or facebook. com/Marquette.Nutrition.And.Fitness

Lorin Mask is a business mentor, coach, trainer, and speaker. You can read all about her at LorinMask.com.

Delores Mason is a Philadelphia-based life coach, author, and educator who enjoys learning and sharing that enthusiasm with others. You can find her at 2YourWell-Being.com.

Liliane Mavridara is a writer, educator, and groupwork facilitator who focuses on spiritual development, holistic health, and right relationships. You can reach her at LiveBrightlyTheBook.com.

Deanna McAdams is a certified paralegal and virtual assistant based in San Diego, Calif. Contact her at DeannaVA.com.

Karen McCarthy is a Reiki Master for people and pets in Maine. Contact her at dragonfly@roadrunner.com.

PC McCullough is a life enthusiast. She is a contributing author of Vibrant Women's Wisdom and author of the novel *Perfect*. Reach PC at PCMcCullough.com.

Doreen Susan McGrath-Smith lives in Columbia, Maryland.

Patricia McKinney-Lins shows non-tech people how to get the photos out of their cameras and share them with family and friends. Find her at MyPhotoSharingSecrets.com.

Nancy McNaughton, coach and founder of Opening Doors to Success Inc., inspires people to let go of impossibility thinking and take steps toward success. Find her at OpeningDoorsToSuccessInc. com.

Heather Meglasson, CMT, Ht, is a mom, author, speaker, relaxologist, and transformation artist who loves to make people smile. Friend her at facebook.com/Heather.Meglasson.

Teena Miller laughs for the "health of it!" She is a life coach and laughter yoga teacher. Contact Teena@Laugh4Health.com.

Tamara Miranda is passionate about dogs, living life to the fullest, and inspiring small business owners to succeed. You can find her at facebook.com/Tamara.B.Miranda.

Roberta Mittman, L.Ac., is a board-certified, licensed acupuncturist, nutritional consultant, and wellness mentor. Roberta empowers individuals to be their own best healers. Visit RobertaMittman. com.

Q Moayad is a highly intuitive and gifted personal transformation leader who helps people create meaningful and fulfilled lives. He can be reached at NakedHealer.com.

Rachel Monde is a peace coach, supporting those who

want a life full of "aliveness" and meaning. Learn more at SpeakingPeaceHearingPeace.com.

Jeanne Huber Morr is an Ohio business owner, and the author of *Under the Hood* and soon-to-be released *From Dust*. Contact jhmTalk.com for more information.

Lynn Morrell helps tennis kids nationwide champion kindness and hone their philanthropic muscle online and on-court. Visit KidsPlayForGood.org.

Cathy Morrissey's Brand YOU–Brand New is smoking hot. Need branding? Her special guests include *Secret* teacher Bob Proctor and Star Ladin. Learn more at CathyMorrissey.com.

Kamala Murphey mentors spiritually minded entrepreneurs to release fear and receive heart, soul, and financial success in their businesses. You can find her at KamalaMurphey.com.

Pam Murphy, M.S., RRT, a holistic nutritionist, actively supports and assists her clients' transition to a "healthstyle" that supports optimal health and well-being. Visit her at OptimizeToHeal.com.

Kathy Nelson lives in San Diego, California.

Martia Nelson, true self mentor and author of *Coming Home: The Return to True Self*, helps motivated professionals lead rich, joyful lives. For a free gift, go to MartiaNelson.com.

Rumyana Nenova is in the business of helping people achieve personal change in an elegant, effective, and fun way. Find her at twitter.com/Alternativz.

Debbie Nichols is the author of *Deployed: Grandparents being Parents*, a true story of parenting her granddaughters while their mother served in Afghanistan. Reach her at GrandparentsBeingParents.com.

Michelle Nightengale is the CEO of The International Association of Health and Wellness Professionals. She lives in West Palm Beach, Fla., with her cat. Learn more at IAHWP.org.

Lynn Workman Nodland, Ph.D., MCC, success coach/psychologist, helps people use strengths personally and professionally to foster good communication, relationships, and positive change. Learn more at LynnNodland.com.

Jenny O'Connell, from Shepparton, Australia, is dedicated to promoting consciousness and creating opportunities to transform trauma into triumph. Contact her at emmakate2@iinet.net.au.

Crystal O'Connor shows businesses and "solo-preneurs" how to get moxie with money and marketing. When you need more moxie you can find her at MoxieMompreneur.com.

Marjorie Old and her husband keep their spirits lifted with a "gratitude board" in their home in Vista, Calif. Marjorie designs training materials and teaches yoga.

Sylvie Olivier is an author and the co-creator of Exploration Gratitude.com, whose mission is to spread and infuse the message of gratitude around the world.

Florence Onochie believes in inspiring and motivating others through inspirational and uplifting messages. You can reach her at FNOBooksCalendarsMagazines.com.

Karen Paris, RPA, is a physician assistant who has practiced integrative medicine for over thirty years. She is located in New York. Reach her at twitter.com/Medicine369.

Kathleen Dakota Parker's career includes work as a TV anchorwoman, reporter, mom, entrepreneur, motivational speaker, philanthropist, stock trader, angel investor, and, most recently, caregiver.

Gail Patterson is "the Women's Envisionary," helping mid-life women meet the changes and challenges they face today. Get to know her at TheWiseWomansWay.com.

Jennifer Peek mentors professional women on aligning their lives with their priorities for greater success in every area. You can find her at PeekCoaching.com.

Carol A. Pena is a Houston-based database technologist with a passion for writing. Find her at twitter.com/capena.

Dr. Eric Pfeiffer is an expert on successful aging, Alzheimer's disease, and caregiving. He is also a published poet. His website is EricPfeifferMD.com.

Colleen C. Phillips is a dynamic speaker, writer, and professional coach helping overwhelmed women have more energy, gain focus, boost profits, and save time. Contact her at PiecesToProfit.com.

Evelyn Pindura is a passionate writer and encourages people to strive for the best through difficult times. You can reach her at EvelynPindura.com.

Matthew Poepsel is the founder of Goals Gone Wild. He's passionate about providing online coaching for individuals and organizations. You can reach Matthew at GoalsGoneWild.com.

Debbie Pokornik helps women who want to "live on purpose" disconnect from negative energies and reconnect to their natural, realistic guidance. Read more at EmpoweringNRG.com.

Joy Porter is the author of the book *GetYourRNFaster.com* and is an online nursing degree advisor to thousands of nursing students around the country. Contact her at JoyPorter.com.

Lois Posner, a "wholistic nurse," is the director of massage of the Run Wholistic Center in Huntington Village, N.Y. She can be reached at HuntingtonMassageTherapy.com.

Carey Powell, ACC, is a PR consultant, helping small and solo business owners attract phenomenal media exposure. Learn more at Fearless-PR.com.

Kathy Preston is known simply as "HiKath" by all who know and love her. She is a warm, wise, witty, courageous traveler.

Jolen Punches supports women with an achy heart from a divorce, breast cancer, or death in their life. You can find her at LighterWithin.com.

Roslyn Rajasingam from Sydney, Australia, is a published article writer who supports the blogging and online business journey of working moms. Find her at RoslynRajasingam.com.

John Rasiej didn't realize how important gratitude was until recently, and is thankful for the realization now. Thank you for reading this! Find John at SpeakLouderThanWords.com.

Luisa Rasiej is a "get you unstuck and embrace your femininity" guide, a world traveler, and a real contessa. Find her online at InnerContessa.com.

John Ready is retired from the Army Reserve, during which he served one year in Iraq. He is currently writing a book about his experiences.

Kimberly Riggins shows women how to feel fabulous in their own skin regardless of shape or size. You can reach her at KimberlyRiggins.com.

Denice Rivera is an architect of the new way of building businesses, helping "women-preneurs" find their passions to build from within. Find her at RareGemEntrepreneurs.com.

Standolyn Kerr Robertson is an organizing expert, coach, big thinker, artist, zydeco Cajun music festival fan, curler, quilter, and vintage camper collector. Find her at Standolyn.com.

Dina Rocha emigrated from Mexico and is a UCSD graduate. She lives in San Diego with her loving family and dogs, Sammy, Jordan, and Angel.

Dr. Robert Ross, a certified coach and Christian clinical counselor specializing in relationships and sexuality, practices in Sarasota, Fla. View his website at RelationshipDynamicsLLC.com.

Coach Louise Rouse, CPPC, is an expert in invisible relationships. Visit AmericasGriefCoach.com for free information via audios, videos, and her blog.

Maryam Nasr Sardari is an art therapist, wannabe writer, blogger

(MyDanglingParticiple.com), jewelry designer, and foodie. Reach her at Maryam@ShopFaso.com.

Gail Schuler is an Alaska-based ADHD Coach. She assists parents and children in building self-advocacy skills. You can find her at CoachingForSelfAdvocacy.com.

Susane D. Schuler is a visionary author and artist whose creations all flow from Source. She can be reached at sds.gin@gmail.com. Much love to all!

Angela Schutz is a career coach, inspirational speaker, and founder of Driven to Succeed Consulting LLC. "I'll help you find the job of your dreams!" Find here at DrivenToSucceed.net.

Michele Scism is a highly motivated, positive and self-driven business woman who helps women business owners get better results. Get great business tips at DecisiveMinds.com.

Susan Secord is a traditional naturopath using mind- and heart-based quantum medicine to help others achieve optimal health and wellness. Here website is AlternativeHealthSuccess.com, and her e-mail is Susan@AlternativeHealthSuccess.com.

Tuck Self, The Rebel Belle, inspires women to live a juicy, joyful, and meaningful life. Meet Tuck, the "rebelicious" coach, speaker, and writer, at TheRebelBelle.com.

Betsy Shands offers exponential transformation at BetsysHands.com. Contact her at betsyshands@gmail.com.

Fiona Shanti provides intuitive counseling and healing to assist you to find your magnificence. You can reach her at VitaminsForTheSoul.com.au.

Ron Shuster and his wife live in Colorado. You can stay at his perfect Summit County Colorado condo: MaryandRonsCondo.com. Ron can be reached at facebook.com/RonShuster.

Beverly Simmons inspires you to confidently stand in your power and speak your truth. You can reach her at TrueTrackCoaching.com.

Anne Skinner is a senior business strategist, coach, and mentor. Her "Practical Solutions" integrates professional experience, creativity, and intuition to guide and enhance you or your business. Contact her at PracticalSolutionsConsultant@gmail.com.

Candace Smith, LCSW, is a psychotherapist and coach in Austin, Texas. She can be contacted at AustinTherapyMom@yahoo.com or through her website, AustinDBT.com.

Marion Smith-Wiason, MD, Ph.D., aka Coach Marion, is passionate about spreading the word that many chronic diseases that lead to heart disease are reversible and can be eliminated.

Stephanie Solaris has developed unique programs to help others achieve optimum health by merging her scientific background and nutrition coaching expertise. You will find her at SolarisWholeHealth.com.

Laura Lee Sparks helps professional services providers escape the chaos of juggling work and life, helping them find balance and productivity. Learn more at TheSimpleSolution.com.

Raissa Spatola lives in Randolph, New Jersey.

Thomas J. "Tom" Starr lives in Milford, Ohio.

Barbara Stuhlemmer lives in Barrie Ontario, Canada.

Edd Sturdevant, 50, lives alone together with his sister, his mother, his cousin, and three adorable dogs in northwestern Pennsylvania.

Carolyn Stys is a business owner, Red Sox fan, sister, daughter, mother to three sons, and wife to her best friend, Mark.

Mok Tuck Sung helps business owners turn around their underperforming and/or financially burdened business to positive cash flow.

Gail Mettler Swain lives in Bishop, Calif. She is a Longaberger™ consultant, creative decorator, great dancer, Science of Mind believer, active hiker, and fun person. Her site is Longaberger.com/gailswain.

Greer Tavel is a coach who can help you identify and achieve your dreams. Read her blog at DareToKeepDreaming.com.

B. E. Thompson is the author of the upcoming book *Creating Marriage* (available February 14, 2011).

Avery Thurman is a nurse and is presently learning about real estate investing and other ventures. She loves friendships, traveling, and animals. Find her at facebook.com/averythurman.

Tracy Tobler helps women turn their talent and passion into a prosperous business so they make money doing what they love. Learn more at TracyTobler.com.

Laurie Tossy helps women achieve their healthy bodies without dieting or excessive exercise. She can be reached at RefuseToDiet.com.

Alice Rosalie Touchette is a gifted healer/textiles artisan, joyfully preparing to reopen Hollyhurst Cottage Inn in Onset, Mass. You can find her at HollyhurstCottageInn.com.

Catherine Traywick lives in Rincon, Georgia.

Jackie Trottmann's St. Louis–based company provides small businesses with practical marketing strategies at LocalBizMentor.com. For individuals, Jackie helps encourage spiritual growth at Guided ChristianMeditation.com.

Cynthia Trygier raises the standard in interior design, elevating her clients' homes to luxury level. She specializes in couture window fashions. Find her at WrapYourselfInLuxury.com.

Erin Tullius is an inspirational wellness trainer and author of *Mind Over Fatter: The Secret to Thinking Yourself Thin*. Find out more at MindOverFatterBook.com.

Vickie Turley mentors virtual assistants by providing them with peer support to create their unique path to business and personal success. Find Vickie at MyVAMentor.com.

Theresa Valade lives in Valparaiso, Indiana.

Wilhelmien van Nieuwenhuizen travels internationally, teaching on fulfilling purpose, call and destiny, and effecting social transformation. You can find her at ClarionCallMinistries.org.

Miguel Vasquez is a Life Coach/Energy Healer and Certified EFT Trauma Specialist who is dedicated to helping Veterans and others. www.SpiritualEFT.com

Susan Veach is a graphic designer living in Southampton, Pa. She is a bibliophile, traveler, art lover, gardener, mother, and wife. You can reach her at SusanVeach.com.

Nicole Vetere is a Toronto-based teacher. She hopes that sharing this book with her students will help to inspire them to maintain an "attitude for gratitude." Contact her at nicvetere@gmail.com.

Milana Vinokur is a highly intuitive and creative woman, artist, photographer, writer, animal empath, spiritual coach, and uniquely fun individual. Contact her at Milana.me.

Barbara G. Wainwright has dedicated her life to helping others. Barbara's personal quest to is help make the world a better place for everyone everywhere.

Marion Smith Waison, MD, Ph.D., is a retired physician and psychologist who now offers health coaching focused on reversing diseases leading to heart disease. Contact her at MarionSmithWaison.com.

Helen Sue Walker lives in Richmond, Va., leads a support group for people with fibromyalgia, and recently published her first book. Find more information at RichmondFibro.org.

Veronica Weeks-Basham, BSN, LMT, practices massage therapy and hypnosis in Hillsboro, Ore., at Northwest Massage and Wellness Center. Her interests are writing, teaching, and speaking.

Ron J. West can always be reached at RonJWest.com.

Jay Westbrook is an award-winning clinician, consultant, clinical director of Compassionate Journey, and amazing national speaker on the constellation of issues surrounding End-of-Life. Contact Jay at CompassionateJourney@hotmail.com.

Laura Westerberg is a professional health and wellness coach. For almost thirty years she has helped people to achieve their goals toward a healthy lifestyle!

Eva Maria Wiesenthal of Vienna is an ambassador of love and political and healing power, and an artist-philosopher-healer-writer. Find her on Facebook and at EvaMariaWiesenthal.com.

Melanie Wilson, Psy.D., is a Philadelphia-based clinical and consulting psychologist in private practice. She can be reached at Melanie@DrMelanieWilson.com.

Ruth Winden is a German-born and UK-based career development professional. She helps ex-pat partners manage and enhance their careers while abroad. Learn more at CareersEnhanced.com.

Amy B. Windham is a travel agent. She plans destination weddings, honeymoons, "conception-moons," "babymoons," family fun, grand trips, and accessible travel. Contact Amy at TheFourCornersTravel.com.

Tziporah Wishky is a certified life coach. Through telecoaching, she helps individuals worldwide who are overwhelmed and facing adversity to fashion new lives. Contact her at IStillHaveMyLife.com.

Corine Wofford is a spirit-rich entrepreneur, a dynamic professional speaker, and an inspired-to-action coach. Join her Be the Difference Brigade at CorineWofford.com.

Jeff Woodard is an expert on effective presentation skills, leadership development, and communication skills. His motto is: "The quality of our communications directly affects the quality of our lives."

Kelly Flynn Zawistowski is a family law attorney in Massachusetts. She can be found at FamilyLawAdvantage.com.

Liz Zed, Ph.D., CMC, is a confidential brainstorm partner to actualize your tremendous ambition and purpose. For a better-quality you in action, go to BetterQualityCoach.com.

Kim Zilliox, MA, MBA, is a San Francisco–based leadership consultant, coach, speaker, and author. Her full bio and description of services can be found at kzleadership.com.

"The Gratitude Book Project" Ambassadors

Thank you to the following people who not only contributed a piece to this book but also put forth time and effort to spread the word about it. We appreciate you!

Deborah Avery
Tracy Allen Baker
Kim Marie Baldwin
Kim Beckett
Michelle A. Beitzel
Rachel Bellack
Jeremy M. Bennett
Nicole Bissett
Dave Block
Jan Blount
Carol A. Boston
Susan Brady
Annie Brandt
Marsha Lee Bressack
Tanya Louise Brown
Susan Brownell
Catherine Bruns
Jenny Bryans
Louise-Annette Burgess
Stefany G. Burrowes
LaVerne M. Byrd
Liana L. Carbón
Allie Casey
Eileen Chadnick
Maureen Charles
Rhonda Chuyka
Laynita Cichy
Heather
   Clarke-Peckerman
Marlene Clay
Louise Ann Cohen
Melinda Coker
Deanna Collins

Kelli O'Brien Corasanti
Sandi Cornez
PC McCullough
Danielle Cousin
Gina M. Crittenden
Lauren L. Darr
Maureen Day
Ronda Del Boccio
Linda Distler
Beverly Dracos
Kristy Dunn Fox
Laurie Dupar
Linda Eaves
Tricia Ebert
Marian Edvardsen
Louise Egan
Deb Farrell
Annie Ferrigno
Michele Flamer
Carol Lynn Fletcher
Di Ana Ford
Alice R. Galassi
Linda Giangreco
Leila Glenn
Linda G. Griffin
Peggy Hanson
Cristy Hayden
Michelle Heinselman
Margaret A. Hicke
Mary Hines
D. Artemas Holden
Gillian Ann Holland
Margaret G. Holmes

Darlene Janke Horwath
Cherry Hsu
Tamra Hughes
Monika Huppertz
Gretchen Iler
Sue Ingebretson
Julie Isaac
Millie Sunday Jett
Amelia Hartfelder-
Johnson
Dawn AV Marie Jordan
Tara Kachaturoff
Louise Morganti Kaelin
Jutta Kastner Leahy
Phyllis A. Klein
Jill Korn
Yardena Krongold
Willie LaBonne
Judy A. LaCroix
Susan Lange
Melissa Anne Lawson
Joyce Layman
Joy Leccese
Gwen L. Lepard
Meredith Liepelt
Annette Denton
   Livingston
Leslie A. Loubier
Margaret (Peg) Loyd
Kris Lozano
Wendy Mackowski
Liliane Mavridara
Nancy McNaughton

Teena Ferris Miller
Roberta Mittman
Lynn Morrell
Cathy Morrissey
Kamala Murphey
Pam Murphy
Maryam Nasr Sardari
Martia Nelson
Kathy Nelson
Lynn Workman Nodland
Crystal O'Connor
Sylvie Olivier
Florence Onochie
Gail Patterson
Carol A. Pena
Christine Peters
Eric Pfeiffer
Colleen C. Phillips
Debbie Pokornik
Carey Powell
Kathy "HiKath" Preston

John S. Ready
Kimberly Riggins
Denice Rivera
Standolyn Robertson
Robert A.K. Ross
Angela Schutz
Susan Secord
Tuck Self
Fiona Shanti
Ron Shuster
Beverly Simmons
Anne M. Skinner
Doreen Smith
Stephanie J. Solaris
Laura Lee Sparks
Barb Stuhlemmer
Gail Mettler Swain
Greer Tavel
Avery Thurman
Laurie Tossy
Alice Touchette

Jackie Trottmann
Cynthia Trygier
Erin Tullius
Vickie Turley
Theresa Valade
Wilhelmien
     Van Nieuwenhuizen
Nicole Vetere
Marion Smith-Waison
Sue Walker
Avenelle Warde
Jay Westbrook
Laura Westerberg
Lois White
Melanie Wilson
Amy B. Windham
Tziporah Wishky
Corine Wofford
Kelly Zawistowski

Want to be a published author?

Book writing, publishing and consulting services provided by Donna Kozik & Associates, Inc.

Write Your Book

"Write a Book in a Weekend" is an online, virtual course that guides you in writing a "short and powerful" book in two days with pre-formatted templates, how-to information, and expert guidance. Find out more and get a FREE AUDIO "12 Strategies to Publishing Success" at WriteWithDonna.com.

Publish Your Book

"Done for You" Publishing Services offers everything from editing, proofreading, interior formatting, and cover design, while providing personal connection and top-rate customer service. Find out more at DoneForYouPublishing.com.

Get Answers to Your Book Writing and Publishing Questions

If you're struggling with what to write about or organizing your material, or if you're frustrated because you can't find answers about how the book publishing process works, get a "Big Breakthrough Session" with two-time award-winning author and publishing expert Donna Kozik. More at MyBigBreakthroughSession.com.

Not sure what you need?

Email business manager Dina Rocha with your questions at Dina@MyBigBusinessCard.com or call us anytime at 619-923-3082 to talk about it.